THE REFERENCE SHELF

Vol. 18   No. 3

REPRESENTATIVE AMERICAN SPEECHES: 1944-1945

Selected by

A. CRAIG BAIRD

Department of Speech, State University of Iowa

THE H. W. WILSON COMPANY
NEW YORK   1945

PS
668
R4
V.18- No3

Copyright 1945
By The H. W. Wilson Company
All Rights Reserved
Published October 1945
Printed in the United States of America

3312

328 p.

PREFATORY NOTE

REPRESENTATIVE AMERICAN SPEECHES: 1944-45 is the eighth in this annual series. Each volume includes about thirty speeches representing important orators on current issues. Together these eight volumes include some one hundred and seventy-five speakers and more than two hundred addresses.

The speeches are grouped according to their content, such as Progress of the War, International Collaboration, Domestic, Economic, Social, Political, Educational, and Religious Problems, and National Ideals.

An alternative classification according to speech forms or audience situations can easily be made. The Introduction which follows classifies the contents of this volume as Congressional speeches, Political Campaign speeches, Eulogies, Committee Hearings, Addresses of Welcome or Reply, Professional Lectures, Sermons, and Radio Commentaries.

This volume, like its predecessors, can be used as a reference for the study of contemporary American thought; as a series of specific arguments or expositions on problems under investigation; as a record of recent history; or as a series of speeches to be studied as models for the student speech-maker. The book, then, should be of special service to students of debate, public speaking, English, history, social science, and to other reference workers.

The Introduction of this volume outlines in detail methods for the systematic criticism of a speech. The introduction to each speech is a further help in the analysis of a given address as the product of the speaker, the occasion, the audience, and of the speech itself with its ideas, evidence, organization, and oral language.

The Tables of Contents and the Indexes of the earlier volumes enable the student to classify the material according to subject-matter. The cumulative author index at the end of this volume will facilitate the survey of the various representatives in their roles as debaters, lecturers, or public orators. Such a guide should open the way to further investigation of any one of these representative American speakers.

A. CRAIG BAIRD

June 30, 1945

CONTENTS

END OF THE EUROPEAN WAR

AMERICA AND INTERNATIONAL COLLABORATION

AMERICA AND NATIONAL DEFENSE

FOURTH TERM CAMPAIGN

End of a Regime

American Ideals

Social and Economic Principles

Education and the War

America and Religion

CONTENTS

INTRODUCTION

The speeches here included are intended to be representative of the kind and quality of speech-making done in the United States during the twelve months ending in June 1945. What are "representative" speeches? By what criteria do we evaluate public addresses? Are they chiefly speeches that read well? Only those that make major headlines? Those most widely heard according to the estimates of radio pollsters? Only those delivered by speakers with a wide reputation as orators?

SOCIAL AND POLITICAL BACKGROUND OF THE SPEECH

The critic of a speech begins by analyzing the social and political background of a given address. Speech-making is oral communication. It arises in a social medium. Like the actor, the speaker is nothing without his audience. Both speaker and audience, however, are the product of the times. The student of speeches, then, should saturate himself with the economic, political, ideological, and psychological backgrounds against which speakers and their audiences do their thinking and talking. Public expression in our United States where, even in wartime, minimum restraints on free utterance are imposed, is especially likely to reflect the wide sweep of events and the corresponding reactions of public temper and opinion.

During 1944-45, to cite the obvious, we have lived exciting history. Our articulate citizens, including those with most vocal skill, have talked freely and intelligently. The speaking has been prolific in quantity and first rate in quality.

On both the military and the civilian fronts, as we mustered and directed our human and material power for the destruction of the Axis, we lived through a succession of crises. In Saipan, Guam, Leyte, Luzon, Mindanao, Iwo Jima, and Okinawa, brilliant amphibious campaigns developed. Major Japanese fleet and air units were shattered. Our flag topped Suribachi.

Rome fell, D-E Day came with national prayers led by the President. Fortress Europe was breached at Normandy, on the Riviera and up the Rhone, at Cherbourg, St Lô, and Caen. Paris celebrated liberation. Aachen was ours. V-bombs demolished sections of London, but the American airmen, with the R.A.F., levelled the cities of Deutschland, pinpointed industrial and military objectives, and demoralized the opposing divisions through tactical support. The Belgian bulge was erased. The West wall collapsed. American armies and their British and other Allies at Remagen and elsewhere leaped the Rhine, executed in the Ruhr one of the greatest enveloping movements in history, plunged to the Elbe, cut to ribbons vast armies, accepted surrender at Reims, and paused while the Allied governments proclaimed V-E Day.

On the political and civilian fronts of America these events produced parallel problems. De Gaulle's government arose, Lublin Poles occupied Warsaw, Greeks clashed with Greeks, the Big Three conferred at Yalta. Conferences took place at Bretton Woods and at Dumbarton Oaks. Argentina about-faced. A reorganized State Department functioned energetically. The Chapultepec Agreement was signed at Mexico City; San Francisco delegates deliberated. High Nazis were corralled, the horrors of Nazi prison and concentration camps shook America. Strikes in hard and soft coal plagued the nation. The Fourth Term campaign gathered momentum, and ended in a triumph for democratic processes. The Political Action Committee boomed. Production, prices, wages, threatened food shortages, black-markets, mounting war debts, accumulating financial surpluses, threatened inflation, reconversion politics, national service legislation, G.I. Bill of Rights—these and similar matters deeply concerned Congressmen and others. Roosevelt died, and Truman took the oath of office. The Japanese war and Russia's role in the Far East and in European and Middle East boundaries and policies overshadowed most other concerns.

Over the radio, in Congress, in pulpits, at community forums, professional and business conferences and dinners, in schoolrooms, and college lecture halls, wherever Americans, young or old met, these events and their accompanying problems were debated, discussed, expounded, recounted. The competent critic of these speeches, then, should view any one discourse as it evolved in such an atmosphere.

THE SPEECH AND THE AUDIENCE

The critic's understanding of the social scene should be attended by a full knowledge of the speaker's audience. Much that the orator thinks and expresses is consciously or unconsciously a reflection of the personality of the auditors. Audience beliefs, attitudes and experiences should color something of the speaker's line of thinking, his language, his adaptations in personality, voice, and bodily action. Critics of speeches, then, will do well to observe closely the education, race, politics, occupation, religion, traditions, economic level, age, and other attributes of a specific audience.

Roosevelt, reporting on Yalta, in the "well" of the House of Representatives, focused on the several hundred Representatives and Senators of this joint session. At Washington, D.C., on September 23rd, the President enthusiastically drove home his political points to a thousand wildly cheering members of the Teamsters' Union. Vandenberg discoursed more formally with those he had long known in the Senate. Commander Harold Stassen held forth in the University of Minneapolis auditorium before a typical Minneapolis-St. Paul audience, reinforced by Minnesota students and his gubernatorial backers. Edward Stettinius and Anthony Eden, at San Francisco, undertook to interpret their League proposals to four thousand, including delegates, their secretaries, and visitors. The visible audience represented almost fifty nations. Most had comparatively little understanding of the English language. Most had outlooks and sentiments "foreign" to those of the platform leaders or of their fellow delegates.

Eric Johnston, at a Waldorf Hotel dinner, spoke vigorously to sympathetic writers, journalists, and radio commentators. Senator Barkley and Quentin Reynolds, at the Chicago Democratic National Convention, struggled against July heat and Stadium clamor, to hold attention and win response from fifteen thousand turbulent convention-infested Democrats. Congressman Karl Mundt argued with his fellow Representatives. Thomas E. Dewey, at Oklahoma City, persuaded an overflowing audience, most of whom were Republican, but representative in their attitudes of that section of the United States. William Hocking, Robert Hutchins, Reinhold Niebuhr, and Robert Redfield conducted a round table for the radio listeners of some eighty-five stations, an educated constitutency, "selected" and pretty well defined after ten years during which this program has operated. H. W. Prentis, Jr., by contrast, had as his audience big industrialists, members of the National Association of Manufacturers. Henry Wallace talked for hours in give-and-take with a Senate Committee, most of whom were hostile to his political principles and ambitions. John D. Rockefeller, Jr., delivered his message to hundreds of Greater New York religious workers; Benjamin E. Mays, President of a Southern Negro college, talked to a Brooklyn audience; and Bernard Iddings Bell, as presiding Canon, held services in St. John's Cathedral in Providence, Rhode Island.

These were "representative" American assemblages. They were American in their cultural and inherited associations. But each group was stamped by its own attitudes and interests that called on the speaker to make appropriate audience adjustments.

The Speech and the Occasion

Speeches are to be studied in their relation to the specific occasion in which they are given. The purpose of the audience in assembling and the kindred purpose of the speaker in talking to them affect character of the subject, ideas, language, delivery, and other elements of the speaking technique. Speeches aim (1) to inform, (2) to entertain, (3) to convince, (4) to persuade, (5) to lead to action, (6) to inspire, or (7) to effect a combination of these ends. More specifically, however, speeches are classified in form or speech type according to the occasion. The contents of this volume, to illustrate this classification according to occasion, may be arranged somewhat as follows:

I. Congressional or Deliberative Speeches: A. H. Vandenberg's "American Foreign Policy"; Karl Mundt's "Peace—If We Want It."

II. Executive Speeches: F. D. Roosevelt's "Yalta Conference"; Harry S. Truman's "V-E Day Proclamation"; Winston Churchill's "Germany Surrenders"; Harry S. Truman's "Address to Congress."

III. Political Campaign Speeches: F. D. Roosevelt's "Keeping Political Faith"; Thomas E. Dewey's "Governmental Integrity."

IV. Nominating Speeches: Quentin Reynolds' "The Campaign and Men In Uniform."

V. Eulogies: Archibald MacLeish's "Tribute to Wendell Willkie"; Bernard Sheil and Hilmar R. Baukhage's "Tributes to Roosevelt"; Winston Churchill's "Humanity's Loss."

VI. Inaugural Speeches: F. D. Roosevelt's "Fourth Inaugural Address."

VII. Anniversary Speeches: H. W. Prentis', "Competitive Enterprise vs. Planned Economy."

VIII. Committee Hearings: Henry A. Wallace's "Charter for Postwar Prosperity."

IX. Community Forum Speeches: Harold E. Stassen's "American World Policy for Peace and Progress."

X. Dinner Speeches: Eric A. Johnston's "Intolerance."

XI. Speeches of Welcome or Reply: Edward Stettinius' "United Nations Security"; Anthony Eden's "A Job to Be Done."

XII. Professional Lectures: Andrew Weaver's "The Challenge of the Crisis"; Harlow Shapley's "A Design for Fighting"; Alexander J. Stoddard's "Education and the People's Peace."

XIII. Professional Conference Speeches: E. J. King's "American Postwar Seapower" Dwight Eisenhower's "The Quality of America's Fighting Men."

XIV. Commencement Speeches: Nicholas Murray Butler's "The Responsibility of Youth."

XV. Radio Talks: William Hocking, Robert Hutchins, Reinhold Niebuhr and Robert Redfield's "The Crisis of Our Time."

XVI. Sermons or Speeches before Religious Groups: John D. Rockefeller's "The Christian Church—What of Its Future?"; Benjamin E. Mays' "The Inescapable Christ"; Bernard Iddings Bell's "Not Taps but Reveille."

These divisions, to be sure, overlap. Most of these talks, for example, could be classified as "radio speeches." The grouping given above is nevertheless advisable and should assist in the analysis of a speech. The introductory notes to the various speeches of this volume give the setting in each case.

THE SPEECH, ITS CONTENT AND FORM

The background of the speech, the audience, and the occasion explain the speech itself—its ideas, forms of support or "proofs," structure, and language.

Ideas. The important address has originality and significance of ideas. It reveals important social and political principles. Its impact upon the problems of the hour may be decisive. The speaker may reveal the character of our national thinking. Thus the addresses of this volume are grouped according to their content. Important subjects were those concerned with the closing days of the European war. Other speeches deal with international government (Dumbarton Oaks proposals and San Francisco deliberations). An increasing amount of hard thinking and speaking channeled in the direction of the endless economic and social problems that loomed up for postwar America. Still another topic that Americans talked about or listened to until November 1944, was the comparative merit of Democratic vs. Republican parties. One subject supplanted all other themes for four days and produced a series of splendid eulogies (a type of speaking of comparative minor import in the preceding years covered by this series of speeches), as America mourned for its lost President.

Forms of Proof. The critic of the speech should examine the concrete details by which the speaker supports and illumines his main ideas. Every speaker weaves a fabric of encompassing material (to change the figure) that gives color, interest, immediate intelligibility, and logical clarity to the central ideas. These amplifying particulars include authorities, statistics, general illustrations, hypothetical or actual cases, events, anecdotes, circumstantial items, figurative or literal analogies or comparisons, definitions, restatements, cause-to-effect chains of reasoning.

The completeness and consistency with which these materials are introduced, their copiousness, their validity as straight thinking, their acceptability to an audience, partly determine the worth of the speech. These details are both "explicit," those that directly enforce the logic, and "implicit," those that enhance the emotional effect. Appeals to patriotism, self-preservation, gratitude, reverence, fear, and similar motives are of the latter sort as contrasted with the more obvious explanatory and argumentative supports.

Organization. Every good speech has organic structure. The successive ideas may be deductively (with propositions preceding details) announced or inductively unfolded. In either case, at the end the auditor should visualize a unified, coherent pattern of the whole discourse.

Language. Since ideas and their accompanying argumentative, explanatory, and persuasive details communicate themselves through language, the vocabulary of the speaker is one index of effectiveness. At their worst words may remain so much "blah-blah," or may create logical pitfalls in which both speaker and audience, sometimes unconscious of the semantic difficulties, flounder. At their best the speaker's phrases open delightful avenues to conviction through the originality, dignity, and even beauty of oral expression. Such power of language characterizes the addresses of Lincoln, Woodrow Wilson, and Winston Churchill.

THE SPEECH AND THE SPEAKER

Finally, the critic looks at the speaker himself, his delivery and his personality.

His voice, enunciation, pronunciation, and bodily action should meet a standard of adequacy. Vocal pitch should be varied, neither unduly high nor low. Rate of utterance should be suited to the theme of the speech and the audience—without undue acceleration or retardation. Loudness (intensity) should be adjusted to the group. Variation in inflection, the use of pauses, and other marks of the "lively sense of communication" should be present. Articulation and pronunciation should meet a satisfactory standard. Tones should be resonant, rich, even beautiful, without undue nasality, flatness, harshness. The speaker's posture, gestures, facial expressions, and bodily movements should be unstudied but appropriate as interpreters of the theme to the audience. Such are the elements of acceptable delivery.

Back of these physiological attributes of good speaking, however, is the personality of the orator, his intellectual power, his emotional equipment and control. What of his humor, sincerity, tact, his conviction, moral persuasiveness? These traits of personal and social adjustment furnish a key to the speaker's ability to dominate audiences and win their repeated approval. Critics, then, should attend carefully to these attributes of the talker.

Rarely does a superior speaker possess all of these traits in high degree. Some orators are excellent in voice but poor in bodily control. Some nervously pace the platform. Others wave their arms without cessation. Some tighten their throats and vocalize harshly. Still others cultivate voice and gesture until artificiality results. Some inflect and pronounce as Southerners, or Midwesterners, or New Englanders. All of the "representative" speakers, however, have repeatedly confronted audiences of various types and have secured notable responses. Each author selected for this volume has a record of repeated achievement on the platform. The critic charts the strong and weak features of the individual delivery, but views these vocal skills and limitations in relation to the strength of the content, including the details of proof, organization, and composition.

EFFECT OF THE SPEECH

Speeches, we may conclude, are gauged according to a combination of these factors of audience, occasion, speech, and speaker. Our judgment of the speech is based on the interplay of these constituents. In the case of one speaker, delivery may count heavily; in another, ideas; in a third, language and audience adaptation. But none of these essentials may be ignored. The speech critic should note their fusion into the total performance. His evaluation, therefore, must reckon with this totality of effect.

Speeches, in the last analysis, emerge from audiences and are to be judged by the audience reaction. Intrinsically the speech and speaker may pass muster with a speech teacher, or student of English composition or logic. The basic question, however, is, Has the speaker stimulated the audience to think or act? How shall we measure the effect of a speech? Shall we do so by noting the applause? By shift-of-opinion ratings? By polling? By the decision of a jury? Size of the radio mail? By headlines? By the number of the preacher's converts? The amount of money donated after the appeal? By November elections? These criteria of response are all pertinent. They are not wholly reliable as tests of effectiveness. Historical and logical techniques must supplement these enumerative approaches. The historian-logician weighs the testimony and views the impact of speaker both upon the immediate visible audience and upon the wider movements of history. His judgments and conclusions are, at best, tentative.

Each orator in this volume had thousands, in some cases millions, of followers. Whatever he said publicly became news. He was literally the voice of many—of the Senate, of the Government, of the Republicans, of industrialists, of the C.I.O., of the secondary school educators, of college presidents, of the United States Armed Forces, of the Negroes of America. Speech-making rises or falls largely by the behavior of the immediate audience, but the evaluative process is complete only as the impress of great speakers on history is traced.

The compiler of these speeches disavows sponsorship for the views of these orators. This book is a collection of representative speeches and not a document aimed to promote a given political or social philosophy.

ACKNOWLEDGEMENT

The editor of this collection is heavily indebted to the various authors of these speeches, for permission to use and reprint their addresses, and to the cooperating publishers and organizations. Specific acknowledgement is made in the footnotes accompanying each speech.

A. CRAIG BAIRD

June 30, 1945

END OF THE EUROPEAN WAR

YALTA CONFERENCE [1]

FRANKLIN D. ROOSEVELT [2]

President Roosevelt gave this address before Congress on Thursday, March 1, 1945, two days after his arrival from the Crimea Conference at Yalta, with Stalin and Churchill.

The "Big Three" met at an "unnamed spot" on the Black Sea in early February 1945, their first meeting since Teheran, in November and December 1943. The aims of the Yalta Conference were to effect agreements for completing the campaign against Germany; to draw plans for political, economic, and other cooperation in the postwar era; and to arrange for a "permanent international organization to maintain peace."

The President's speech was a crucial one in his campaign for postwar world collaboration. Ratification of any international organization depended, of course, on Senate approval. The speaker's problem, then, was to establish rapport between the executive and legislative branches. Under a governmental system that automatically sets up a gap between these branches, Roosevelt attempted to fuse the thinking, understanding, and purpose of the two to the end that world government be accepted by the American people and by the large majority of the Senate.

The Chief Executive, like Churchill before Parliament during the same week, reported as soon as practicable after his return. Roosevelt displayed frankness and high respect for his audience. He spoke informally, often departing from his set manuscript. His seated position in the "well" of the House of Representatives (he entered in a wheelchair) emphasized his effort at intimacy, his attempt to speak from the level of his audience and in close contact with them. His jests on his physical infirmity and the proclivity of the Roosevelts to travel, further created an atmosphere of friendliness and informality. Although the address was broadcast, the speaker talked primarily to those before him and in a low conversational tone. The President sat relaxed, sometimes with hands on the chair arms, sometimes with arms extended across the table, as if at his desk. He frequently tapped the loose-leaf notebook from which he read.

[1] The text was from a transcription by Robert Ray. The text was printed in the *New York Times*, March 2, 1945. The official White House version, as printed in the *Congressional Record* for March 1, 1945, omitted the extempore additions and changes. See *Congressional Record*. 91, No. 39:1652-6 (daily edition) March 1, 1945.

[2] For biographical note see Appendix.

The speech contained a minimum of oratory and fervid appeal, and a maximum of restrained statement of fact and logic. No challenges to his opponents, no appeals for political solidarity were included. By inference he reminded the Senators of their power to make or break any treaty to establish international government.

This report to Congress furnished a striking example of audience adaptation, both in delivery and in composition.[3]

Reaction to the speech was highly favorable—both by the legislative audience and by the millions who listened or read the extensive message. The Republican "loyal opposition" either approved (for example, Senator Wallace White, of Maine) or mildly tempered their criticism (for example, Senator Taft). The address undoubtedly contributed heavily to the consolidation of American public opinion behind the San Francisco conference.

Mr. Vice President, Mr. Speaker and Members of the Congress: I hope that you will pardon me for an unusual posture of sitting down during the presentation of what I want to say, but I know that you will realize it makes it a lot easier for me in not having to carry about ten pounds of steel around on the bottom of my legs and also because of the fact that I have just completed a 14,000-mile trip.

First of all, I want to say that it is good to be home. It has been a long journey and I hope you also will agree that it has been, so far, a fruitful one.

Speaking in all frankness, the question of whether it is entirely fruitful or not lies to a great extent in your hands. For unless you here, in the halls of the American Congress—with the support of the American people—concur in the general conclusions reached in the place called Yalta, and give them your active support, the meeting will not have produced lasting results.

And that is why I have come before you at the earliest hour I could after my return. I want to make a personal report to you, and at the same time to the people of the country. Many months of earnest work are ahead of us all, and I should like to feel that when the last stone is laid on the structure of international peace, it will be an achievement for which all of us in America have worked steadfastly and unselfishly—together.

I am returning from this trip, which took me so far, refreshed and inspired. I was well the entire time. I was not ill for a

[3] See Richard Wilson in the *Des Moines Register*, March 2, 1945.

second until I arrived back in Washington. And I heard all of the humors which occurred in my absence. Yes, I returned from the trip refreshed and inspired—the Roosevelts are not, as you may suspect, averse to travel; we seem to thrive on it.

And far away as I was, I was kept constantly informed of affairs in the United States. The modern miracle of rapid communications has made this world very small; we must always bear in mind that fact when we speak or think of international relations. I received a steady stream of messages from Washington, I might say not only from the executive branch with all its departments, but also from the legislative branch—its two departments. And, except where radio silence was necessary for security purposes, I could continuously send messages any place in the world. And, of course, in a grave emergency we could even have risked the breaking of the security rule.

I come from the Crimean Conference with a firm belief that we have made a good start on the road to a world of peace.

There were two main purposes in this Crimean Conference. The first was to bring defeat to Germany with the greatest possible speed and with the smallest possible loss of Allied men. That purpose is now being carried out in great force. The German army, and the German people, are feeling the ever-increasing might of our fighting men of the Allied armies and every hour gives us added pride in the heroic advance of our troops in Germany, on German soil, toward a meeting with the gallant Red Army.

The second purpose was to continue to build the foundation for an international accord which would bring order and security after the chaos of the war and would give some assurance of lasting peace among the nations of the world. In that goal, toward that goal, a tremendous stride was made.

After Teheran, a little over a year ago, there were long-range military plans laid by the chiefs of staff of the three most powerful nations. Among the civilian leaders at Teheran, however, at that time, there were only exchanges of views and expressions of opinion. No political arrangements were made and none was attempted.

At the Crimean Conference, however, the time had come for getting down to specific cases in the political field. There was on all sides at this conference an enthusiastic effort to reach an agreement. Since the time of Teheran, a year ago, there had developed among all of us a—what shall I call it—a greater facility in negotiating with each other, which augurs well for the peace of the world. We know each other better.

I have never for an instant wavered in my belief that an agreement to insure world peace and security can be reached. There are a number of things that we did at the conference that were definite. For instance, the lapse of time between Teheran and Yalta without conferences of civilian representatives of the three major powers have proved to be too long—fourteen months. During this long period local problems were permitted to become acute in places like Poland and Greece and Italy and Yugoslavia.

Therefore we decided at Yalta that, even if circumstances made it impossible for the heads of the three governments to do it, to meet more often in the future, and to make that sure by arranging that there would be frequent personal contacts for the exchange of views between the Secretaries of State, the Foreign Ministers of these three powers.

We arranged for periodic meetings, at intervals of three or four months. I feel very confident that under this arrangement there will be no recurrence of the incidents which this winter disturbed the friends of world-wide cooperation and collaboration.

When we met at Yalta, in addition to laying our strategic and tactical plans for the complete, final military victory over Germany, there were other problems of vital political consequence.

For instance, there were the problems of occupational control of Germany after victory, the complete destruction of her military power, and the assurance that neither the Nazis nor Prussian militarism could again be revived to threaten the peace and the civilization of the world.

Secondly, again for example, there was the settlement of the few differences which remained among us with respect to the international security organization after the Dumbarton Oaks Conference. As you remember, at that time, I said afterward we had agreed 90 per cent. That's a pretty good percentage. I think the other 10 per cent was ironed out at Yalta.

Thirdly, there were the general political and economic problems common to all of the areas that would be in the future, or which had been, liberated from the Nazi yoke. There are special problems—we over here find it difficult to understand the ramifications of many of these problems in foreign lands. But we are trying to.

Fourth, there were the special problems created by a few instances, such as Poland and Yugoslavia.

Days were spent in discussing these momentous matters. We argued freely and frankly across the table. But at the end, on every point, unanimous agreement was reached. And more important even than the agreement of words, I may say we achieved a unity of thought and a way of getting along together.

Of course we know that it was Hitler's hope—and German war lords,—that we would not agree, that some slight crack might appear in the solid wall of Allied unity, a crack that would give him and his fellow-gangsters one last hope of escaping their just doom. That is the objective for which his propaganda machine has been working for many months.

But Hitler has failed.

Never before have the major Allies been more closely united —not only in the war aims but also in their peace aims. And they are determined to continue to be united—to be united with each other—and with all peace-loving nations—so that the ideal of lasting peace will become a reality.

The Soviet, British and United States Chiefs of Staff held daily meetings with each other, they conferred frequently with Marshal Stalin, with Prime Minister Churchill and with me, on the problem of coordinating the strategic and tactical efforts of the Allied powers. They completed their plans for the final knockout blow to Germany.

At the time of the Teheran Conference the Russian front, for instance, was removed so far from the American and British fronts that, while certain long-range strategic cooperation was possible, there could be no tactical, day-by-day coordination. They were too far apart.

But Russian troops have now crossed Poland, they are fighting on the eastern soil of Germany herself, British and American troops are now on German soil close to the Rhine River in the west. It is a different situation today from what it was fourteen months ago. A closer tactical liaison has become possible—for the first time in Europe—and, in the Crimean Conference, that was something else that was accomplished.

Provision was made for daily exchange of information between the armies under command of General Eisenhower, on the western front, and those armies under the command of the Soviet marshals on that long eastern front, and also with our armies in Italy—without the necessity of going through the Chiefs of Staff in Washington or London, as in the past.

You have seen one result of this exchange of information in the recent bombing by American and English aircraft of points which are directly related to the Russian advance on Berlin.

From now on, American and British heavy bombers will be used—in the day-by-day tactics of the war—and we have begun to realize, I think, that there is all the difference in the world between tactics on the one side and strategy on the other. Day-by-day tactical war, in direct support of the Soviet armies, as well as in the support of our own in the Western Front.

They are now engaged in bombing and strafing in order to hamper the movement of German reserves, German materials, to the Eastern and Western Fronts from other parts of Germany or from Italy.

Arrangements have been made for the most effective distribution of all available material and transportation to the places where they can best be used in the combined war effort—American, British and Russian.

Details of these plans and arrangements are military secrets, of course. But they are going to hasten—this kind of working together is going to hasten—the day of the final collapse of Germany. The Nazis are learning about some of them already, to their sorrow, and I think all three of us at the conference felt that they will learn more about them tomorrow and the next day —and the day after that.

There will be no respite for these attacks. We will not desist for one moment until unconditional surrender. You know I have always felt that common sense prevails in the long run, quiet overnight thinking. I think that's true in Germany, just as much as it is here. The German people, as well as the German soldier, must realize, the sooner, the sooner they give up and surrender, surrender by groups or by individuals, the sooner their present agony will be over. They must realize that only with complete surrender can they begin to re-establish themselves as people whom the world might accept as decent neighbors.

We made it clear again at Yalta, and I now repeat—that unconditional surrender does not mean the destruction or the enslavement of the German people. The Nazi leaders have deliberately withheld that part of the Yalta declaration from the German press and radio. They seek to convince the people of Germany that the Yalta declaration does mean slavery and destruction for them—they are working at it day and night—for that is how the Nazis hope to save their own skins, how to deceive their people into continued and useless resistance.

We did, however, make it clear at the Conference just what unconditional surrender does mean for Germany.

It means the temporary control of Germany by Great Britain, Russia, France and the United States. Each of these nations will occupy and control a separate zone of Germany—and the administration of the four zones will be coordinated—coordinated in Berlin by a control council composed of representatives of the four nations.

Unconditional surrender means something else. It means the end of nazism. It means the end of the Nazi party—and all of its barbaric laws and institutions.

It means the termination of all militaristic influence in public, private and cultural life of Germany.

It means for the Nazi war criminals a punishment that is speedy and just—and severe.

It means the complete disarmament of Germany, the destruction of its militarism, of its military equipment; the end of its production of armament; the dispersal of all armed forces; the permanent dismemberment of the German General Staff, which has so often shattered the peace of the world.

It means that Germany will have to make reparations—reparations in kind for the damage which has been done to the innocent victims of its aggression.

By compelling reparations in kind—in plants, in machinery, in rolling stock and raw materials—we shall avoid the mistake that we and other people—other nations—made after the last war, the demanding of reparations in the form of money, which Germany could never pay.

We do not want the German people to starve, or to become a burden on the rest of the world.

Our objective in handling Germany is simple—it is to secure the peace of the rest of the world, now and in the future. Too much experience has shown that that objective is impossible if Germany is allowed to retain any ability to wage aggressive warfare.

Now these objectives will not hurt German people. On the contrary it will protect them from a repetition of the fate which the General Staff and Kaiserism imposed on them before and which Hitlerism is now imposing upon them again a hundredfold. It will be removing a cancer from the German body politic, which for generations has produced only misery and only pain for the whole world.

During my stay in Yalta I saw the kind of reckless, senseless fury, this terrible destruction, that comes out of German militarism. Yalta, on the Black Sea, had no military significance of any kind. It had no defense.

Before the last war it had been a resort, a resort for people like czars, princes and aristocracy, and their hanger-ons. However, after the war, after the Red Revolution, until the attack on the Soviet Union by Hitler a few years ago, the palaces, the villas of Yalta had been used as a rest and recreation center by the Russian people.

The Nazi officers took these former palaces and villas, took them over for their own use. They are the only reasons that the so-called former palace of the Czar was still habitable when we got there. It had been given, or had thought to have been given, to a German general for his own property and his own use. And when Yalta was so destroyed he kept soldiers there to protect what he thought would become his own nice villa.

It was a useful rest and recreation center for hundreds of thousands of Russian workers, farmers and their families, up to the time it was taken again by the Germans.

The Nazi officers took these places for their own use, and when the Red Army forced the Nazis out of the Crimea, just almost a year ago—last April, I think it was—all the villas were looted by the Nazis, and then nearly all of them were destroyed by bombs placed on the inside. And even the humblest of homes of Yalta were not spared.

There was little left of it except blank walls, ruins, destruction.

Sevastopol, that weather-fortified port, about forty or fifty miles away—there again was a scene of utter destruction—a large city with its great navy yards, its fortifications. I think less than a dozen buildings were left intact in the entire city.

I had read about Warsaw and Lidice and Rotterdam and Coventry—but I saw Sevastopol and Yalta. And I know that there is not room enough on earth for both German militarism and Christian decency.

Of equal importance with the military arrangements at the Crimean Conference were the agreements reached with respect to a general international organization for lasting world peace.

The foundations were laid at Dumbarton Oaks. There was one point, however, on which agreement was not reached. It involved the procedure of voting, of voting in the Security Council. I want to try to make it clear by making it simple. It took me hours and hours to get the thing straight in my own mind at many conferences. At the Crimea Conference the Americans made a proposal on this subject which, after full discussion, I am glad to say, was unanimously adopted by the other two nations.

It is not yet possible to announce the terms of it publicly, but it will be in a short time.

With respect to voting, when the conclusions reached are made known, I think and I hope, that you will find them a fair solution of this complicated and difficult problem. You might almost say it's a legislative problem. They are founded in justice, and will go far to assure international cooperation in the maintenance of peace.

There is going to be held—as you know—after we have straightened that voting matter out, there is going to be held in San Francisco a meeting of all the United Nations of the world, on the 25th of April, next month. There, we all hope, and confidently expect, to execute a definite charter of organization upon which the peace of the world will be preserved and the forces of aggression permanently outlawed.

This time we are not making the mistake of waiting until the end of the war to set up the machinery of peace. This time, as we fight together to win the war finally, we work together to keep it from happening again.

As you know, I have always been a believer in the document called the Constitution of the United States. I spent a good deal of time in educating two other nations of the world in regard to the Constitution of the United States.

The charter has to be, and should be, approved by the Senate of the United States under the Constitution. I think the other nations all know it now—I am aware of that fact, and now all the other nations are, and we hope that the Senate will approve of what is set forth as the Charter of the United Nations, when they all come together in San Francisco, next month.

The Senate of the United States, through its appropriate representatives, has been kept continuously advised of the program of this Government in the creation of the International Security Organization.

The Senate and the House will both be represented at the San Francisco Conference. The Congressional delegates will consist of an equal number, and the Senatorial will consist of an equal number of Republican and Democratic members. The American delegation is—in every sense of the word—bipartisan.

But I think that world peace is not exactly a party question—I think that Republicans want peace just as much as Democrats. It is not a party question any more than is military victory—the winning of the war.

When our republic was threatened, first by the Nazi clutch for world conquest back in 1939 and 1940, and then by the Japanese treachery in 1941, partisanship and politics were laid aside by nearly every American; and every resource was dedicated to our common safety. The same consecration to the cause of peace will be expected, I think, by every patriotic American, by every human soul overseas, too.

The structure of world peace cannot be the work of one man, or one party, or one nation, it cannot be just an American peace, or British peace, or a Russian, or a French or a Chinese peace. It cannot be a peace of large nations—or of small nations. It must be a peace which rests on the cooperative effort of the whole world.

It cannot be what some people think—a structure of complete perfection at first. But it can be a peace, and it will be a peace, based on the sound and just principles of the Atlantic Charter —on the concept of the dignity of the human being—and on the guarantees of tolerance and freedom of religious worship.

As the Allied Armies have marched to military victory, they have liberated peoples whose liberties had been crushed by the Nazis for four long years, whose economy had been reduced to ruins by Nazi despoilers.

There have been instances of political confusion and unrest in these liberated areas—that is not unexpected—as in Greece or in Poland or in Yugoslavia, and maybe more. Worse than that, there actually began to grow in some of these places queer ideas of "spheres of influence" which were incompatible with the basic principles of international collaboration. If allowed to go on unchecked these developments might have had tragic results, in time.

It is fruitless to try to place the blame for this situation on one particular nation or on another. It is the kind of development which is almost inevitable unless the major powers of the world continue without interruption to work together and assume joint responsibility for the solution of problems that may arise to endanger the peace of the world.

We met in the Crimea determined to settle this matter of liberated areas. Things that might happen that we can't see at this moment might happen suddenly, unexpectedly, next week or next month. And I am happy to confirm to the Congress that we did arrive at a settlement—and incidentally, a unanimous settlement.

The three most powerful nations have agreed that the political and economic problems of any area liberated from Nazi conquest, or any former Axis satellite, are a joint responsibility of all three governments. They will join together during the temporary period of instability after hostilities, to help the people of any liberated area, or of any former satellite state, to solve their own problems through firmly established democratic processes.

They will endeavor to see—to see to it that interim governing, and the people who carry on the interim government between occupation by Germany and true independence—that such an interim government will be as representative as possible of all democratic elements in the population, and that free elections are held as soon as possible thereafter.

Responsibility for political conditions thousands of miles away can no longer be avoided, I think, by this great nation. Certainly, I don't want to live to see another war. As I have said, the world is smaller—smaller every year. The United States now exerts a tremendous influence on the cause of peace.

What we people over here are thinking and talking about is in the interest of peace, because it's known all over the world. The slightest remark in either house of the Congress is known all over the world the following day. We will continue to exert that influence only if we are willing to continue to share in the responsibility for keeping the peace. It would be our own tragic loss, I think, if we were to shirk that responsibility.

Final decisions in these areas are going to be made jointly, therefore, and therefore they will often be a result of give-and-take compromise.

The United States will not always have its way 100 per cent, nor will Russia, nor Great Britain. We shall not always have ideal answers, solutions to complicated international problems, even though we are determined continuously to strive toward that ideal. But I am sure that under the agreements reached at Yalta there will be a more stable political Europe than ever before.

Of course, once there has been a true expression out of the people's will in any country, our immediate responsibility ends, with the exception only of such action as may be agreed on by the international security organization we will set up.

The United Nations must also begin to help these liberated areas adequately to reconstruct their economy—I don't want them starving to death—so that they are ready to resume their places in the world. The Nazi war machine has stripped them of raw materials and machine tools, and trucks and locomotives and things like that. They have left the industry of these places stagnant, and much of the agricultural areas are unproductive— the Nazis have left a complete ruin, or a partial ruin, in their wake.

To start the wheels running again is not a mere matter of relief. It is to the national interest that all of us see to it that these liberated areas are again made self-supporting and productive, so that they do not need continuous relief from us. I can say that as an argument based on plain common sense.

One outstanding example of joint action by the three major Allied powers was the solution reached on Poland. The whole Polish question was a potential source of trouble in postwar Europe, as it had been some time before, and we came to the conference determined to find a common ground for its solution, and we did, even though everybody doesn't agree with us, obviously.

Our objective was to help create a strong, independent and prosperous nation. That's the thing we must always remember, those words, agreed to by Russia, by Britain and by me, the objective of making Poland a strong, independent and prosperous nation, with a Government ultimately to be selected by the Polish people themselves.

To achieve that objective it is necessary to provide for the formation of a new government, much more representative than had been possible while Poland was enslaved. Accordingly, steps were taken at Yalta to reorganize the existing provisional government in Poland on a broader democratic basis, so as to include democratic leaders now in Poland and those abroad. This new reorganized government will be recognized by all of us as the temporary government of Poland. Poland needs a temporary government in the worst way. An ad interim government, I think, is another way of putting it.

However, the new Polish provisional government of national unity will be pledged to holding a free election as soon as possible on the basis of universal suffrage and a secret ballot.

Throughout history Poland has been the corridor through which attacks on Russia have been made. Twice in this generation Germany has struck at Russia through this corridor. To insure European security and world peace a strong and independent Poland is necessary to prevent that from happening again.

The decision with respect to the boundaries of Poland was practically a compromise. I didn't agree with all of it by any means, but we didn't go as far as Britain wanted in certain areas, go as far as Russia wanted in certain areas and we didn't go so far as I wanted in certain areas. It was a compromise. The decision was a compromise under which the Poles will receive compensation in territory in the north and west in exchange for what they lose by the Curzon line in the east.

The limits of the western border will be permanently fixed in the final peace conference. We know roughly that it will include in the new strong Poland quite a large slice of what now is called Germany. And it was agreed also that the new Poland will have a large and long coastline and many a new harbor. Also that East Prussia, most of it, will go to Poland and the corner of it will go to Russia. Also (what shall I call it) that the anomaly of the Free State of Danzig, I think Danzig would be a lot better if it were Polish.

It is well known that the people east of the Curzon Line are predominantly White Russian and Ukrainian. They are not Polish, to a very great majority. And the people west of the line are predominantly Polish, except in that part of East Prussia and East Germany which will go to new Poland. As far back as 1919 the representatives of the Allies agreed that the Curzon Line represented a fair boundary between the two peoples. You must remember also there was no Poland before, there had not been any Polish Government, before 1919, for a great many generations.

I am convinced that this agreement on Poland, under the circumstances, is the most hopeful agreement possible for a free, independent and prosperous Polish state.

Now the Crimean conference was a meeting of the three major military powers on whose shoulders rest the chief responsibility and burden of the war. Although, for this reason, another nation was not included—France was not a participant in the conference—no one should detract from the recognition that was accorded there to her role in the future of Europe and the future of the world.

France has been invited to accept (on second thought, this was on my motion), France has been invited to accept a zone of control in Germany, and to participate as a fourth member of the Allied control council of Germany.

She has been invited to join as a sponsor of the international conference at San Francisco next month.

She will be a permanent member of the International Security Council together with the other four major powers.

And, finally, we have asked that she be associated with us in our joint responsibility over the liberated areas of Europe. Of course there are a number of smaller things which I haven't got time to go into on which argument was had. We hope these things will straighten out.

Agreement was reached on Yugoslavia, as announced in the communiqué, and we hope that it is in process of fulfillment. But it is not only there, but in some other places we have to remember there are a great number of prima donnas in the world, who all wish to be heard. Before anything becomes fact, we may have a little delay while we listen to more prima donnas.

Quite naturally, this conference concerned itself only with the European war and with the political problems of Europe, and not with the Pacific war.

In Malta, however, our combined British and American staffs made their plans to increase the attack against Japan.

The Japanese war lords know that they are not being overlooked. They have felt the force of our B-29's, and our carrier planes. They have felt the naval might of the United States, and do not appear very anxious to come out and try it again.

The Japs now know what it means to hear that "The United States Marines have landed." And I think I can add, having Iwo Jima in mind, that "the situation is well in hand."

They also know what is in store for the homeland of Japan now that General MacArthur has completed his magnificent march back to Manila, and that Admiral Nimitz is establishing his air bases right in their own back yard.

But, lest somebody else lay off work in the United States, I can repeat what I have said, a short sentence, even in my sleep, "We haven't won the wars yet," with an "s" on wars.

It is a long tough road to Tokyo. It is longer to go to Tokyo than it is to Berlin, in every sense of the word.

The defeat of Germany will not mean the end of the war against Japan. On the contrary, we must be prepared for a long and costly struggle in the Pacific. But the unconditional surrender of Japan is as essential as the defeat of Germany. I say that advisedly, with the thought in mind that that is especially true if our plans for world peace are to succeed. For Japanese militarism must be wiped out as thoroughly as German militarism.

On the way back from the Crimea I made arrangements to meet personally King Farouk of Egypt, Haile Selassie, the Emperor of Ethiopia, and King Ibn Saud of Saudi Arabia. Our conversations had to do with matters of common interest. They will be of great mutual advantage because they gave me and a good many of us an opportunity of meeting and talking face to face, and of exchanging views in personal conversation instead of formal correspondence.

Of the problems of Arabia, I learned more about that whole problem, the Moslem problem, the Jewish problem, by talking with Ibn Saud for five minutes than I could have learned in exchange of two or three dozen letters.

On my voyage, I had the benefit of seeing the Army and Navy and Air Force at work.

All Americans, I think, would feel proud, as proud of our armed forces as I am, if they could see and hear what I did.

Against the most efficient professional leaders, sailors and airmen of all history, our men stood and fought and won.

I think that this is our chance to see to it that the sons and grandsons of these gallant fighting men do not have to do it all over again in a few years.

The conference in the Crimea was a turning point, I hope, in our history, and therefore in the history of the world. It will soon be presented to the Senate and the American people, a great decision that will determine the fate of the United States, and I think therefore of the world, for generations to come.

There can be no middle ground here. We shall have to take the responsibility for world collaboration, or we shall have to bear the responsibility for another world conflict.

I know that the word "planning" is not looked upon with favor in some circles. In domestic affairs, tragic mistakes have been made by reason of lack of planning, and, on the other hand, many great improvements in living, and many benefits to the human race, have been accomplished as a result of adequate, intelligent planning—reclamations of desert areas, developments of whole river valleys, provision for adequate housing, and a dozen different topics.

The same will be true in relations between nations. For the second time in the lives of most of us, this generation is face to face with the objective of preventing wars. To meet that objective, the nations of the world will either have a plan or they will not. The groundwork of a plan has now been furnished, and has been submitted to humanity for discussion and decision.

No plan is perfect. Whatever is adopted at San Francisco will doubtless have to be amended time and again over the years, just as our own Constitution has been.

No one can say exactly how long any plan will last. Peace can endure only so long as humanity really insists upon it and is willing to work for it and sacrifice for it.

Twenty-five years ago American fighting men looked to the statesmen of the world to finish the work of peace for which they fought and suffered. We failed them then. We cannot fail them again, and expect the world to survive again.

I think the Crimean conference was a successful effort by the three leading nations to find a common ground of peace. It spells, it ought to spell, the end of the system of unilateral action and exclusive alliances and spheres of influence and balances of power and all the other expedients that have been tried for centuries, and have always failed.

We propose to substitute for all these a universal organization in which all peace-loving nations will finally have a chance to join.

And I am confident that the Congress and the American people will accept the results of this conference as the beginning of a permanent structure of peace upon which we can begin to build, under God, that better world in which our children and grandchildren, yours and mine, the children and grandchildren of the whole world, must live and can live.

And that, my friends, is the only message I can give you, but I feel very deeply, and I know that all of you are feeling it today and are going to feel it in the future.

V-E DAY PROCLAMATION [4]

HARRY S. TRUMAN [5]

Grand Admiral Doenitz, in charge of all German military forces, surrendered unconditionally to the Allies, in a little red schoolhouse, at Reims, France, at 8:41 P.M., Eastern War Time, on May 6th, 1945. The end of the war in Europe was officially announced at 9 A.M. Eastern War Time, May 8th, by President Harry S. Truman, in a broadcast from the oval room, of the Executive Mansion. Previous to his broadcast, he read to the press the address and proclamation; he interpolated comment.

Prime Minister Winston Churchill followed immediately on the air. Marshall Stalin postponed his announcement until the afternoon of May 8th after a second surrender ceremony had been carried out in Berlin.

Throughout that day America and Great Britain gave thanks and celebrated. Russia observed the following day. Large enemy forces in Czechoslovakia and scattered units elsewhere continued to resist. But the organized war was formally ended after five years and eight months of enormous destruction and bloodshed, dating from Germany's invasion of Poland on September 1, 1939.[6]

Edward Kennedy, of the Associated Press, announced the surrender before the official authorization, and received wide condemnation.

President Truman's address was probably heard by more American listeners than any other broadcast in the history of radio. According to C. E. Hooper, a radio polling expert, the address had a record high of 64.1, which meant that at least "36,500,000 adults" in this country heard the President. The previous high, according to Hooper, was a rating of 59.6, given to President Roosevelt's speech on December 8, 1941 when, addressing a joint session of Congress, he called for a declaration of war against Japan.[7]

To radio listeners the President's V-E Day speech may have sounded somewhat perfunctory. The references to rejoicing over peace, our debt to the dead, and gratitude to God (referred to five times) were what the listeners would expect. The "speech behind the speech," however, had strong implications not to be missed. The President's own interpretation, in his preliminary reading and comments to two hundred newsmen in his office, reinforced the speech and the accompanying proclamation.

[4] Recorded by the editor of this volume and by Robert Ray, from the broadcast. For text see also *Congressional Record,* Vol. 9, No. 92, p. 44-5, May 10, 1945 (daily edition).

[5] For biographical note see Appendix.

[6] See *Representative American Speeches: 1939-40,* p. 21 ff.

[7] See *Representative American Speeches: 1941-42,* p. 15 ff.

This is a solemn but a glorious hour. I only wish that Franklin D. Roosevelt had lived to witness this day. General Eisenhower informs me that the forces of Germany have surrendered to the United Nations. The flags of freedom fly all over Europe.

For this victory we join in offering our thanks to the Providence which has guided and sustained us through the dark days of adversity.

Our rejoicing is sobered and subdued by a supreme consciousness of the terrible price we have paid to rid the world of Hitler and his evil band. Let us not forget, my fellow-Americans, the sorrow and the heartache which today abide in the homes of so many of our neighbors—neighbors whose most priceless possession has been rendered as a sacrifice to redeem our liberty.

We can repay the debt which we owe to our God, to our dead and to our children only by work—by ceaseless devotion to the responsibilities which lie ahead of us. If I could give you a single watchword for the coming months that word is—work, work, and more work.

We must work to finish the war. Our victory is but half won. The West is free, but the East is still in bondage to the treacherous tyranny of the Japanese. When the last Japanese division has surrendered unconditionally, then only will our fighting job be done.

We must work to bind up the wounds of a suffering world—to build an abiding peace, a peace rooted in justice and in law. We can build such a peace only by hard, toilsome, painstaking work—by understanding and working with our allies in peace as we have in war.

The job ahead is no less important, no less urgent, no less difficult than the task which now happily is done.

I call upon every American to stick to his post until the last battle is won. Until that day, let no man abandon his post or slacken his effort.

And now, I want to read to you my formal proclamation of this occasion:

BY THE PRESIDENT OF THE UNITED STATES OF AMERICA

A PROCLAMATION

The Allied armies, through sacrifice and devotion and with God's help, have won from Germany a final and unconditional surrender. The western world has been freed of the evil forces which for five years and longer have imprisoned the bodies and broken the lives of millions upon millions of free-born men. They have violated their churches, destroyed their homes, corrupted their children, and murdered their loved ones. Our armies of liberation have restored freedom to these suffering peoples, whose spirit and will the oppressors could never enslave.

Much remains to be done. The victory won in the west must now be won in the east. The whole world must be cleansed of the evil from which half the world has been freed. United, the peace-loving nations have demonstrated in the west that their arms are stronger by far than the might of dictators or the tyranny of military cliques that once called us soft and weak. The power of our peoples to defend themselves against all enemies will be proved in the Pacific war as it has been proved in Europe.

For the triumph of spirit and of arms which we have won, and for its promise to the peoples everywhere who join us in the love of freedom, it is fitting that we, as a nation, give thanks to Almighty God, who has strengthened us and given us the victory.

Now, therefore, I, Harry S. Truman, president of the United States of America, do hereby appoint Sunday, May 13, 1945, to be a day of prayer.

I call upon the people of the United States, whatever their faith, to unite in offering joyful thanks to God for the victory we have won and to pray that He will support us to the end of our present struggle and guide us into the way of peace.

I also call upon my countrymen to dedicate this day of prayer to the memory of those who have given their lives to make possible our victory.

In witness whereof, I have hereunto set my hand and caused the seal of the United States of America to be affixed.

HARRY S. TRUMAN.

GERMANY SURRENDERS [8]

WINSTON CHURCHILL [9]

Mr. Churchill, in his radio proclamation, spoke in quiet, firm tones, increasing the intensity only with his final, "Advance Brittannia! Long live the cause of freedom! God save the King!" The Prime Minister, following his radio talk, addressed a joyful House of Commons and then the multitudes in Whitehall. In the evening King George also addressed the British Commonwealth and the world; his excellent address was also heard by millions in America.

Yesterday morning at 2.41 A. M. at General Eisenhower's headquarters General Jodl, the representative of the German High Command and of Grand Admiral Doenitz, the designated head of the German State, signed the act of unconditional surrender of all German land, sea and air forces to the Allied Expeditionary Force and simultaneously to the Soviet High Command.

General Bedell Smith, Chief of Staff of the United States Army, and General François Sevez signed the document on behalf of the Supreme Commander of the Allied Expeditionary Force and General Susloparoff signed on behalf of the Russian High Command.

Today this agreement will be ratified and confirmed at Berlin where Air Chief Marshal Tedder, Deputy Supreme Commander of the Allied Expeditionary Force, and General de Lattre Tassigny will sign on behalf of General Eisenhower and General Zhukoff will sign on behalf of the Soviet High Command.

The German representatives will be Field Marshal Keitel, Chief of the High Command, and the Commander in Chief of the German Army, Navy and Air Forces.

Hostilities will end officially at one minute after midnight tonight, Tuesday, the 8th of May.

[8] Recorded by Robert Ray, of the Speech Department, State University of Iowa.
[9] For biographical note see Appendix.

But in the interest of saving lives, the cease fire began yesterday to be sounded all along the front and our dear Channel islands are also to be freed today.

The Germans are still in places resisting the Russian troops, but should they continue to do so after midnight they will, of course, deprive themselves of the protection of the laws of war and will be attacked from all quarters by the Allied troops.

It is not surprising that on such long fronts and in the existing disorder of the enemy, the commands of the German High Command could not in every case have been obeyed immediately. This does not, in our opinion, with the military advice at our disposal, constitute any reason for withholding from the nation the facts communicated to us by General Eisenhower of the unconditional surrender already signed at Reims nor could it prevent us from celebrating today and tomorrow, Wednesday, as Victory in Europe Day. Today, perhaps, we shall think mostly of ourselves. Tomorrow we shall pay a particular tribute to our heroic Russian comrades whose prowess in the field has been one of the grand contributions to the general victory.

The German war is therefore at an end.

After years of intense preparations, Germany hurled herself on Poland at the beginning of September, 1939, and in pursuance of our guarantee to Poland and, in common with the French Republic, Great Britain, the British Empire and Commonwealth of Nations declared war upon this foul aggressor.

After gallant France had been struck down, we from this island and from our united empire maintained the struggle single-handed for a whole year until we were joined by the military might of Soviet Russia and later by the overwhelming power and resources of the United States of America.

Finally almost the whole world was combined against the evil doers who are now prostrate before us. Our gratitude to all our splendid allies goes forth from all our hearts in the island and throughout the British Empire.

We may allow ourselves a brief period of rejoicing, but let us not forget for a moment the toils and efforts that lie ahead.

Japan, with all her treachery and greed, remains unsubdued. The injuries she has inflicted upon Great Britain, the United

States and other countries and her detestable cruelties call for justice and retribution.

We must now devote all our strength and resources to the completion of our task both at home and abroad.

Advance Britannia! Long live the cause of freedom! God save the King.

AMERICA AND INTERNATIONAL COLLABORATION

AMERICAN FOREIGN POLICY [1]

Arthur H. Vandenberg [2]

Senator Vandenberg debated the issue of foreign policy before the Senate on January 10, 1945. The argument was evidently timed and designed to support President Roosevelt's address to Congress four days before, in which the President argued that the United Nations should be organized effectively this year to promote and protect peace. The President revealed his fear of the Senate's deep-seated tendency to avoid international commitments.

The Michigan Senator spoke boldly and directly for an alliance with our allies to guarantee against World War III. Mr. Vandenburg thus repudiated his isolationist voting record, and with utmost candor declared that no nation "can immunize itself by exclusive action." Furthermore, the Senator proposed not only an immediate alliance to present overwhelming military might against a German or Japanese outbreak, but one that would operate militarily without Congressional action.

Such courageous utterance was an astonishing reversal of dominant Republican sentiment since 1919. Coming from a spokesman of the Republican "middle of the road" bloc, proclaimed just before the historic Stalin-Churchill-Roosevelt meeting of February 1945, the address probably marked the permanent collapse of isolationism as a basic American policy. With such Republican underwriting of an "alliance," the passage of an appropriate treaty of collaboration by the Senate was reasonably well assured.

Senator Vandenberg spoke with his usual vocal impressiveness. He has an excellent voice, inclines to an oratorical pattern, but controls well his intensity, rate, and pitch. His gestures are numerous but emphatic and appropriate. He ranks in the upper group of effective Senate speakers.

The address was restrained in its argumentative approach. Only after the Senator had carefully reasoned the need for constructive action did he expound his startling program. He frequently quoted with approval the President's address. His criticism of the recent eclipse of the

---

[1] Reprinted from the *Congressional Record*, Vol. 91, No. 6, p. 169-73, January 10, 1945 (daily edition), proceedings and debates of the 79th Congress, first session.

[2] For biographical note see Appendix.

Atlantic charter was moderate and persuasive. Dramatic here and there was the phrasing, but typical of the Senator's oral style.[3] Emotional proofs accompanied every logical argument, appeals to self-interest, co-operation, need for immediate action, precedent, fear, justice, patriotism, duty, respect for official leaders (e.g., Roosevelt, Churchill).

Appointed as two of the American delegates to the San Francisco conference were Senators Connally and Vandenburg. After Senator Connally gave an impressive farewell address to the Senate on April 20, 1945, Mr. Vandenburg followed.

"Mr. President, I am glad to join in the sturdy statement made by my distinguished colleague from Texas," he said. "In taking temporary leave of my dear friends in the Senate this afternoon, I do so with a sense of deepest dedication to a supreme cause. No cause could be greater than the hopes and aspirations of human souls everywhere for permanent peace with justice in a free world of free men.

"I have no illusions that the San Francisco Conference can chart the millennium. Please do not expect it of us. I have no illusions that we can bring back to you a treaty which will be free of all the frictions that our widely differing personal convictions inevitably invite.

"But, Mr. President, I have faith that we may perfect this charter of peace and justice so that reasonable men of good-will shall find in it so much good, so much emancipation for human hopes, that all lesser doubts and disagreements may be resolved in its favor.

"As did the distinguished and able Senator from Texas, I pledge you my total efforts in this unreserved and indispensable direction; and once more I am asking that your prayers for this great enterprise shall fail neither it nor us.

"Mr. President, we go to San Francisco and the Golden Gate. I hope there is significance and prophecy in the latter phrase. I hope we may justify the bitter sacrifices of our soldier sons, and justify the deepest aspirations of America and United Nations by opening the Golden Gate upon a better, a happier, and a safer world."

The Senators rose and applauded.

Mr. President, I shall detain the Senate less than thirty minutes. I desire to speak about some phases of foreign policy. Because of the solemnity of the subject itself I ask the indulgence of my colleagues that I be permitted at least to make my preliminary statement without interruption.

Mr. President, there are critical moments in the life of every nation which call for the straightest, the plainest, and the most courageous thinking of which we are capable. We confront such a moment now. It is not only desperately important to

[3] See the "Memorial Day Address," *Representative American Speeches*: 1937-38, p. 39-44.

America. It is important to the world. It is important not only to this generation which lives in blood. It is important to future generations if they shall live in peace.

No man in his right senses will be dogmatic in his viewpoint at such an hour. A global conflict which uproots the earth is not calculated to submit itself to the dominion of any finite mind. The clashes of rival foreign interests, which have motivated wars for countless centuries, are not likely suddenly to surrender to some simple man-made formula, no matter how nobly meditated. Each of us can only speak according to his little light—and pray for a composite wisdom that shall lead us to high, safe ground. It is only in this spirit of anxious humility that I speak today. Politics, in any such connection, would be as obnoxious at home as they are in manipulations abroad.

Mr. President, we still have two major wars to win. I said "We." That does not mean America alone. It means the continued and total battle fraternity of the United Nations. It must mean one for all and all for one; and it will mean this, unless somewhere in this grand alliance the stupid and sinister folly of ulterior ambitions shall invite the enemy to postpone our victory through our own rivalries and our own confusion. The United Nations, in even greater unity of military action than heretofore, must never, for any cause, permit this military unity to fall apart. If it does, we shall count the cost in mortal anguish, even though we stumble on to a belated, though inevitable victory. And, getting down to what Mr. Churchill would call the bare bones of the matter, this is an obligation which rests no less upon our allies than upon us, and no less upon us than upon our allies. First things must come first. History will not deal lightly with any who undermine this aim ere it is achieved. Destiny will one day balance any such ghastly accounts.

We not only have two wars to win, we also have yet to achieve such a peace as will justify this appalling cost. Here again an even more difficult unity is indispensable. Otherwise we shall look back upon a futile, sanquinary shambles and—God save the mark—we shall be able to look forward only to the curse of World War No. 3.

Unfortunately, Mr. President, the morale of unity in war is often threatened by sharply clashing and often disillusioning disclosures which threaten this unity in peace. The two considerations cannot be disassociated. President Roosevelt correctly said in his annual message that "the nearer we come to vanquishing our enemies the more we become inevitably conscious of differences among the victors." He also correctly said that "nations like individuals do not always see alike or think alike, and international cooperation and progress are not helped by any nation assuming that it has a monopoly of wisdom or of virtue." That applies to us. It applies to each of our allies. But when "differences among the victors"—to use the White House phrase —when "differences among the victors," before they have clinched their victory, threaten both the victory and the peace, the hour cannot much longer be postponed when any such trends shall be reversed. We shall not reverse them by our silence upon the issues that are clearly involved; nor, and I say it with great respect, shall we reverse them merely by a generalized restatement of the high aspirations revoiced in the recent Presidential message. Certainly we shall not reverse them by a snarling process of international recrimination in which every United Nation's capital tries to outdo the other in bitter back talk about the infirmities of each. Such bickering is dangerous—over there or over here. It is water on the Axis wheel. Again I agree whole-heartedly with President Roosevelt when he says:

We must not let such differences divide us and blind us to our more important common and continuing interests in winning the war and building the peace.

On the other hand, I hold the deep belief that honest candor, devoid of prejudice or ire, is our greatest hope and our greatest necessity; and that the Government of the United States, above all others, is called at long last to exercise this honest candor not only with its allies but also with its own faithful people.

I hesitate, even now, to say these things, Mr. President, because a great American illusion seems to have been built up— wittingly or otherwise—that we, in the United States, dare not publicly discuss these subjects lest we contribute to international dissension and thus encourage the very thing we all need to cure. But I frankly confess that I do not know why we must be the only silent partner in this grand alliance. There seems to be no fear of disunity, no hesitation in Moscow, when Moscow wants to assert unilateral war and peace aims which collide with ours. There seems to be no fear of disunity, no hesitation in London, when Mr. Churchill proceeds upon his unilateral way to make decisions often repugnant to our ideas and our ideals. Perhaps our allies will plead that their actions are not unilateral; that our President, as Bevin said, has initialed this or that at one of the famous Big Three conferences; that our President, as Churchill said, has been kept constantly "aware of everything that has happened"; in other words, that by our silence we have acquiesced. But that hypothesis would only make a bad matter worse. It would be the final indictment of our silence—the final obituary for open covenants. We, of course, accept no conception that our contribution to unity must be silence, while others say and do what they please, and that our only role in this global tragedy is to fight and die and pay, and that unity for us shall only be the unity which Jonah enjoyed when he was swallowed by the whale.

I hasten to say that any such intolerable conception would be angrily repudiated by every American—from the President down to the last citizen among us. It has not been and is not true. Yet it cannot be denied that our government has not spoken out—to our own people or to our allies—in any such specific fashion as have the others. It cannot be denied, as a result, that too often a grave melancholy settles upon some sectors of our people. It cannot be denied that citizens, in increasing numbers are crying: "What are we fighting for?" It cannnot be denied that our silence—at lease our public and official silence—has multiplied confusion at home and abroad. It cannot be denied that this confusion threatens our unity—yes, Mr. President, and already hangs like a cloud over Dumbarton Oaks. So I venture to repeat, with all the earnestness at my command, that a new rule of honest candor in Washington—as a substitute for mystifying silence or for classical generalities—honest candor on the high plane of great ideals—is the greatest contribution we can make to the realities of unity at this moment when enlightened civilization is our common stake.

Let us not mistake the meaning of unity. Unity does not require universal and peremptory agreement about everything. It does not demand a meeting of all minds now in respect to all the minutiae of a postwar world which will take years to stabilize. The President is wholly right in pleading for tolerance upon this score and to warn that we must not expect what he calls perfectionism overnight. Here in the Senate we do not have perpetual agreement between two sides of the aisle, but we have never failed to have basic unity when crisis calls. The unity I discuss is the over-all tie which must continue to bind the United Nations together in respect to paramount fundamentals. We had it once in the original spirit of the Atlantic Charter, and we must get it back again before it is too late.

When Mr. Churchill spoke in the British Parliament last December 15, defending his own current course in Greece and Mr. Stalin's proposed partition of Poland, he said:

There is no doubt that when the time comes the United States will make its own pronouncement upon these matters, bearing in mind, as it will, the practical aspects which these matters assume and also how much failure on the part of the three greatest powers to work together would damage all our hopes for the future structure of a world government which, whatever else it might fail to do, will at any rate be equipped with all powers necessary to prevent outbreak of future war.

I do not like one of the implications in this quotation. It seems to say that unless we acquiesce in these self-serving unilateral arrangements now being made by great European powers, we shall be the scapegoats to be made responsible for the next war. I would respond categorically to any such abortive thesis by saying that, regardless of the future structure of a world government, an unjust peace, built upon the age-old frictions of international power politics, is the most fatal of all threats which our hopes for the future can possibly confront. But that is not the reason I use the quotation at this point. Of even greater importance is the other implication—namely, that the United States has not spoken; that her official attitude is not dependably recorded; and that, until she does speak, the world cannot find its bearings.

There is no doubt—says Mr. Churchill—that when the time comes the United States will make its own pronouncement.

When the time comes! Mr. President, is the time not here right now?

If it is, Mr. President, what shall we say that we have not already said in the Connally resolution in the Senate and the Fulbright resolution in the House and in the Presidential utterances?

It seems to me, Mr. President, that the first thing we must say, beyond misunderstanding, is that we have not altered our original commitments; that we have not lowered our sights; that we have not diluted our dedications; that we are not fighting to pull ancient chestnuts out of alien fires; that the smell of victory is not an anaesthetic which puts our earlier zeals to sleep. We still propose to win this war, come what may. We are fighting to defend America. We still propose to help create the postwar world on a basis which shall stop aggressors for keeps and, so far as humanly possible, substitute justice for force among free men. We propose to do it primarily for our own sake. We still propose also, to substitute justice for force—if we can—in writing the peace which terminates this war when we deal with the victims of Axis tyranny. That is the road to permanent peace. We still propose that none of the United Nations shall seek aggrandizement, territorial, or otherwise—though conceding that all change is not necessarily aggrandizement. We still propose, outside the Axis, that there shall be no territorial changes which do not accord with the freely expressed wishes of the people concerned. Similarly we still propose to respect the right of all peoples to choose the form of government under which they will live. We still propose to see sovereign rights and self-government restored to those who have been forcibly deprived of them, if it lies within our power.

In a word, Mr. President, it seems to me that the first thing we must do is to reassert, in high places, our American faith in these particular elemental objectives of the so-called Atlantic Charter, which was officially issued as a signed document by the State Department on August 14, 1941; which was officially communicated to the Congress as a signed document by the Presi-

dent of the United States in his message of August 21,1941;
which was embodied in a joint resolution of all the United
Nations on January 1, 1942; which was commemorated by the
President on August 14, 1943 in a proclamation on the second
anniversary of its "signing"—his word—which had a tragic sink-
ing spell when its formal authenticity was amazingly depreciated
in a White House press conference a fortnight ago, but which
the President re-embraced in his message of January 6, 1945.

I am sure the President did not anticipate the shocking results of his recent almost jocular, and even cynical, dismissal of
the Atlantic Charter as a mere collection of fragmentary notes. It
jarred America to its very hearthstones. It seemed to make a
mere pretense out of what has been an inspiringly accepted fact.
It seemed almost to sanction alien contempt. It seemed
to suggest that we have put too much emphasis upon a fighting creed which did not deserve the solemnity which we
have been taught to ascribe to it. Coming at a particularly critical moment when these pledges seemed to be at least partially
paralyzed in Moscow—and when even Mr. Churchill's memory
about the charter was proving to be admittedly fickle—the President's statement was utterly devastating in its impact. He has
since sought to repair this damage. I hope he has succeeded.
With justification he reminds us in his annual message that there
are no rules of easy application—of the charter—to each and
every one of this war-torn world's tangled situations. He now
says correctly and bravely, "We shall not hesitate to use our
influence—and use it now—to secure so far as is humanly possible the fulfillment of these principles." That is the indispensable point. These basic pledges cannot now be dismissed as
a mere nautical nimbus. They march with our armies. They
sail with our fleets. They fly with our eagles. They sleep with
our martyred dead. The first requisite of honest candor, Mr.
President, I respectfully suggest, is to relight this torch.

The next thing we need to do, Mr. President, if I may be so
bold, in this spirit of honest candor, is to appeal to our allies,
in the name of reason, to frankly face the postwar alternatives
which are available to them and to us as a means to preserve tomorrow's peace for them and for us. There are two ways to

do it. One way is by exclusive individual action in which each of us tries to look out for himself. The other way is by joint action in which we undertake to look out for each other. The first way is the old way which has twice taken us to Europe's interminable battlefields within a quarter century. The second way is the new way in which our present fraternity of war becomes a new fraternity of peace. I do not believe that either we or our allies can have it both ways. They serve to cancel out each other. We cannot tolerate unilateral privilege in a multilateral peace. Yet, that seems to be the fatalistic trend today. I think we must make our choice. I think we must make it wholly plain to our major allies that they, too, must make their choice.

I hasten to make my own personal viewpoint clear. I have always been frankly one of those who has believed in our own self-reliance. I still believe that we can never again—regardless of collaborations—allow our national defense to deteriorate to anything like a point of impotence. But I do not believe that any nation hereafter can immunize itself by its own exclusive action. Since Pearl Harbor, World War No. 2 has put the gory science of mass murder into new and sinister perspective. Our oceans have ceased to be moats which automatically protect our ramparts. Flesh and blood now compete unequally with winged steel. War has become an all-consuming juggernaut. If World War No. 3 ever unhappily arrives, it will open new laboratories of death too horrible to contemplate. I propose to do everything within my power to keep those laboratories closed for keeps. I want maximum American cooperation, consistent with legitimate American self-interest, with constitutional process and with collateral events which warrant it, to make the basic idea of Dumbarton Oaks succeed. I want a new dignity and a new authority for international law. I think American self-interest requires it. But, Mr. President, this also requires whole-hearted reciprocity. In honest candor I think we should tell other nations that this glorious thing we contemplate is not and cannot be one-sided. I think we must say again that unshared idealism is a menace which we could not undertake to underwrite in the post-war world.

Now, I am not so impractical as to expect any country to act on any final motive other than self-interest. I know of no reason why it should. That is what nations are for. I certainly intend that intelligent and loyal American self-interest shall be just as vigilantly and vigorously guarded as is amply obvious, from time to time, in their own behalf by the actions of our allies. The real question always becomes just this: Where does real self-interest lie?

Here, Mr. President, we reach the core of the immediate problem. Without remotely wanting to be invidious, I use one of many available examples. I would not presume, even under these circumstances, to use it except that it ultimately involves us. Russia's unilateral plan appears to contemplate the engulfment, directly or indirectly, of a surrounding circle of buffer states, contrary to our conception of what we thought we were fighting for in respect to the rights of small nations and a just peace. Russia's announced reason is her insistent purpose never again to be at the mercy of another German tyranny. That is a perfectly understandable reason. The alternative is collective security. Now, which is better, in the long view? That is the question I pose. Which is better, in the long view, from a purely selfish Russian standpoint: To forcefully surround herself with a cordon of unwillingly controlled or partitioned states, thus affronting the opinions of mankind, as a means of postwar protection against a renaissance of German aggression, or to win the priceless asset of world confidence in her by embracing the alternative, namely, full and whole-hearted cooperation with and reliance on a vital international organization in which all of us shall honorably participate to guarantee that Axis aggression shall never rise again? Well—at that point, Russia, or others like her, in equally honest candor, has a perfect right to reply, "Where is there any such alternative reliance until we know what the United States will do? How can you expect us to rely on an enigma?"

Now we are getting somewhere. Fear of reborn German aggression in years to come is at the base of most of our contemporary frictions. It is a perfectly human and understandable fear on the part of all neighboring nations which German militarism has twice driven to the valley of the shadow within one generation. Fear of reborn German aggression in years to come is the cause assigned to unilateral plans for Russian postwar expansion. Fear of reborn German aggression is the reason assigned to the proposed partition of Poland. Fear of reborn German aggression gave birth to the Anglo-Soviet agreement of 1942, the Soviet-Czechoslovak agreement of 1943, the Franco-Soviet Treaty of 1944, and to similar unilateral and bilateral actions inevitably yet to come. Fear of reborn German aggression is our apple of discord. This Second World War plagues the earth chiefly because France and Britain did not keep Germany disarmed, according to contract, after World War No. 1. In other words, when we deal with Europe's fear—her justified fear—of another rebirth of German military tyranny in some future postwar era, we are at the heart of the immediate problem which bedevils our Allied relationships.

I propose that we meet this problem conclusively and at once. There is no reason to wait. America has this same self-interest in permanently, conclusively, and effectively disarming Germany and Japan. It is simply unthinkable that America, or any other member of the United Nations, would allow this Axis calamity to reproduce itself again. Whether we Americans do or do not agree upon all the power that shall reside in an ultimate international council to call upon us for joint military action in behalf of collective security, surely we can agree that we do not ever want an instant's hesitation or doubt about our military cooperation in the peremptory use of force, if needed, to keep Germany and Japan demilitarized. Such a crisis would be the lengthened shadow of the present war. It would be a direct epilogue to the present war. It should be handled as this present war is handled. There should be no more need to refer any such action back to Congress than that Congress should expect to pass upon battle plans today. The Commander in Chief should have instant power to act, and he should act. I know of no reason why a hard-and-fast treaty between the major allies should not be signed today to achieve this dependable end. We need not await the determination of our other postwar relationships. This problem—this menace—stands apart by itself. Regardless of what our later decision may be in respect to the power that shall be delegated to the President to join our military force with others in a new peace league—no matter what limitations may commend themselves to our ultimate judgments in this regard, I am sure we can agree that there should be no limitations when it comes to keeping the Axis out of piracy for keeps. I respectfully urge that we meet this problem now. From it stem many of today's confusions, doubts, and frustrations. I think we should immediately put it behind us by conclusive action. Having done so, most of the reasons given for controversial unilateral and bilateral actions by our allies will have disappeared; and then we shall be able, at least, to judge accurately whether we have found and cured the real hazard to our relationships. We shall have closed ranks. We shall have returned infinitely closer to basic unity.

Then, in honest candor, Mr. President, I think we have the duty and the right to demand that whatever immediate unilateral decisions have to be made in consequence of military need—and there will be such even in civil affairs—they shall all be temporary and subject to final revision in the objective light of the postwar world and the postwar peace league as they shall ultimately develop. As President Roosevelt put it in his annual message:

> During the interim period, until conditions permit a genuine expression of the people's will, we and our Allies have a duty, which we cannot ignore, to use our influence to the end that no temporary or provisional authorities in the liberated countries block the eventual exercise of the peoples' right freely to choose the government and institutions under which, as free men, they are to live.

I agree to that. Indeed, I would go further. I would write it in the bond. If Dumbarton Oaks should specifically authorize the ultimate international organization to review protested injustices in the peace itself, it would at least partially nullify the argument that we are to be asked to put a blank-check warrant behind a future status quo which is unknown to us and which we might be unwilling to defend.

We are standing by our guns with epic heroism. I know of no reason why we should not stand by our ideals. If they vanish under ultimate pressures, we shall at least have kept the record straight; we shall have kept faith with our soldier sons; and we then shall clearly be free agents, unhampered by tragic misunderstandings, in determining our own course when Berlin and Tokyo are in Allied hands. Let me put it this way for myself: I am prepared, by effective international cooperation, to do our full part in charting happier and safer tomorrows. But I am not prepared to guarantee permanently the spoils of an unjust peace. It will not work.

Mr. President, we need honest candor even with our foes. Without any remote suggestion of appeasement—indeed, it seems to me that it is exactly the contrary—I wish we might give these Axis peoples some incentive to desert their own tottering tyrannies by at lease indicating to them that the quicker they unconditionally surrender the cheaper will be unconditional surrender's price. Here again we need plain speaking which has been too conspicuous by its absence, and, upon at least one calamitous occasion, by its error.

Mr. President, I conclude as I began. We must win these wars with maximum speed and minimum loss. Therefore we must have maximum Allied cooperation and minimum Allied frictions. We have fabulously earned the right to be heard in respect to the basis of this unity. We need the earliest possible clarification of our relations with our brave Allies. We need this clarification not only for the sake of total Allied cooperation in the winning of the war but also in behalf of a truly compensatory peace. We cannot drift to victory. We must have maximum united effort on all fronts. We must have maximum united effort in our councils. And we must deserve the continued united effort of our own people.

I realize, Mr. President, in such momentous problems how much easier it is to be critical than to be correct. I do not wish to meddle. I want only to help. I want to do my duty. It is in this spirit that I ask for honest candor in respect to our ideals, our dedications, and our commitments, as the greatest contribution which government can now make to the only kind of realistic unity which will most swiftly bring our victorious sons back home, and which will best validate our aspirations, our sacrifiecs, and our dreams.

AMERICAN WORLD POLICY FOR
PEACE AND PROGRESS [4]

HAROLD E. STASSEN [5]

Commander Harold E. Stassen, of the United States Navy, gave this address in the auditorium of the University of Minnesota, at Minneapolis, before the Minnesota United Nations Committee, on March 7, 1945. The talk was broadcast in a nation-wide distribution. It was Commander Stassen's first public address on world policy since he resigned as Governor of Minnesota to enter the Navy in 1943. Before entering the Navy, he had repeatedly expressed himself in favor of America's joining an international organization. (See, for example, his address of January 7, 1943.) President Roosevelt had selected him as one of the seven representatives of the United States to participate in the United Nations Conference at San Francisco, on April 25, 1945, to frame a program for a United Nations World Organization.

The address may be examined as a reflection of the thinking and attitude of a considerable body of military leaders of this date. The introduction follows the Ciceronian pattern of rendering the audience attentive and well disposed toward the speaker and his theme. The discussion proper expounds clearly the seven cardinal points of our future world policy. The conclusion is especially persuasive. Notable is the directness of style and the constant military-naval imagery.

The speaker stressed the need for reconciling realism and idealism in determining a policy of international government. He would face realities, talk of things as they are, have a maximum national defense, and yet move toward the realization of splendid cooperation.

The over-all effect of the speech was pleasing to the supporters of the San Francisco Conference aims. As a Midwesterner who championed a world outlook, as a peace advocate who had a successful military record, as a successful governor of an important state, Stassen possessed the personality, background, and political outlook that promised for him an outstanding position with the Republican party of 1946.

Mr. Stassen was an intercollegiate debater and orator at the University of Minnesota, one of the outstanding students under the guidance of Professor Frank Rarig, Head of the Speech Department.

[4] *Congressional Record,* Vol. 91, No. 45, A1196-8, March 9, 1945 (daily edition). By permission of Commander Stassen.

[5] For biographical note see Appendix.

Professor Rarig[6] stated, "Harold E. Stassen as a participant in college activities, and particularly in debate and oratory, demonstrated that he had well established and sound habits of work. . . . He maintained an attitude of responsibility, not only for getting the job done but also for doing it in a workmanlike fashion. His outstanding intellectual trait was a habit of forming objective, balanced judgments which he reached as the result of mental processes that included an objective consideration of the most relevant factors in a given situation. He early demonstrated his concern for the public interest as opposed to partisan and factional interests and his immunity from the incitements of zealots, either doctrinaire or opportunistic. As a student, he was able to pick issues, balance the arguments on both sides, and arrive at a conclusion based on assumptions of the general welfare. . . . Stassen made some of the most closely reasoned rebuttal speeches I ever heard made by a college debater."

In these last three years America, with her allies, has won a long series of brilliant historic victories in this war. The names stand out as grim markers of our march toward victory, from Guadalcanal and Casa Blanca to Iwo Jima and the Rhine. These battles will be symbols for generations of how Americans, who love peace, can and will fight when they must.

The superb productive power of our country has played a heavy part in these victories and has contributed to the strength of the other United Nations. American labor, management, capital and agriculture are entitled to high commendation for their performance. The flow of supplies and munitions and ships and planes and guns has been nothing short of a miracle.

The victories have been actually won by the unbelievably heroic and effective fighting of those wise-cracking, good-natured, beloved American sons of yours on the battle fronts of the world.

They take off from rolling carrier decks or advanced airfields, penetrate thick, soupy weather, fight their way to enemy strongholds and deal devastating blows. They wade into beaches in wave after wave regardless of the whir of machine guns, the wham of mortars and the blast of bombs. They slog and worm their way up to blast and burn pillboxes and caves. They stand by their guns and pour out their fire in the face of diving planes or roaring counter-fire or charging tanks. They take their guns, their planes, their tanks, their ships, their subs, their small boats, anywhere and everywhere to strike an enemy or support a pal.

[6] Letter to compiler, May 17, 1945.

They die doing these things. They die, and others like them take their places.

With splendid military leadership from the Commander in Chief, and from generals like Marshall, Eisenhower, MacArthur and Arnold and Vandegrift, and from admirals like King, Leahy, Nimitz and Halsey, they have brought us within sight of the final victory.

That final victory must be our No. 1 aim until the last enemy has surrendered. Nothing must divert us from following through to early, complete winning of the war. Each new quota of supplies and munitions and men to meet the fluctuating needs of the shifting types of battle must be promptly met. We must not listen to the siren call of reconversion until we can reconvert together in peace. Each new battle must be fought with vigor and with skill.

But it is right and proper and urgent that we in service, when the opportunity presents itself, and you at home, proceed to think through the world policy of America for peace, lest we lose much of what we are fighting for.

As you know, the President has invited me to serve as a member of the United States delegation to the San Francisco conference of the United Nations, and I have accepted.

It will be my endeavor to study and to learn as much as possible of the information, ideas and viewpoints of the people of America on the questions coming up at this conference. I have consulted and will consult with leaders of our government and of my Republican party; of Church; of labor, agriculture and business; of women, of youth and of veterans. But I will not seek to, nor claim to, represent any of them as special groups at San Francisco. I will consider it my duty to represent my country as a whole as I see its best welfare, and to be individually responsible for my actions. It will be my aim to assist in securing a result of this crucial conference which will be supported by the overwhelming majority of the people of America, and by substantially all of the other United Nations. This means, of course, that the result will not be, and can not be, entirely in accord with any nation's or any person's individual views. But, I cannot say too emphatically, that the alternative to finding the areas of agreement is to do nothing at all. And nothing at all would start us on our way along the short road of inaction, to world-wide depressions and to the next and most tragic world war. That is not an acceptable alternative.

It is of tremendous importance that the principles which will guide our actions in the years to come be formulated and clarified and tempered in the heat of free discussions now, so that they may be clearly and definitely set before the world.

To stimulate this search, speaking only for myself, I frankly state what I consider should be the seven cardinal points of our future world policy.

First: That as a nation we will join with our present allies at San Francisco to build a definite continuing organization of the United Nations of the World, based on justice and law and insured by force. That we will seek to gradually develop a new and higher level of government, with legislative, judicial and executive functions, and with world-wide jurisdiction, for the future peace, progress and well-being of mankind. That we are and will continue to be interested in what happens in every other part of the globe. That this is one world.

Nor can I speak those last two words without pausing to pay a tribute to him who made them mean more than mere words, more than a symbol, the veritable keystone to a living cause and hope for mankind—Wendell Willkie.

Second: That we do not subscribe to the extreme view of nationalistic sovereignty, that we realize that neither this nation, nor any other nation can be a law unto itself in the modern world, and that we are willing to delegate a limited portion of our national sovereignty to our United Nations organization, so that it may be effective in the tasks we expect it to accomplish. That we hold that true sovereignty rest in the people, and that there is and must be a law of humanity above and beyond the narrow rule of nationalistic, absolute sovereignty.

Third: That we consider that the future welfare and peace and happiness of the people of America is inseparably intertwined with the future welfare and peace and happiness of the men and women and children of the world.

Fourth: That we will use the enormous productive capacity of America and the reservoirs of capital and credit and technical skill to contribute to the gradual advancement of the standards of living of the peoples of the world, not as recipients of charity, but as self-respecting men and women of dignity and of pride.

Fifth: That we believe in the freedom of information through press and radio and school and forum as a vital factor in the peace and progress of the world and in the fulfillment of the dignity of man.

Sixth: That those who were aggressors in this war shall be stripped of all means to make war and shall remain so stripped. That we propose to remain strong on land, at sea, and in the air, and will join with Russia and Great Britain, China and France, and the other United Nations in furnishing police power in the world.

Seventh: That we are and propose to remain a democracy of free citizens with an economic system of private capital and individual enterprise. That we will constantly seek to improve the functioning of our system, both as to freedom and equality of our citizens and as to the success and adequacy of our economy. That we will explain our system to the world, but will leave it to the peoples in each nation to decide for themselves their own form of government so long as they do not trample on basic human rights, or threaten the peace of the world, or transgress upon their neighbors. That we will permit our own citizens to learn of any other form of government they wish to study, but will not permit any other government to actively seek to undermine our own.

Obviously each of these cardinal points could well be the subject of a major address. Within the limits of my time this evening I will discuss them in turn.

It is very generally agreed now that an international organization should be formed and that the United Nations should be the basis of such an organization.

I am not one of those who feel that the organization must take some certain detailed, exact form. I believe there are many forms that would be a definite step forward and would make a constructive contribution.

I hope that it will include some method of developing basic world-wide law. It should make possible the future enactment of a fundamental code of human rights. The beginning may be very small. But even if we started with the enactment of one law, a law that no country, in time of peace, shall execute a human being without just trial, it would be a significant step. We sometimes fail to realize that there is no such world law today. The Nazi storm troopers and Gestapo who dragged civilians from their houses in Germany and summarily shot them were violating every moral code we know of, but they were not violating any international law, because there is none to protect a human being within a nation. This starkly silhouettes the tragic slowness of the development of society on the world level.

We know full well that Nazi aggression actually started, not when Hitler marched across his borders but rather when he first ruthlessly trampled the rights of men within Germany.

From small beginnings, gradually the rights of freedom of worship, of fair trial, of freedom of speech and press, the right of the worker to organize, and the prevention of discrimination should be developed. With it should be stated the world-wide laws or rules against aggression, for the flight of aircraft, for the use of ports and canals, the restriction of armaments, the availability of resources, the advancement of health and education, and the prevention of unjust confiscation of property.

Obviously, if we are to have laws, we must have a court to administer these laws. Clearly, then, a United Nations court of some type with world-wide jurisdiction is essential.

It is equally clear that a police force of some nature is mandatory to enforce the decisions of the court if order and justice is to be respected and maintained. This definitely does not mean an all-powerful international police force of a superstate.

Let us clarify our thinking. If either the United States, or Russia, or Great Britain decide in the next twenty-five years to make war, then there will be another world war, and no organization, or league, or union, or treaties will stop it. But I do not believe any of these countries will want to make war. Each knows the horrors of war. Each has so much to gain by not making war. Each has a great future in the peaceful development of its resources and its standing in the world.

They will not always see problems alike. They will not always please each other. But in the main, they must and should work out their differences of views and find the way for joint action. The Yalta Conference was a very important indication that this can and will be done. Clearly, then, our policies should be based on the development of the world with these three desiring peace.

A note of caution should also be sounded, however, that we should definitely envisage a system of laws and justice and a moral code supported by police force, and must not permit the development of a continuing system of world power and force without law.

The United Nations should also develop an effective and just method of trusteeships for use in governing territories that for reasons of extreme military importance, or inability of self-government, or peculiar economic position, or seizure from an enemy, can best be held in a form of joint United Nations title, rather than in the title of any individual nation. The enlightened interest of the world and the human rights of the people concerned should both be carefully safeguarded. The trustee may be either one of the United Nations, or the United Nations organization itself.

Let us also make it clear that the United Nations organization does not mean breaking up any of the stable associations of nations and peoples now in existence. It is definitely not adverse to the British Commonwealth of Nations, nor to the Union of Soviet Socialist Republics, nor to the United States of America, nor to the various associations of nations through treaties and friendships. On the contrary, we seek to build on these cornerstones of stability a world-wide beginning for order and justice and peace in place of chaos and tragedy and war.

Tremendous steps have been taken in recent months toward the fulfillment of this first cardinal point of our world policy.

So it will be, and must be at San Francisco. The results of a successful conference will be of incalculable importance, but they will not be the final answer to our world problems for peace. They will only be the first step. Continuing interest of the American people, continuing devotion of their government, the approval and support of the proposals by the Senate, and then the steady growth and development of the United Nations organization, will be essential if we are to have anything more than a precarious beachhead.

In a discussion of the development of a new and higher level of government you frequently hear the rejoinder, yes, that would be a good step but it would violate the rule of absolute nationalistic sovereignty.

Let us meet this issue squarely. I do not want my country to face another generation of youth marching off to the horrors of war and say: "We could have prevented the development of this conflict but we had to cling to the extreme principle of absolute nationalistic sovereignty."

There may be many diplomats who do not know it; there may be many political leaders who are afraid to admit it; there may be people who do not understand it, but the extreme principle of absolute nationalistic sovereignty is of the Middle Ages and it is dead. It died with the airplane, the radio, the rocket and the robomb.

In its place we must develop the new principle of the rights, duties and responsibilities of each nation to the other nations and of each man and each woman to the other people of the world.

No nation has any right in the modern world to do as it pleases without regard to the effects of its actions upon the peoples of other nations. True sovereignty rests in the people, and the people know that for their own future welfare they must exercise a portion of that sovereignty on a world level in place of the nationalistic level.

Just as each free man must limit his liberty of action so that he does not injure his neighbor, so each nation must limit its action so that it does not injure its neighbor. And in one world today, the nations of the world are all neighbors.

One of the most striking facts which has been demonstrated in this war is the enormous productive capacity of America. It has been a huge power for destruction and for victory.

It can be an equally great power for world construction and progress after the war if we but lift our eyes to its opportunities and responsibilities and take the necessary steps for world stability.

This will require increased investments by American capital in the resources and facilities of other nations, and increased trade with lower tariffs throughout the world. We must explode the narrow view that if we develop production in other parts of the world we will pre-empt our own markets. We will create markets as we develop means to produce. Producers are consumers. The capacity of the human race to consume is just as great as the capacity of the human race to produce. Of course there are and will be acute problems of distribution. But we can either fight over a shrinking wealth, or work together to participate in an expanding production and the wealth of the future.

Vast sums of charitable assistance will be needed in the immediate postwar period, but this should be definitely separated from the careful investment of capital in the long-term development of other nations. It is better that American capital be invested and reinvested in various countries of the world to assist in raising their standards of living, and indirectly develop jobs in America in the process, than that it be sterile and stagnant in America.

This does not mean a Santa Claus role. Most of the peoples of the world do not want charity beyond the war emergency conditions. They want to be self-reliant. They want to rebuild their own homes and develop their own economy. It is healthy and wholesome for them and for the world that they should. But it will mean long-term investments and reinvestments.

Nor is this all just an idealistic dream. Never did a country for its own sake more need to clear the cobwebs from its thinking. Never did a country for its own sake more need to appraise the value and the purpose of its great productive strength.

If it does not lift its eyes and use its brain and its brawn for progress of the world it will wither and deteriorate in petty internal struggles over the division of a shrinking economy.

But if it contributes to the progress of the world it will itself share in that progress in high standards of living, a richer life and peace.

This is also true of other peoples. Any attempt to profit by one nation at the expense of other peoples will fail. If it meets with temporary success it will soon be lost in either the whirlpool of depression or the cauldron of war. We cannot have continued economic warfare and continued military peace. The world must advance together and there is room in the world for all the peoples who live in it.

World opinion is almost unanimous that the Germans and the Japanese must be stripped of their means of making war. This can best be done by joint action of the victorious nations through the United Nations organizations, with a continuing joint occupation and inspection.

Under that military rule all indemnities and penalties and reparations should take place. Then and only then the gradual development of self-government should be permitted to arise. It should begin in the localities and in the schools and slowly develop as the capacity and desire for non-aggressive, peaceful and successful administration is demonstrated.

Freedom of information to the citizens of these countries must be a fundamental rule. Open to the children of Germany and Japan and Italy the full access to the radios and publications and books of the world, and if we are right in our basic concepts in America, and I believe we are, in a generation or two we will have a different Germany and a different Japan. When the change is demonstrated, they should be permitted to become self-governing and be granted membership in the world organization, but even then there is no reason why they should be permitted to rearm, and there is every reason to prevent them from rearming. We will be saying in effect to the conquered nations, "We will permit you to rise again as successful, self-governing constructive nations, if you so desire, but we will not permit you to rise again as a military power, whatever may be your protestations of intentions."

We, ourselves, should remain strong. We should maintain a powerful, modern navy. We should keep an alert up-to-date air force. We should constantly train an efficient land force.

We should do this to fulfill the police force responsibility which will be ours in enforcing and supporting the world code of justice and the United Nations organization, and also to assure our own future security and progress. We should make it plain that much as we want peace we will fight again and will fight anyone who basically violates world justice and seeks to flaunt our policies and tries to make might right. This position, I am convinced, is more likely to maintain peace than an announced policy of making ourselves weak and of not fighting, even though provoked.

To those who scoff at thoughts like these expressed tonight as abstract idealism I simply ask that you look out upon the world-wide tragedy of war today. When the terror of war has reached the grand scale that it has today, it is time for some thinking for peace on a grand scale. And I add that I will work with you with just as much hard-shelled realism on the emergency of today and with just as much down-to-earth practicalism on the problems of tomorrow.

But our ideals will determine the all-important question of the basic course that we take. We need no scoffers today. We need men. Men to assault the pillboxes of lethargy—the emplacements of prejudice—the spitting guns of intolerance. Men who are willing to fall in the assault so that others may carry the day. It will take that to biuld the world. It will take that to raise the standards of mankind—to make freedom and liberty and peace living symbols to men and women and children—and not mere words in speeches or in charters.

Our fighting men want America to have a world policy for peace that is as big, as definite and as successful as has been our strategy of war. It will take time and it will cost. But the alternative makes it worth the cost. They do not want you to surrender before the counter-attacking assault waves of cynicism this best hope of enduring peace on earth.

Some people say that our democracy is not perfect and that there is discrimination and inequality and apathy and corruption.

They are right. Some say that our economic system has not functioned perfectly and that here are maladjustments and sufferings and faulty distributions. They are right.

But neither of these facts is any reason for waiting for the correction of these imperfections before we step forward to fulfill the world leadership which it is mandatory that we exercise. We must advance on both the world front and the domestic front at the same time. In fact, they are in large measure interdependent.

I speak not of a utopia. I speak not of a human race suddenly turned angelic. There will be selfishness and greed and corruption and narrowness and intolerance in the world tomorrow and tomorrow's tomorrow. But pray God, we may have the courage and the wisdom and the vision to raise a definite standard that will appeal to the best that is in man, and then strive mightily toward that goal.

With the background of the Atlantic Charter and the commitments of Secretary Hull's conference at Moscow, the declarations of Teheran, the proposals of Dumbarton Oaks, the decisions at Yalta, the President's excellent message to Congress last week, and the never-ending wholesome study and discussion throughout America have brought us to the eve of the San Francisco Conference for the drafting of a definite framework for continuing United Nations action in peace, with the overwhelming support of the people of the country and of the United States Senate for the steps proposed.

We should look, therefore, upon the San Francisco Conference as a golden opportunity to win a beachhead in the battle for a just and lasting peace. The beachhead is of crucial importance and requires many sacrifices and never-ending determination. And, also, the beachhead is not the final goal, but only the jumping-off place for the long, hard drive toward victory.

THE UNITED NATIONS SECURITY CONFERENCE [7]

Edward R. Stettinius [8]

President Harry S. Truman opened the United Nations Security Conference at San Francisco, on April 25, with an address of welcome telephoned from the White House to the San Francisco Opera House and then broadcast throughout the world. Governor Earl Warren, of California, and Mayor Roger Lapham, of San Francisco, followed with appropriate greetings, also broadcast.

Some eight hundred and fifty delegates, advisers, and secretaries of forty-six participating nations assembled to organize a league, based on the Dumbarton Oaks proposals. From August 21, 1944, to October 7, 1944, the representatives of Great Britain, the Soviet Union, and the United States (joined later by China after the departure of the Russian delegates), held exploratory discussions at Dumbarton Oaks in Georgetown, Washington, D.C. to devise means of preventing World War III. Basic principles of international cooperation were agreed to.

At Yalta, in February 1945, the Big Three (Roosevelt, Churchill, and Stalin) endorsed the international organization as drawn up at Dumbarton Oaks, and tentatively agreed upon an early conference of United Nations to complete the work.

The issues before the Conference were chiefly, (1) Was the threat of future wars sufficiently great to demand some effective international government? (2) Would the Security Council, as proposed, be merely another combination of the Big Powers, a continuation of a military alliance of the Big Three to dominate the world and support imperialism? (3) Was the Assembly a mere debating society without power to significance? In any case, should each nation have only one vote? (4) Was the veto power, by which any one member of the Security Council could veto a proposal for action in a dispute to which that member might be a party, a means of blocking any effective program for preventing war? (5) If war was to be waged against any aggressor, what constituted aggression and how, when, and where should the military forces be selected and set in motion? (6) Would the new court displace the old World Court? (7) Should regional pacts, such as the Chapultepec (Mexico) Agreement, give way to a United Nations league? And what of treaties of alliance, such as those between France and Russia?

The second session was held on April 26. Mr. Stettinius, speaking first, had already come to grips with these problems through his experi-

[7] Text furnished by the Department of State.
[8] For biographical note see Appendix.

ence at Dumbarton Oaks, at Mexico City, and at San Francisco during the preceding twenty-four hours. His address was a tactful definition of the aims of the Conference, a skilful, if indirect and diplomatic statement, calculated to secure conciliation and over-all cooperation of the many nations with their conflicting ideologies, interests, and sharply differing answers to the issues.

His remarks were supplementary to his highly effective "welcoming" speech given on the preceding night. In that earlier address, however, he had persuasively quoted or cited with impressiveness the unseen personalities that created the Conference and were intended to dominate it: the late President, the former Secretary of State Cordell Hull, in a hospital, and the new President, who remained in Washington but who in his radio appeal to the delegates made clear his whole-hearted support of the aims.

Mr. Stettinius spoke with measured solemnity and oratorical rhythm. His tones lacked the vocal warmth or conversational directness of Roosevelt. But Stettinius had sufficient vocal vitality and earnestness to dominate and persuade. He succeeded in his difficult role of oral spokesman for the United States in these international deliberations.

Fellow-Delegates to the United Nations Conference on International Organization:

Three years ago the forces of tyranny and aggression seemed on the very point of conquering the world. Today, on every front, they are face to face with defeat—utter and complete defeat.

It has taken years of toil and sacrifice to bring us to this moment. But the doom of the aggressor nations was sealed long ago. It was sealed in Washington on January 1, 1942, when the United Nations Declaration was signed.

Our enemies could conquer only by keeping us divided. Instead we confronted them with a free and voluntary association of nations united in purpose and without equal in human and material resources. This unity neither force nor subterfuge has broken. Against the common will and the common strength of the United Nations, our enemies have hurled their propaganda and their armed might in vain.

For centuries to come, men will point to the United Nations as history's most convincing proof of what miracles can be accomplished by nations joined together in a righteous cause. It is a unity achieved in spite of differences of language and custom, of cultural tradition and of economic structure. It is a unity which proves that no differences of race, color, creed, history or geography can divide peoples united in a higher community of interest and purpose.

Our first objective has been the defeat of our enemies. But from the beginning the United Nations have pursued another objective—one which is equally necessary to each one of us. It is the objective which gives ultimate meaning to all the sacrifice and suffering of these tragic years. We are united not only for survival, not only for military victory. We are united above all in the necessity to assure a just and enduring peace in which the peoples of the world can work together to achieve at last freedom from fear and from want.

We have made a better beginning toward the fulfillment of this purpose than nations have ever made before.

For this purpose the responsible leaders of our nations and their representatives have met in Moscow and in Teheran, in Cairo, in Quebec, at Dumbarton Oaks and in the Crimea.

Because of our common understanding that economic security goes hand in hand with security from war, United Nations conferences were held in Atlantic City, Hot Springs and Bretton Woods on cooperative measures for relief, to meet common problems in food and agriculture and to prepare the financial basis for economic reconstruction and an expanding world economy in the postwar world.

At Mexico City the inter-American conference on problems of war and peace strengthened the ties between the republics of the Western Hemisphere and prepared the way for a close integration of the inter-American system with the world organization.

Yes, the United Nations have long been at work together on many preparations required in building the structure of lasting peace.

Here at San Francisco we have come to the decisive point in these preparations. The purpose of this conference is to prepare the charter of an international organization to maintain peace with justice in a free world of free men.

I believe that it was a wise—indeed, a necessary—decision to limit the work of this conference to that great task.

It was a wise decision because writing the constitution of a world organization to maintain peace in the future is a task wholly separate from the punishment of the international gangsters who started this war.

It was a necessary decision because establishment of the world organization must be kept above and apart from the peace settlements if the organization is to be able to deal freely and justly with future threats to the peace that may arise from any cause, including these settlements.

Preparation of the charter of the world organization should not, therefore, be entangled with the many and complex political and economic issues involved in the defeat of Germany and Japan. And the imminent collapse of organized German resistance makes it all the more important that the world organization be established at the earliest possible moment.

To deal with these other issues there will have to be many other conferences, and many other decisions, both national and international. We have no time to lose.

Success at this conference will not of itself assure enduring peace. The whole structure will take years to build. But without agreement on a charter of the world organization, the structure of peace cannot be built at all.

A house cannot be built without a plan or without a foundation. Here at San Francisco the United Nations must draw the plan and lay the foundation.

Upon this foundation and in accordance with this plan the framework of the structure will be erected when the United Nations have ratified the charter by their respective constitutional processes and brought the world organization into being. It is only around this framework that we can complete the structure of peace with all the other agreements on political, economic and social problems which we must reach together.

At this conference we have, therefore, undertaken a responsibility on which all else depends. We have undertaken to draw up the charter of an international organization strong enough to prevent war and flexible enough to allow for peaceful development and change.

The outlines of such a charter are contained in the proposals formulated at Dumbarton Oaks last fall by the representatives of the Republic of China, the Union of Soviet Socialist Republics the United Kingdom and the United States of America.

These proposals were formulated after years of preliminary study. They represent in their essentials the common denominator of thought among the four sponsoring nations. They are being presented to this conference as affording the basis of the charter of an international organization.

The proposals were submitted months ago to the most searching examination by the governments and peoples of all the United Nations. Since then many constructive suggestions have been made toward their improvement. Some of these suggestions, and others which may emerge from our discussions here, will undoubtedly be reflected in the final draft of the charter. And the charter itself should be open to whatever later amendment experience may dictate as wise.

We must always bear in mind, however, that there are at least two conditions essential to the establishment of a world organization which can successfully maintain peace.

One of these conditions is that these peace-loving nations which have the military and industrial strength required to prevent or suppress aggression must agree and act together against aggression. If they do not agree and act together, aggression cannot be prevented or suppressed without a major war. This fact has certainly been spelled out by our experience in this war.

That is why the first step toward establishment of the world organization was to prepare proposals on which the nations sponsoring this conference could agree. That is why, in the structure and powers of the security council of the world organization proposed in the Dumbarton Oaks plan, provision was made for this essential agreement and unity of action by the major nations. Without this, we cannot hope to build a world organization which will provide security to all nations, large and small. Without this we cannot hope to develop enduring institutions in which all free nations may participate on a basis of sovereign equality and in which justice and respect for law will apply to the powerful as well as to the weak.

The second essential condition of success in our endeavor is the voluntary cooperation of all peaceful nations, large and small, acting with full respect for the equal sovereignty of each, to promote justice among nations, to foster respect for basic human rights and to solve those common problems upon which the security and the economic and social advancement of their peoples so largely depend. There can be no end to the tyranny of fear and want unless the proposed world organization commands the allegiance of both the mind and the conscience of mankind.

The International Court, the Assembly and the Economic and Social Council and its related agencies are the institutions proposed at Dumbarton Oaks which would have the major responsibility in these fields. They are of the utmost importance. Widespread economic insecurity and poverty, ignorance and oppression breed conflict and give aggressors their chance. Measures for security against aggression, no matter how effectively contrived, will not alone provide the assurance of lasting peace. We have also to work effectively in close cooperation together toward rising standards of living, and greater freedom and opportunity for all peoples, of every race and creed and color.

In the preparations for this conference we have sought from the beginning to build with vision and with justice, but to build always upon the realities and upon hard-won experience.

To build upon a millennial idealism, however fine in theory, would be to build upon quicksand. To build only on the collaboration and interests of the major nations would be to deny the community of interests of all nations.

We have sought instead to assure that the strength of the major nations will be used both justly and effectively for the common welfare, under the law of a world charter in which all peaceful nations are joined together.

We began by seeking common understanding among the sponsoring nations on basic objectives and on the essential machinery for action. These are the nations which have united their strength against the aggressors so successfully in this war. We proceed now by seeking agreement among all the nations, large and small, which have been united against the common enemy.

This is a conference of United Nations, the nations that loved peace and freedom enough to fight for them. The international organization we seek to build is one that is based upon this inescapable fact of our time—that peace and security will be the right of these nations which are willing to share in the responsibility for keeping them. Tyranny and barbarism have never recognized neutrality. They never will. We do not intend to build a world organization that will overlook this cardinal fact. We do propose that after it is established, the organization be open to membership of all other nations which have demonstrated their willingness and ability to fulfill their obligations under the charter.

I have reviewed briefly the preparations for this conference and our thinking on some of the major problems that we must meet here.

We cannot expect at this conference to produce a charter which will answer all the questions or resolve all the problems. No charter, no constitution, no basic document was ever drafted that was not open to improvement.

We Americans have a convincing proof of that in our own history. Our Constitution, under which the Republic has grown and prospered for a hundred and fifty years was by no means satisfactory to all the citizens when it issued from the Constitutional Convention of Philadelphia in 1787, or even satisfactory to all the delegates to that convention. It lacked many provisions which numerous Americans of that day believed to be essential. Yet it was adopted by the requisite number of states in 1789. Only four years after the Constitution was written the first ten amendments went into effect, and eleven other amendments have been made since then.

What was true of the thirteen states which joined to form the United States is true also of the nations which have met in this conference to consider the proposed organization of the world for security and peace. Let us construct the charter of the world organization as soundly as we can. But let us not sacrifice approval to perfection.

Let us act now in the sure knowledge that our work can be improved upon with time but that if we fail to act, we are likely to lose altogether the opportunity which has been given us to prevent another World War.

Fellow delegates, as we enter upon our great task, we cannot forget the millions of men of our armed forces who have given their lives to this cause, nor the other millions of men, women and children who have suffered the cruel agonies of starvation, torture and death. We cannot forget the untold destruction that has been wrought. Nor can we forget how close our whole civilization has come to utter ruin.

It is our supreme responsibility, at this conference and afterwards, to see to it that this calamity never again falls upon the world.

Vision we must have to see clearly that without peace and security for all nations, there will be no peace and security for any one of us.

Courage we must have to carry us through trying delays and temporary misunderstandings and lesser differences to the fulfillment of our common purpose.

Faith we must have in the ability of mankind to make peace with the same resolute devotion that the United Nations peoples have given to fighting this war.

That vision, that courage, that faith inspired the great American leader whose life was given to the cause for which we have here met—Franklin Delano Roosevelt.

It is only with such vision, courage and faith, expressed in a thousand different ways, that the United Nations have been able to travel so far along the hard road to final victory. It is only with this vision, courage and faith that we shall make peace secure for ourselves, and for succeeding generations.

A JOB TO BE DONE [9]

ANTHONY EDEN [10]

Anthony Eden, representing the British Empire, followed Edward Stettinius in addressing the second general session of the United Nations Security Conference, at San Francisco, on April 26, 1945. These opening statements by the spokesmen for each of the four sponsoring nations were addressed both to the Opera House audience of nearly four thousand and to a radio audience throughout the United States and the rest of the world.

Eden's address, like that of Stettinius, was a tactful and yet forthright presentation, designed to motivate the audience toward concerted and constructive deliberation. His logical and psychological plan in the speech was one especially adapted to his audience and the occasion. His introduction was attention-getting and persuasive; he appropriately responded to the welcome of Governor Warren and Mayor Roger Lapham; he paid tribute to Roosevelt, unified his listeners as they reflected on the spirit of the late President; and he outlined again the purposes of the conference. His argument proper, clothed in simple and unpolemic terms and details, established the necessity of this organization. (It was a case of either international organization or the destruction of civilization. San Francisco was the "world's last chance.") Impressing his listeners with the need, he then convinced them of the practicability of the undertaking. Here the speaker's method was one of meeting obvious objections. (1) It was not, as alleged, a perfect—but rather a compromise—plan; (2) it was not a mere dictatorship by the four Great Powers; (3) furthermore it was not, as alleged, to spring forth full fledged, but rather was to emerge only in outline. The listeners were persuaded to accept an *attainable* goal.

With this need and this practicable goal approved by his auditors, he then developed one more proposition of his argument proper: the political and economic responsibilities of the league framers, especially the four sponsoring powers and their Security Council. Eden would persuade his listeners that Russia, Great Britain, and the United States, for example, would use their immense power unselfishly in the interests of *all* nations. His conclusion was an appeal for action (agreement upon a charter "within four weeks"), an appeal topped off by vivid illustration.

Mr. Eden, British Foreign Secretary, was also Leader of the House of Commons and thus was in direct line for the Prime Ministry. Winston

[9] Text supplied by the British Information Services.

[10] For biographical note see Appendix.

Churchill had described him as "the one fresh figure of magnitude" among Britain's younger generation to survive World War I. In 1931, he became undersecretary of foreign affairs. He fought consistently and vigorously against the policies of Hitler, Mussolini, and Franco. When the young Englishman became convinced that he would not be supported, he resigned from the Chamberlain cabinet in 1938. Churchill, coming to power in 1940, made his protege head of the Foreign Office.

Mr. Eden, at San Francisco, was a highly skilled public speaker. He had extempore skill, effective audience adaptation in substance, in language, and in delivery. Although no Churchill in oratory, Eden ranks high as a parliamentary debater and defender of his political principles and programs. [11]

No more suitable setting could have been found for this assembly than the splendid city of San Francisco, one of the main centers of the United Nations war effort. San Francisco, whose confidence in the future is only equaled by its sense of comradeship today.

Our deep gratitude is due to the city itself and to the whole State of California, which with traditional hospitality has opened its gates to us, and also to the Government and the people of the United States who in a wider sense are our hosts at this momentous conference.

We are met here in the shadow of a grievous loss. No one can speak in this assembly without recalling the memory of Franklin Roosevelt, the friend of free peoples, the good neighbor. He looked forward to continuing in peace that close association of the free nations which has brought us to the very edge of victory and from which the meeting of today has sprung. It was he who named us the United Nations, and we shall best honor his memory by proving ourselves worthy of that proud title.

Let us be clear about the purpose of this conference. We are not met here to draft the terms of the treaty of peace. We are met to agree to set up a world organization which will help to keep the peace when victory is finally won over Germany and Japan.

At intervals in history mankind has sought by the creation of international machinery to solve disputes between nations by

[11] For further comment on Anthony Eden as a speaker in the United States, see Representative American Speeches: 1942-43, p. 131-41.

agreement and not by force. Hitherto all these endeavors have failed. Yet no one here doubts that despite these earlier failures a further attempt must be made, and this time we must succeed. All the causes that made some form of international machinery desirable after the last war make it indispensable today.

In the last hundred years, and in particular the last twenty-five years, the discoverers of science have served to enrich and sometimes endanger the world, but above all to contract it. We have entered an age when no natural barrier, whether mountain or ocean, can guarantee security against the new weapons which science has placed at the disposal of mankind. This hard fact is now biting deeply into the consciousness of all peoples, and they are, I believe, ready to accept its implications and to shoulder the responsibilities which it imposes.

Herein lies the main difference between today and the lost opportunity at the end of the last World War. Today this fact is patent to us all. Whether we will or not we are all now one another's neighbors. San Francisco is as close to Berlin or Tokyo as New York to Washington a century ago.

The world of today is one large city and our countries are its several parishes. We are the citizens. Either we must find some means of ordering our relations with justice and fair dealing while allowing nations great and small full opportunity to develop their free and independent life, or we shall soon head for another world conflict which this time must bring the utter destruction of civilization in its train. It is, therefore, no exaggeration to say that the work on which we are making a start here may be the world's last chance.

That is why the governments of the four powers who sponsored the invitations to this conference asked their representatives to meet and work out proposals which might later form the basis of an international agreement. They did so, at Dumbarton Oaks. Their work was examined and completed in the Crimea. The final outcome is now before you.

Here there are a few general observations which I would make. In the first place these proposals admittedly constitute a compromise. In the second place they do not constitute an attempt by the four powers to dictate to the rest of the world what form the future world organization should take. They are the suggestions which we unitedly present to you, for your consideration. Nor are they intended to stand unchanged until the end of time.

For our own part His Majesty's Government and the United Kingdom are prepared to accept and to endorse them and to do their best to give them life because we believe that they can form a basis for a future world organization which will help to provide that security which is today mankind's greatest need.

Security is not itself a final end. But it is indispensable if we are to make true freedom possible. Not otherwise can we hope to realize a world in which justice for nations as well as for individuals can prevail.

But this security cannot be created in a day nor by any document however admirable. It must be the product of time and of constant effort, of learning to work together, of practicing and upholding accepted standards of international conduct. The important thing is to begin now.

Here let me sound a warning note and make a suggestion. Let us not attempt too much. We cannot hope here to produce a complete scheme perfect in all its elaborate details for future ordering of the world. I am persuaded that we should be wise to set ourselves a goal more within the compass of our immediate possibilities.

We shall have taken the indispensable first step if we can now draw up a charter within the framework of our principles. The details can then be left to be filled in in the light of experience. I know that this is an Anglo-Saxon conception, which may possibly be challenged by others, but I am convinced that in this particular case it is right, and I would claim that its merit is capable of proof by reference to historical facts.

Now let me turn briefly to the proposals themselves which we are met to discuss. They impose obligations equally on all powers great and small. But I am conscious that a special responsibility lies on great powers in these days when industrial potential is so decisive a factor in military strength.

Great powers can make a twofold contribution. They can make it by their support of this organization. They can make it also by setting themselves certain standards in international conduct and by observing those standards scrupulously in all their dealing with other countries. The greater the power any state commands the heavier its responsibility to wield that power with consideration for others and with restraint upon its own selfish impulses.

What was the most sinister feature of the years which preceded the present struggle? It was the deliberate debasement of international conduct in which Germany, Italy and Japan engaged to further their own selfish plans. It was the practice of these powers not only persistently to violate their engagements, but to use the new engagements they so readily undertook after each aggression as a cloak to cover their next crime. This was their technique.

But what was the result? There came a time when the outraged forces of civilization had to call a halt to these practices and so inevitably the world was plunged into another war. Great powers have a special responsibility to guard against the recurrence of such practices.

I have laid emphasis on that portion of our task which is concerned with the provision of international machinery for the settlement of political disputes. But of equal importance with this is the solution of economic problems, which, if untended, can themselves sow the seeds of future wars. This will be the task of the social and economic council which finds its place in the proposals now before you. It is our duty to insure that this council shall be well adapted to play its full part in our new structure of peace.

Here then are our two immediate tasks, political and economic. Let us press them vigorously to a conclusion. World events of unprecedented magnitude both in the east and in the west crowd upon us every hour.

If we order our labors efficiently and work to the utmost of our strength, it should surely be possible for us to agree upon our charter within four weeks from now. We cannot afford to delay. Sir, I hope that we shall set ourselves such a target date and determine to reach it. This conference bears heavy responsibilities. It has also splendid opportunities. Let it seize them now.

In the early days of this war I went to Egypt to greet soldiers from Australia and New Zealand who had come to that country to protect the Suez Canal against the imminent threat of Mussolini aggression. On the evening of their arrival I was speaking to a number of the men of the motives which had made them volunteer for this adventure. Of the group one man remained silent. At last I turned to him and said, "And what made you come here?" He replied, "I guess there is a job of work to be done."

In the last six terrible years unnumbered men have died to give humanity another chance. We too have a job of work to do if we are not to fail these men. Let us do it with courage, modesty and dispatch. Let us do it now.

AMERICA AND NATIONAL DEFENSE

AMERICAN POSTWAR SEAPOWER AND CONTROL OF PACIFIC BASES [1]

ERNEST J. KING [2]

Admiral Ernest J. King, United States Navy, Commander in Chief of the United States Fleet and Chief of Naval Operations, gave this address at the Hotel Astor in New York City under the auspices of the Academy of Political Science and the Carnegie Endowment for International Peace, on April 4, 1945. The speech was given at a dinner that closed the first all day meeting of a two-day session on the political, social, and economic aspects of postwar international relations.

The Admiral's strong recommendations for a mighty navy and for control of Pacific bases which the armed forces had won in the Pacific raised fundamental issues to be faced at the San Francisco Conference and at other early meetings of Russia, Great Britain, and the United States, and suggested the legislative policy to be followed by early sessions of Congress.

Such issues confronted Admiral King as he spoke. He presumably reflected the attitude of the Navy. His speech was compact. He enumerated the requirements for an effective naval power and indicated (as a minor premise) that only by controlling such Japanese bases could our seapower be genuinely effective in safeguarding our interests and those of world peace.

Admiral King has a reputation for economy of language. His address, nevertheless, was concrete at every turn in illustration of his point. Somewhat the tone of a naval communique was present, the straightforward vocabulary of his naval reports since 1941.

He frequently addresses public gatherings and radio audiences. He is regarded as one of the outstanding speakers of the armed forces.[3]

I wish to thank the Academy of Political Science for affording me this opportunity to speak. I propose to discuss the influence of certain phases of seapower as it has shaped some of

[1] By permission of Admiral King. Text supplied by the Navy Department.
[2] For biographical note see Appendix.
[3] See his addresses on Navy Day, October 27, 1943 and November 27, 1944.

the events of the war up to this time. I shall also touch upon the role seapower may play in our future national security.

For almost three and one-half years we have been fighting an intense global war. During these months of combat, American seamen have proved themselves the rightful inheritors of naval traditions almost forgotten. During this same period our fleet has been multiplied in spite of war's bitter attrition. By now, however, sufficient evidence has been accumulated to warrant our drawing a few observations and conclusions. They are more than this—they are lessons.

Although seapower contributed much in the founding of our Republic, although it fought to preserve the nation after its birth, the passage of time records that we neglected our birthright. Somewhere along the line we lost the pioneer's vision. Particularly during the latter decades of the nineteenth century and until recent years the American public thought of this nation primarily as a land power. Several factors influenced that thought. Millions of our people lived inland—our territory was contiguous and it was located in a peaceful hemisphere.

But today, the United States is the leading maritime power in the world. And events of this war have proved—if proof were needed—that where international affairs are concerned, seapower is of maximum significance.

Seapower means precisely what it implies: the power to gain and hold control of the seas. It does not mean ships—and ships alone; neither does it mean planes—and planes alone. The term is collective, denoting the sum total of all those instruments by which control of the seas is gained and exercised.

Composed of seven essential elements, we may express seapower as an equation: Seapower equals surface ships, *plus* submarines, *plus* aircraft, *plus* merchant ships, *plus* naval bases, *plus* trained personnel, *plus* the productive capacity to build, equip, operate and fight them. To be fully effective, seapower must have all of these seven vital elements. The omission of any one tends to upset the equation and renders seapower that much less efficient.

In the present war there have been several instances in which one or another of the belligerents failed to pay sufficient attention to all of the elements of seapower. By neglecting surface ships, submarines, aircraft, merchant ships, bases, trained personnel, or productive capacity, serious consequences were suffered.

Foremost in making such a costly blunder is Germany. The Germans, who have never been effectively sea-minded, launched their program of world conquest in 1939 without providing adequate means for projecting their massive land forces across intervening stretches of water. They placed their reliance upon the plane and the submarine. The submarine is intended, not so much as a means to gain control of the sea, but to deny its use to the enemy. German U-boats attacked the Allied lifeline to Britain, and the Battle of the Atlantic ensued. The result is well known to all.

Again, by placing their major confidence upon the airplane, the Nazis failed to thrust across the English Channel. Their planes wreaked havoc on British cities, but they could not occupy that defended land. The Germans massed tanks and infantry at the water's edge—and there they stopped. Their provisions for amphibious warfare, which we have since so highly developed, were inadequate. Our mastery of this kind of warfare and our control of the waters adjacent to Europe enabled Allied armies to do in 1944 what the Nazis were incapable of doing in 1940— cross the English Channel.

Japan too blundered. Perhaps the weakest link in her naval armor was the inability to protect her merchant marine. In their lightning offense of 1941-42, the Japanese sprawled their forces over an expanse greater than their merchant marine could effectively serve. Means were not available to them to prevent our submarines, and, later our planes, from whittling down Japanese shipping. This deficiency was further accentuated by the inadequacy of trained personnel and shipbuilding facilties to replace these losses. Thus the Japanese found themselves incapable of exploiting their conquered empire; they had no way of linking it with their industrial centers on Honshu and the Asiatic mainland.

In pointing to the mistakes of our enemies, we must also examine our own shortcomings. An inadequate merchant marine was one of our prewar weaknesses. After the last war, we dissipated our store of merchant shipping. We compounded the error by not maintaining our shipbuilding capacity. Consequently, at the outbreak of this war, we found it necessary to construct swiftly what has come to be a stupendous tonnage of cargo ships. But so great was the demand and so heavy our shipping losses in the early days of the conflict that new construction could not keep pace with our needs.

For many anxious months, it was a nip-and-tuck affair trying to fulfill the shipping needs and at the same time attempting to meet the requirements for offensive and protective operations both in the Atlantic and Pacific.

As you know, the appetite of war is said to be all but insatiable. The demands of this war have almost continuously exceeded the supply. Always, from the first day of hostilities, there seemed to be highly desirable operations that might have been conducted had we but possessed a sufficient pool of supporting cargo vessels. Even with the unparalleled accomplishments of our cargo shipbuilding efforts, severe shortages have made it necessary from time to time to delay operations. We have paid the price in retarded progress.

Recalling the shipping difficulties encountered in this war, and contemplating the armada of bottoms and the expanse of shipyards we have built, we now face a vital question. How much shipping should be retained in fairness to ourselves? Shall we again risk the impact of total war without adequate shipping to deliver the tremendous quantity of materials needed by our forces and those of our allies? Shall we again permit our goods to be carried in foreign bottoms to the detriment of our own shipping needs in time of emergency? In the light of our foreign trade and our naval needs what should we do? This will be one of the knottiest postwar problems—a problem in which the Navy is vitally interested.

But more than an adequate merchant marine, we must have bases. Of all the elements of seapower, the United States Navy suffered most at the war's outbreak from the lack of overseas bases. We lacked operating bases in the Alaskan area; had none in the Far East, except for isolated and inadequate Cavite; none in the Central Pacific, except Pearl Harbor, and only those recently acquired in the North and Central Atlantic outside of Cuba and continental United States. The bases we did possess were not equipped with the requisite guns and planes and men to stem the enemy's initial onslaughts.

I make this point because it is well to remember that the mere ownership of outlying bases means little, if these bases are not maintained and implemented by an appropriate fleet ready for action.

Up to the present, the Pacific war has been largely a battle for bases. Our primary efforts so far have been directed toward wresting from the enemy advance territory from which our naval and military forces can rain body blows upon the inner Japanese empire. At the war's termination we shall have bases serving our task forces in most areas of operations.

These atolls, these island harbors, will have been paid for by the sacrifice of American blood. They will have been scooped out of sand and rock, coral and volcanic ash, by a generation of Americans giving their service, their ingenuity, and their money.

Failure to maintain these bases essential for our defense raises the fundamental questions: How long can the United States afford to continue a cycle of fighting and building and winning and giving away—only to fight and build and win and give again? Rich as we are, we do not have the human or physical resources to dissipate our patrimony, generation after generation, in this manner.

The United States Navy now possesses a balanced fleet containing all the essential elements by which control of the seas can be attained and retained. How this concentration of power has been applied against the enemy—the actions of our fleets speak for themselves. But as forceful as they have been, there are several basic achievements worthy of mention, accomplishments that may not have received sufficient emphasis.

In all wars, the Navy's strategy and tactics have revolved around those weapon-bearers that hit hardest and farthest. Our fleet's adaptation of the airplane to sea warfare may be rated as one of the major military achievements of our age. The air arm of the United States Navy is the envy of other navies throughout the world. By utilizing air, our fleet has been able to make long advances, instead of having to doggedly batter the enemy mile by mile. Without our highly developed and closely integrated air arm, we would, in all probability, still be operating in Allied territory today. Particularly is thus true in the Pacific where distances count for so much.

The significant aspects of naval aviation are not only the technological advances that have been made in airplane and carrier, but also the manner in which the plane has been integrated with the fleet. It is this high degree of integration that explains much of our sea-air success in the present war. The process of integration began in 1913 when the plane was coming to be recognized as a potent military weapon. In assimilating the plane, the Navy treated it as any other new weapon or new weapon-bearer—just as it had previously treated the submarine.

When the effective submarine first came into being shortly after the turn of the century, the Navy did not create a separate submarine, or underwater corps, commanded by officers who knew submarines and little else. Instead, those naval officers of the line who volunteered for submarine duty were considered to have additional qualification above and beyond the normal line requirements.

So it was with the airplane a decade or so later. In accepting the plane, the Navy did not junk its other weapons; nor did it give the plane an independent or semi-independent status. Instead, the plane was added to the arsenal of the many weapons that are necessary to gain and to exercise control over the seas. Naval aviators are naval officers who are additionally qualified for the management and operation of aircraft. That has been the practice down to this day. The Japanese, uniquely among other powers, have copied our methods in the matter of naval aviation development. Had the Japanese carried out such a development independently of our example and had we failed to develop an efficient integrated naval aviation arm, I can assure you that our country would have been confronted with disastrous probabilities.

Wartime developments in the employment of various other instruments of sea warfare are significant. The battleship and cruiser are types in point. The advent of the plane materially altered the technique of their employment, but far from destroying their usefulness made them more than ever, essential elements of seapower.

Weapons, however, are not enough to win a war. They must be used with skill and employed in new ways. Although amphibious warfare is as old as history, we have through hard work and battle experience developed and perfected the technique of amphibious operations, in which the Japanese were apparently so proficient in the early days of the war. Such operations have, however, achieved a new importance because of certain geographic factors of this war; and also, because modern weapons have made the defense so strong that amphibious attack has become one of the most difficult forms of the offensive. In former times, landing on an enemy shore was a fairly simple matter. Those afloat had more mobility than those ashore. The classic technique was to fool the enemy by a surprise landing where his defenses were weak or nonexistent.

However, in recent years it has become more difficult to outguess the defenders. This is due to the development of mechanized land forces which permit the defenders to move with great speed, and the reconnaissance of aviation which precludes surprise attacks. In the special case of the war in the Pacific, we frequently have had to make frontal attacks against small islands where no soft spots could be found and there was no possibility of surprise. Consequently, new types of vessels and new types of weapons and equipment have been devised. We are still improving, with some of the ablest officers in the armed forces working continuously in applying the dearly bought lessons of the war. In all such operations the cornerstone of our success has been the proven ability of the Army and Navy to fight as one team. It is significant that amphibious operations have initiated practically all of the Allied successes during the past three years.

I do not have the time to mention all the other uses to which instruments of seapower have been put in this war. But one of great importance is our development of the task force or task fleet. The idea was conceived by the United States Navy years before the outbreak of war. It was tested and found to be sound in the various hit-run raids on the Marshalls and Gilberts, Marcus and Wake, in early 1942.

Another significant naval development has been in the field of supply. By speeding up the flow of men and materials to the fighting fronts, our fleets have been able to operate against the enemy over protracted and unprecedented periods of time. Never in the history of naval warfare have fleets remained away from their bases so long. Without such logistical support, the Pacific war could not have progressed so far or so fast.

Improvement in naval gunnery has been another outstanding achievement of the war. Prior to the war, the world's prevailing naval thought was that surface craft could not successfully challenge shore batteries. Our fleet has proved that view wrong. The big guns of our battleships and cruisers have successfully slugged it out with coastal guns on several beachheads in both the European-African and Pacific areas. In effect, the guns of the fleet have extended the area of sea control inland from the sea.

Spectacular as have been the achievement of the United States Navy during this war, I wish to add this sobering thought: We cannot patent or copyright them for our exclusive future use. Our successes and our mistakes, our tactics and strategy will be studied and copied or avoided by other navies for years to come. Today, we are truly writing the naval textbooks of tomorrow.

It therefore behooves this nation to keep abreast—no, *ahead* of the time—in war and peace alike. We must, therefore, continue scientific research in the military field on a sustained basis even after the final victory. We must go still further. If we are to maintain our naval position in future years, we must augment the study of the science of war that has guided us in the past during peace. This has special application, of course, to the officers of our military and naval establishments. It seems unnecessary to expand on this point.

We are today confronted with two powerful warrior nations that have made the scientific conduct of war a continuing study, one of them for more than seventy-five years. When they struck, they struck swiftly and effectively, while their selected opponents were mentally and materially unprepared. Only because of our favorable geographic position and the brave delaying actions fought by our allies were we spared even greater reverses that we might have sustained. Never again can we afford to let future aggressors versed in the art of war take advantage of us.

Today there are people who gaze into the future and confidently predict that seapower—control of the seas—will not be a significant factor in determining the outcome of another war. Some of these prognosticators are the same as those who, earlier in this war, sang the swan song of the battleship and consigned the foot soldier to oblivion.

Throughout the ages centers of civilization and power have gravitated toward the water. Access to the seas has made nations prosperous in times of peace. Control of the seas has made them powerful in times of war. There are no developments in this war that controvert the fundamental importance of the sea. Neither is there anything that depreciates the value of seapower —at least, nothing that need concern us of this generation or in the foreseeable future.

Because of the exercise of our seapower in this war, a significant two-fold result has been accomplished. First, even at the lowest ebb of our naval strength, we were able to keep the conflict two thousand miles from our shores. The battles to protect the United States from invasion were fought in the Solomons, the Coral Sea, at Midway, and in the Aleutians—not off San Francisco, or Seattle, or San Diego. Second, our seapower has enabled us to maintain at all times the vital sea communications without which we could not support our allies. This gave us an advantage that is not sufficiently understood or appreciated. This is an advantage we must never relinquish.

I wish to point out particularly that the success of international agreements in the settlement of international disputes, especially in the early phases, will rest on world appreciation and recognition that these decisions can be—probably will be—enforced. Seapower will be an essential means to this end.

Moreover, it is well to take thought of the human factor. Just as in this day of mechanized warfare, the machines, ships, planes, tanks guns, which make was so deadly are as nothing without the men who man them and give them life. So it is with agreements and treaties. Without human will to make them work, or without the physical means to make them effective, they become and are in fact "more scraps of paper." Theodore Roosevelt was, I think, quite right when he said: "Speak softly, but carry a big stick."

Possessed as we are for the moment with naval greatness, it is difficult to believe that we will permit this power to be squandered or bartered away thoughtlessly. We will never do this, I am sure, if we understand what it might mean in terms of America's future in the world of tomorrow.

Hence our seapower should be maintained. Furthermore, it should be dedicated, in war and peace alike, to promoting the security and well-being of our people and to the peaceful stabilization of an improving world orderliness. We who have gone through this war have paid the penalty of forgetting the lessons of the years between wars. This time we shall win the victory despite our past mistakes. But next time, the penalty of forgetting may be the loss of America, and of liberty as we have known it.

PEACE—IF WE WANT IT [4]

Karl D. Mundt [5]

Representative Karl D. Mundt, of South Dakota, gave this argument for a world air patrol, before the House of Representatives, on January 30, 1945. Under a previous order of the House the speaker was recognized for one hour.

Warm applause and favorable comment followed the presentation of the argument.[6] The speaker faced and answered the question: To what extent should the world organization have control over the military might of the world? Mr. Mundt, commenting later on his own argument, stated, "What is desperately needed today is greater attention to the details and mechanics of a program appropriately devised to make the recurrence of great wars a complete impossibility. This can be achieved. But it can only be achieved if and when great nations as well as small are willing to dedicate an effective portion of their armed might to preventing war rather than simply and only engaging in rival armament races. . . . Today's most devasting falcons of war can become the world's most effective harbinger of peace, if we exercise sufficient moral courage now to dedicate military power to the task of preventing future wars." [7]

This speech should be analyzed and briefed as an example of extended argument. It has the best qualities of complete forensic. The introduction, for example, includes a highly personal narrative by which the speaker establishes the good-will of the listeners and justifies his one-hour argument, outlines the goals of any postwar international program, and defines terms (e.g., *isolationism* and *interventionism*). The issues are not directly stated, but the field of argument is clearly mapped out. The main argument treats in turn, (1) the need for some specific program to safeguard national security, solvency, self-government and sovereignty; (2) the solution of that need in the establishment of an international police patrol; (3) the practical details and working of such patrol; (4) the ten aspects of the program that would assure its satisfactory results in achieving the goals mentioned at the outset; (5) the realization of these results without impairing national sovereignty (the refutation phase of the argument). Finally the conclusion reinforces the arguments and appeals for action ("let us now set up the pattern").

[4] By permission of Representative Mundt. Text furnished by the author.

[5] For biographical note see Appendix.

[6] See, for example, *New York Times*, January 31, 1945, p. 3; also *Congressional Record*, Vol. 91, No. 46, p. A 1227-8 (daily edition) March 12, 1945.

[7] *Congressional Record*, Vol. 91, No. 46, p. A 1227-8 (daily edition) March 12, 1945.

Representative Mundt is a seasoned and personable platform speaker. He is lively and easily holds audience attention and interest. He has had training and experience as a debater at Iowa University and Carleton College, has taught speech and directed debate teams, has had wide speaking experience in political campaigns and before educational audiences. On December 28, 1944, he gave an extemporaneous address before the National Association of Teachers of Speech, at Chicago, as a last minute substitute for Senator-elect Wayne Morse, of Oregon. Mr. Mundt demonstrated full effectiveness in extempore address.

Mr. Speaker, late last August the gentleman from South Carolina, Congressman James Richards, and I went to Europe as two members of the House Foreign Affairs Committee in an effort to bring back what information we could on three matters which are frequently before our committee. First, the effectiveness in the battle areas of lend-lease and lend-lease in reverse; second, the needs and the administrative efficiency of U.N.R.R.A.; and, third, the problems which will confront the United States in the postwar era, together with the possibilities of developing ways and means for establishing and enforcing permanent peace.

The gentleman from South Carolina [Mr. Richards] and I spent nearly five weeks in the United Kingdom and in Europe. We conferred with a great many officials and private citizens, not only of England and France but of other members of the United Nations. We talked with literally hundreds of officers and men in the United States armed forces. We visited battle areas, bombing bases, barracks behind the lines, hospitals, and other places where G.I.'s were eager to talk to us and we were eager to talk with them. We talked with businessmen and taxi drivers, with cabinet officers, and street-corner orators, with prominent citizens and members of Parliament as well as the common run of citizens assembled in the pubs and crowded in the underground bomb shelters.

To the best of our ability we tried to bring back a cross-section of what our men in uniform are thinking and of the prevailing lines of thought running through the various strata of the economic life of our associates in this war. We did not limit our study to the grandiose plans of the great men in public office although we did counsel long and profitably with these public men of affairs. We were also interested, however, in the opinions and plans of the little men in the shops and on the streets who comprise the great background of community thought which, in the final analysis in any democratic government, nourishes and supports or nullifies and stifles the proposals made by public men.

Both the gentleman from South Carolina [Mr. Richards] and I, in our own way and on earlier occasions, have expressed ourselves in regard to the operations of lend-lease and concerning our findings in connection with U.N.R.R.A. We shall probably have more to say, each in our individual capacity, on these subjects when they once again become matters for legislative consideration by Congress.

Today, therefore, I want to limit my remarks to the third of our objectives in visiting Europe last September and October, namely, the problems of the postwar era and the paths which seem most clearly to point to permanent peace. Obviously, I speak for myself alone and in the main I have not even discussed the proposals I am about to make with my good and respected traveling companion, the great and able Democrat, the gentleman from South Carolina, Congressman James P. Richards.

Let me say, first of all, that it is with deep humility and considerable hesitation that I take the time of the House to discuss what I consider to be the outline of a program which can make for permanent peace. Far abler men than I have voiced their ideas on the building of a lasting peace, and I am encouraged to add my thoughts to the growing collection of testimony on the subject only because, first, it is the most important problem confronting humanity at this juncture of history; second, in a republic such as ours it is only by the free exchange and the critical examination of many ideas that we can finally arrive at the optimum course of action for preserving peace; and, third, since the men who should have most to say about the plans for peace—the men fighting in the battle areas—are not here to express themselves, I think it only right that I should bring to you some of the thoughts on the subject which they conveyed to me as I talked with them last fall in England, in France, and elsewhere overseas.

Let me say, further, that the proposals which I am about to make do not represent a finished and completed plan of action but rather they are suggestions for an approach to world peace which I consider workable, which are of the type that almost immediate action can be taken on them, and which are amenable to refinement and development as they are given further study should sufficient citizens deem them to have merit enough to warrant continued examination.

Mr. Speaker, we hear much these days in the nature of debate as to whether the United States should join this or that type of world organization to preserve the peace of the world, following victory in this war. I believe it fair to say that today the vast majority of our citizens, the genleman from South Dakota now addressing you among them, favor the United States exerting in the field of peaceful postwar relations the same type of sturdy and effective leadership our armed forces are now so successfully exerting in the field of battle. Most of us feel that cooperation with other nations of the world is essential after the war. Most of us believe and hope that some type of world organization can be created which will provide for the adjustment of differences between nations without resort to war. All of us hope that war may be forever outlawed as a means of settling international disputes once victory crowns our efforts in this conflict.

There is little difference among us, Mr. Speaker, concerning the heart hunger of all Americans—it is for a just and permanent peace. Where the differences arise is over the details of establishing a world organization, the authorities to be given to it, the recognition which it will give to smaller nations and the peoples of races colored other than white.

Disputes take place over how much sacrifice or sovereignty our Republic can make and still remain secure in its defense and sure that its influence can be sufficiently exercised to move the world upward rather than finding ourselves submerged in a universal whirlpool pulling humanity downward. Who shall have the voting power? Who shall control the police force? Shall imperialism, or self-determination, or enforced democracy, or unchallenged communism, or universal capitalism, or recognized monarchies, or diluted fascism either be the universal order or be specifically denied to individual nations within or outside the new world organization? How large should the police force be?

All agree, of course, that it should be large enough to stop Japan or Germany or Italy from ever charging across their new postwar borders again to start a career of aggression. But should it be large enough to combat the British or American navies or to defeat the Russian armies should any of these, through some weird distortion of future objectives, ever engage in aggressive acts?

The answers to these questions are not all clear, Mr. Speaker, and men of good will still disagree among themselves about the imposition of international rules of cooperation, good behavior, and police power when they apply to present members of the United Nations. Yet, all but the most unrealistic must recognize that the greatest fallacy in international logic is the assumption that we can have permanent world peace merely by making certain that those against whom we are presently arrayed shall not start another war. If such illogical reasoning had dominated our thinking for the last quarter of a century, we would indeed be in a sorry fix in our war with Japan since the Japanese Empire was one of our allies in World War No. 1, and in that conflict Italy also fought on our side.

Nations have a habit of changing both friends and foes in the bloody history of battles. At any stage of history it is always tragically true that today's friends may become tomorrow's foes. To assure permanent peace we must devise methods which not only hold in check our present enemies but which also make certain that they operate with equal effectiveness when applied to all present members of the United Nations, including the United States.

While we in the United States are of one mind that imperialism and aggression shall never form a part of our national policy we must realize that no matter how sacred our own good intentions the citizens of other lands need more than that to induce them to accept for themselves restrictions and regulations which we in this republic might prefer to see applied only to others and not to ourselves. Self-interest is still a prime rule of survival for all nations, great or small.

While the problems that must yet be solved are prodigious in the matter of developing an international organization which we can all support, I am not one of those who hold the pessimistic view that it cannot be done. We shall and we must continue trying. No recital of pious platitudes and glittering principles no matter how long or eloquent will assure the world of lasting peace. It is the method and machinery for putting those pretty phrases into actual operation which puts reality into our rhetoric. It is here that a world-wide area of agreement is actually needed. It is also the specific proposals, the concrete plans, the devilish little details that make or mar the achievements of idealism.

A hundred resolutions of intent are not as important as a single resolution in support of a specific step in the colossal job of weaving a pattern of good international behavior in the postwar world. Resolutions of good intention such as we have already passed in Congress too greatly resemble a general reformation against sin which studiously avoids detailing any of the personal vices which we propose to correct. They sound well, but they accomplish little in this world of stern reality.

A great philosopher, Seneca, once said, "If you would speak with me, define your terms." We Americans should recognize, and I am sure we do, that neither our domestic policy nor our foreign policy can operate successfully without consideration for the other. Neither can operate in a vacuum. Each should supplement and reinforce the other. When the one conflicts with the other it must result, sooner or later, in the one nullifying the other. Consequently, one or both is certain to fail unless they have been developed coordinately. As we proceed with each we must define our terms.

There are some who say, "What is good for America is good for the world," and others who argue, "What is good for the world is good for America." I presume the former group represents what is called nationalism or isolationism and the latter group what we call interventionists or extreme internationalists. In my opinion, both isolationism and interventionism have ceased to mean anything significant in this country and have ceased to define important groupings of public opinion.

For my own part, in the pre-Pearl Harbor days I never considered myself either an interventionist or an isolationist. I did not fit comfortably under either of the then prevailing labels.

So, for lack of a better designation, I then called myself an "insulationist." I favored making America and the Western Hemisphere as strong and effective a modern military establishment as possible, and I favored keeping the United States from taking steps which would needlessly involve it in two great wars simultaneously and before we were prepared. As I said many times in those pre-Pearl Harbor days, I favored full international cooperation for maintaining peace and promoting progress but I favored "insulating" ourselves as much as possible from the ravages and cruelties of war. Thus the term "insulationist."

In earlier days, when the decision was an issue, I was known with reservations as a League of Nations Republican. Yes, Mr. Speaker, before Pearl Harbor, I was an internationalist in peace and an "insulationist" in war. I still am. There is, however, no guaranty that either intervention in foreign affairs or isolation from them will bring permanent peace and tranquility to America. Neither is a patent medicine with a miraculous cure-all for international problems. Either of them can do more to wreck than to win human happiness, if intelligence is not exercised in their application.

Simply to commit ourselves to international organization without analyzing carefully its mechanics of operation, its controls, its objectives, and its infringements upon self-determination may, actually, purchase more of future war than it does of sustained peace.

Thus it seems the acme of human folly to proclaim we are for or against participation in an international organization to preserve peace unless at the same time we weave into the fabric of our resolution something of the pattern of procedure and purpose we would have such an organization undertake. Again, sir, I say we must define our terms.

As for me, I am convinced today, as I have always been, that the United States as a nation cannot enjoy permanent good health surrounded by a world which is seriously ill nor can we enjoy permanent peace in a world which finds a large part of itself repeatedly at war with other substantial parts of it. I think that it is also an accurate corollary of that statement to say that neither can the world enjoy permanent peace and good health in an era in which the United States is seriously ill in an economic, social, or political sense.

I, therefore, favor a program of international cooperation—exercised through an international organization if it can be appropriately developed—which within our means and to the full extent of our ability will help bring better government, tolerant attitudes, sustained peace, and improved economic conditions to other portions of the world. While remembering that our first patriotic concern must be for America, we should also recognize that in nations as in neighborhoods, what helps others helps us, and what helps us helps others.

I stated on May 10, 1943, in an address in Constitution Hall here in Washington when I participated in a public forum sponsored as part of the United Nations discussion series:

> I believe the United States should extend the hand of Christian fellowship and friendly helpfulness as far and as fast as other nations will reach out to take it in a firm and sincere resolve to work together to preserve peace and to eliminate the evils and inequalities which provide the seeds of resentment and of war.

That, Mr. Speaker, is my creed and conviction. I had earlier expressed it in an address in Baltimore commemorating the diamond anniversary of the Elks Lodge of that city and on several occasions I have reaffirmed it on the floor of this House.

In determining what the earmarks of "an organization appropriately developed" should be, I believe there are four factors which our statesmen should bear in mind as we begin shaping the actual details and defining the specific mechanics of such an organization. These four factors are:

1. Our national security must be safeguarded. We must avoid anything in the postwar world which would endanger the security of this republic. We must pray and we must work for the best, but we must be prepared for the worst. Our army, navy, and air corps must ever be strong enough to protect the position of the United States while we strive to perpetuate the peace of the world. We must always be willing to do our part to keep the world from engaging in a crazy contest of armament building, but we must not permit our good faith to induce us to weaken ourselves so that, relatively, we lose the prestige and

the power which now are ours. As the mightiest armed force in the world today which is contributing the most to winning this war we have a duty and a right to maintain our position in the years to follow victory.

2. Our solvency must be safeguarded. A bankrupt, insolvent America can do little to influence world behavior wisely. We must be strong financially to be influential idealistically. Thus, our ambition to help others must never exceed our ability to finance what we undertake. If it does, we help nobody, but we hurt ourselves and destroy the confidence which others have in our integrity. We must always cut our pattern to fit our financial cloth.

3. Our system of self-government must be safeguarded. Believing as we do in freedom, we must protect here at home that which we seek to project abroad. We cannot inspire others to follow the processes of democracy unless we retain the *functions* as well as the *forms* of self-government in the United States. It follows, therefore, that the people of America must participate in the formation of a people's peace and that due constitutional procedures must be relied upon in the development of any postwar program which is to be effective. It is also essential that the men who are actually fighting this war should be given something to say about the type of program and/or the international organization that is to follow the victory which their sacrifices will have won.

The pagan philosophy that young men should fight the wars and old men in high places safe at home should alone exercise the judgment which either involves countries in war or promises to prevent future conflicts has no part in a republic dedicated to the principles of self-government. It is well that we plan and prepare now for world cooperation to follow this war, but it is a wretched point of view to hold that completely firm commitments should be made at this time by those at home without an opportunity for consultation with or ratification by the men whose heroism on the field of battle is making possible our free decisions in the postwar world. I, for one, have little sympathy with the idea that those whose blunderings may have been responsible for the failure to avert this total global war should now have a monopoly on making the decisions of the future.

In this republic there should not be those who, when 11,000,-000 citizens are in uniform away from home, would arrogate unto themselves the sole right to determine what dividends should flow from the sacrifices of those now making them on the field of battle. This time let us hope that the young men who fight the wars will also be given something to say about what is to result from their fighting.

4. Our sovereignty must be safeguarded. We in the United States number less than 140,000,000 human beings. The world had a prewar population of 2,140,000,000. It is axiomatic, therefore, that if the United States is to exert its rightful influence upon the other peoples of the world, it must exert that influence as a unit rather than through its separate citizens acting and voting as single individuals, in a world-wide association in which each citizen's influence is equal to each of the other 2,140,000,000 human beings inhabiting the world.

With more than 2,000,000,000 citizens living outside the United States it is clearly obvious that our power for good would be comparatively insignificant if national sovereignty were to be sacrificed to the point where a mere counting of noses or of votes were to determine policies in any world-wide organization. As a national *unit,* as the richest and most powerful nation in the world, the United States can and should exert a tremendous influence for human betterment, world peace, and economic advancement, but with all sovereignty submerged we could exert virtually no directive strength in world leadership.

To protect what we have, and to promote what we feel to be right, the United States must retain its sovereignty if it is to work effectively with other nations to raise the world's levels of human decency and civilized conduct. To merge this country into world citizenship without protecting the power of this great country to exert its united influence for good would do more to set back human progress than to stimulate it.

In working with others, we may well have to forego certain prescribed functions of sovereignty and we must learn to exercise certain of these functions in harmony with other right-minded nations, but while we reach for the stars we must keep our feet on the ground. Otherwise we deceive ourselves and defraud others of the dividends which can accrue from world leadership by the United States but which cannot be produced by the unorganized and unharnessed efforts of 140,000,000 individual citizens of the United States regardless of their good intentions and their high ideals.

Mr. Speaker, I come now to the immediate problem of maintaining lasting peace for which all of the foregoing is but a background for my reasoning. I come, too, to the plans for peace and for preparedness which I mentioned in the beginning of this address and having discussed with men and women in uniform overseas when I was in England and France last fall. I now want to discuss my proposals for the establishment of permanent peace as they have developed from my own study and from these observations and these conferences and as they fall within the framework of the considerations set forth thus far in this discourse.

Mr. Speaker, I believe the establishment of an international peace patrol of the air can successfully, definitely, and permanently avert another major war. I say this categorically and without reservation. I believe the time is here when the world can have permanent peace if it wants it. It can have it without nations seriously sacrificing their sovereignty, without their foregoing their cultural or political ideals, and without the expenditure of such enormous sums for national armaments that economic progress and human happiness are denied to common citizens.

Mr. Speaker, by making a realistic approach to the problem of lasting peace the world now has an opportunity of turning the most awful falcons of war into effective doves of peace. The airplane which has brought death and disaster to so many as an implement of war can now be utilized to bring security and peace to all humanity for all future time to come.

I propose, Mr. Speaker, that the United States take the initiative in requesting the other members of the United Nations to join it in establishing without delay the basic foundations for operating an international peace patrol of the air after this war. This peace patrol of the air can be staffed and manned by volunteers from among the fighting pilots and their officers who are now using airpower so effectively in helping to turn the tides of war in our favor on every battle front.

The details of operating the peace patrol of the air, its size, its rates of compensation, its home bases, the extent of its prerogatives, its directive agency, and the like can be determined by experts in the art of national defense and can be easily agreed upon because they require no serious encroachments upon national sovereignty and they avoid the perplexing problems growing out of agreements for complicated international organizations.

Reduced to its simplest, though not necessarily its optimum form, but still comprising the nucleus of a force sufficient to sustain a permanent peace, it could operate as follows. At the start, five thousand military planes could be selected from the best now being operated by the armed services of the United Nations with a thousand planes being home based on each of five strategically located air bases in the world.

Depending on what progress the world makes in regulating and controlling its postwar armaments, both in the air and on the land and sea, the size of this international peace patrol of the air can and should be expanded to many times more than five thousand planes if necessary to enforce the peace.

More bases could be dedicated to this purpose as it becomes wise or necessary. But for the purpose of explaining my proposal, I am using five thousand planes and five bases as an illustrative figure to demonstrate the way the peace patrol of the air would work.

Due consideration should be given to selecting a wise ratio of fighter and bomber planes, of superbombers and of transports, of photographic observation planes, of amphibious and land-based planes, and of all modern types of military planes. Suggested quotas for volunteers to man these planes and officer their operation might well follow the general percentages of men whom the respective members of the United Nations now have engaged in the aviation services.

Where any nation fails to fill its quota by volunteers or by any other method it uses to select them, the quotas should be opened to other nations desiring to supply the manpower.

Until and unless some other more comprehensive world organization is developed and entered into by all of the major members of the United Nations, I would place the directing control of this International Peace Patrol of the Air in the hands of the Joint Chiefs of Staff of the United States, England, Russia, China, and France, which would set up some type of supreme control headquarters for this purpose similar to the existing pattern represented by the supreme headquarters of the Allied Expeditionary Forces now operating in Europe under the able direction of General Eisenhower. One member of this staff would serve as chairman, with the office rotating among the five members, and the vote of three of the five members would control the policies of the peace patrol and determine when and where it should strike should use of the force become necessary with unexpected promptitude.

On matters of policy, each member of the joint staff would secure his instructions from the properly constituted authority of his own country—which in this country would be Congress—but where immediate use of the police force became necessary the supreme control headquarters would be authorized to strike at once in conformity with clearly defined policies governing the extent of its activities and determined upon in advance by the governments thus cooperating.

Mr .Speaker, I propose this International Peace Patrol of the Air might originally be based on the airports now located as follows: Stephenville, Newfoundland; Preswick, Scotland; Cairo, Egypt; Natal, Brazil; and on one of the great air bases in China which American Army units have built. These bases have been built by the money of American taxpayers either as a direct part of the expense of this war or under lend-lease agreements and I suggest this country donate these ports for the use of the air peace patrol and that the countries in which they are located donate the land on which they are located for the same purpose. Thus internationalized, these great airports could be used to win the peace with the same effectiveness that they are now being used to win the war. They could also be used for commercial air traffic by all of the nations of the world but they would be under the direct management of the International Peace Patrol of the Air.

As to the financing of the activities of this patrol, whatever its ultimate size, I propose that each country contribute to the cost in direct proportion that it contributes personnel to the international peace patrol. The cost, at worst, will be infinitesimal as compared with the cost of war or even with the cost of maintaining military establishments of the vast size necessary if nothing tangible and direct is done to make future wars impossible.

It is my thought that the joint chiefs of staff of the United Nations as heretofore defined and which will direct the activities of this air patrol should be authorized by their respective governments to select, train, and deploy the units of this patrol so that it can operate to literally make future aggressive wars impossible. I would give the directing heads of this police force of the air the authority to order it into immediate action against any country which sent its armies or navies into war against any other country in the world. With no more than twenty-four hours' notice to the offending country, this air force should be empowered to fly military formations over the borders of any nation starting its war machines out beyond its own borders with instructions to bomb into oblivion any military units and establishments found within ten miles of that border after the notice to cease and desist warlike actions had been served on the offender.

So much for the actual activity of this peace patrol of the air in making future wars impossible. Now, Mr. Speaker, let me elaborate a bit on why and how this peace patrol would achieve its sacred responsibility of putting an end to war. Here are the reasons based on the lessons of this war, together with the collateral stipulations which would make the starting of a future war a virtual impossibility or at worst a short-lived suicidal effort on the part of its instigator.

1. While airpower has not proved sufficient to permit any nation in this war to win victory with it alone, airpower has demonstrated its strength sufficiently so that it is now obvious that any nation which lacks both defensive and offensive air weapons is helpless in modern warfare.

2. As part of this program to outlaw all future war by use of quick and immediate air force rather than by relying only on pious promises and glib sounding international compacts, I propose that after victory is won in this war our enemy countries be entirely stripped and kept divested of all offensive and defensive airpower. This must include anti-aircraft defenses as well as planes themselves together with the factories and equipment designed for making weapons of these types. It must of course include the new air weapons of this war such as the robot bombs, the great V-2 rocket bombs, and other offensive and defensive inventions capable of defense against airpower or of carrying destruction to others in the form of winged death or long-distance missiles. It must also include poisonous gas and implements for using it since gas is an airborne weapon and its potentialities as a weapon of war are too great to trifle with if the world wants permanent peace.

3. The personnel of the International Peace Patrol of the Air, in addition to its volunteer flyers and ground crew, should include from each country able and mature men in like ratio to the volunteers, assigned with diplomatic rank and from among specialists experienced in inspecting, evaluating, and analyzing weapons of war and factories capable of manufacturing them. These men should carry appropriate identification credentials cloaking them with authority to visit all factories and testing laboratories for military equipment in all countries of the world, including the United States. Thus we could be assured that our present enemy countries were being kept completely disarmed from the standpoint of all offensive and defensive air equipment including poisonous gas, and the world could be assured that among present friendly powers there was developing no maniacal race of armaments.

At least quarterly, these representatives of the peace patrol should publish reports written in every language and made alike available to every country of the world showing the status of military preparedness in every country, not only from the standpoint of defensive and offensive air weapons of war, but encompassing all implements of war.

4. Planes of this air patrol should be painted a distinctive color reserved for them alone and they should be authorized to land without charge on any public airport in the world at any time.

5. Members of the air peace patrol should wear distinctive uniforms save for some of the specialists in the inspecting service who could operate in plain clothes, when desirable, but only when supplied with proper identifying credentials.

6. With all present enemy countries permanently stripped of all offensive and defensive weapons and planes for air war, the other nations of the world should enter into collective agreements regulating the extent to which they, themselves, would be permitted to expand their own armaments of the air and their other military establishments.

A working rule of thumb for determining the size and scope of future airpower and preparedness might well be that at any future time the comparative air war strength and military might of each nation in the world should be relatively the same as it is at the conclusion of World War II, except for the aforementioned provision that the countries presently at war against the United Nations shall never again be permittted to develop any offensive and defensive air weapons. The quarterly reports by international military experts which I propose will prevent any nation, friend or foe, from secretly developing a dangerous and disproportionate military might.

7. Whatever decision the world makes concerning other future armaments, however, the airpower of all nations should be regulated as above suggested so that air force can be used primarily for the prevention of future wars and to give security to nations which have demonstrated their willingness and intention of living as good neighbors without aggressive acts of war. The functions of airpower should be reserved essentially to patrol the peace.

8. The International Peace Patrol of the Air should emerge immediately following this war while the men and equipment now being used in the fighting are readily available. This proposal neither demands nor denies the necessity of forming a comprehensive international organization to preserve the peace

and to better international living conditions. If such an international organization eventuates, the direction of the International Peace Patrol of the Air can gradually be turned over to the directing agency of that organization. If such an international organization, on the other hand, fails to eventuate, fails to attract the membership of all major nations, or fails to develop promptly after the war, the joint chiefs of staff as presently constituted are in position to begin directing the activities of the peace patrol the day after peace arrives.

9. Participation in the International Peace Patrol of the Air should be open to all present members of the United Nations and to all present neutrals in the ratios already outlined. No nations should be compelled to participate but if many do eventually, a sixth or seventh representative can be added to the chiefs of staff comprised of the members from the smaller nations selected by them on a rotating basis. If either the United States, England, Russia, France, or China should fail to join in the formation and functioning of this peace patrol the remaining major powers should proceed without it and that country's representation should be given to other nations desiring to participate.

Should any such nation refuse to participate, which now seems highly improbable, its acceptance should still be sought for permission to inspect its armament plants and use its airports. Only where such permission is denied should a country be excepted from those receiving the quarterly reports.

Denial of such permission would be notice to the world that that nation had something to conceal. It would be an advance warning signal of trouble. It would afford right-minded nations an opportunity to consult together to take stock of the situation before trouble veered into warfare and to take whatever protective or corrective steps might be necessary. As part of the articles of peace, however, it should be specifically provided that representatives of the peace patrol should have access to the airports and the armament plants of our vanquished foes for all time to come.

10. Much of the work of policing the peace and of ordinary armed forces of occupation could be undertaken by this peace

patrol. It is foolhardy to believe that once we have defeated the Axis we can withdraw all our forces and depend upon our enemies to establish order, maintain equity, and conform with the articles of peace.

On the other hand, American soldiers, sailors, and airmen will not want to be stationed for long periods of time in foreign countries doing a gigantic police job far away from home. However, members of the air forces are eager to continue flying. They will welcome the opportunity to volunteer to become members of the peace patrol, since this will permit frequent visits home and will assure them a distinguished career of flying and of public service. Within twenty-four hours a great portion of this vast flying police force could converge on a certain trouble spot and without modern defense against airpower an offending country can be forced to give up war as a means of settling international disputes or of satisfying international pride. For a nation to start a war without adequate offensive and defensive airpower would be to invite quick and certain disaster for itself.

Mr. Speaker, I have discussed these proposals with many people both in this country and in Europe. I have advised with distinguished American airmen such as my good friend Col. Roscoe Turner of Indianapolis and they have assured me that by reserving to airpower the missions of peace we can prevent nations from acquiring the essential machinery for war. Many a G.I. in France and England has told me that he does not want to be assigned as a member of an army of occupation for any length of time. Americans do not take to soldiering in peace and are not candidates in large number for membership in a mercenary army. Once war is ended they want to return to their homes, their schools, and their various means of livelihood.

On the other hand, tens of thousands of our young flying heroes are eager to take up careers in aviation. Ordinary peacetime flying opportunities will accommodate only a small percentage of these ambitions. I am confident that many over ten times as many volunteers will petition for membership in the International Peace Patrol of the Air as it can possibly utilize.

In discussing this plan while overseas, many a young airman told me, "I would jump at the chance to serve in such a peace patrol of the air." One especially enthusiastic young flyer in France told me, "Congressman, go back and tell America that this is the G.I. plan for permanent peace."

Other G.I.'s might not share so radiant an enthusiasm, but I am sure we can get the cream of the crop of able flyers of every country in the world, and these young men can be provided with permanent careers at good pay, and with the satisfaction of knowing they are engaged in the most important business in the world—the business of making future wars impossible.

Mr. Speaker, it is not my idea that this peace patrol of the air alone can fill the needs of the postwar world for international cooperation. Disputes between nations and international differences will still arise. The use of arbitration, the orderly development of an appropriate international organization to give countries the opportunity to work together in the solution of great problems, a world court in which to adjudicate, peacefully, the arguments which used to lead to war—all of these will still be desirable and utilitarian. But all of these without the use of force to make their decisions effective will not prevent a future war. This is the job for a police force with ability to act promptly and effectively. The International Peace Patrol of the Air would comprise such a force.

For the first time in history the world has access to a police force which can operate both on land and sea and which can cross continents and oceans in pursuit of its duties. It can secure peace without establishing the hazard that in our desire for peace we shall instead reap only the frightful dividends of more frequent war. It does not infringe upon the constitutional rights of the free people of this country to determine when and against whom we shall go to war and it does not delegate to one man the fateful decision of when or whether the young men of this country are to risk another rendezvous with Mars. Instead it sets up an international police force of the air, dedicated to a specific purpose defined by clear-cut policies shaped by the constitutional governing bodies of all participants.

It does this, Mr. Speaker, while preserving for the United States and every other country the four essential factors of security, solvency, self-government, and sovereignty which I mentioned earlier in this address.

Members of this peace patrol would function not as Americans or as Russians or as Britons but as members of an international police force, directed by an international control board, striking down wars virtually before they have had a day in which to get under way.

This force would strike not as a war commitment by any of the participating powers but as an avenging force for peace, representing the convictions of all countries that war is never again to be used as a means for aggrandizement or as a device for seeking justice against real or imaginary wrongs.

Countries could still resort, if they must, to disputes with their neighbors, to name calling, even to economic strife, but war would have been completely outlawed by dedicating to the patrolling of the peace the use of airpower. Without such weapons for either defensive or offensive use, any nation, great or small, is powerless to wage effective war against neighbors, near or far.

Out of this war has truly come the lesson which can prevent all future war. The world is now able to secure permanent peace if it wants it. As we go along in our thinking, refinements and additions to this proposal will steadily develop and in this we should call freely upon the experience and ideas of men now in uniform, but the working, operative, effective nucleus of a program to preserve peace permanently is now at hand.

An international peace patrol of the air set into motion at the end of this war can prevent our ever again being either participants or witnesses in another great war. It can stop wars at their source by driving warlike hordes back inside their own boundary lines before the march of Mars gets under way. When those now in uniform return we should also advise with them not only concerning the extended and expanded use of this air patrol but with regard to more comprehensive forms of world organization and cooperation.

There can never be a big war without having it originate somewhere by some nation striking out across its borders or beyond its shores on a mission of destruction and no country lacking offensive and defensive weapons for air warfare in this modern world can withstand the devastating attacks which a peace patrol of the air could bring down upon it. The only way to prevent big wars is to stop little wars at the very start if it is impossible to stop them from beginning.

It is well that we now discuss plans for the postwar world and that we argue the great opportunities and the troublesome details of international organizations for cooperative effort and for striving toward the goal of permanent peace. Let this continue and let us all prayerfully hope for perfection in these endeavors but without delay and with realistic determination let us now set up the pattern for an international patrol of the air and prepare to put it into operation with the dawn of peace.

We should do this so that never again may a disillusioned world be plunged into the suffering of war because men have planned too slowly or too short-sightedly or because their glorious dreams of peace have lacked a satisfactory method of enforcement.

We can now have peace—permanent peace— if we want it!

QUALITY OF AMERICA'S
FIGHTING MEN [8]

Dwight D. Eisenhower [9]

General Dwight D. Eisenhower, Supreme Commander of the Allied
Expeditionary Forces, delivered this address before a joint session of the
United States Congress, on June 18, 1945.

Fresh from Europe, the General was greeted by "a million men,
women, and children," perhaps the greatest and most enthusiastic throng
ever to welcome a national leader to Washington.

The immediate audience, besides the Senators and Representatives,
included members of the Supreme Court, ambassadors and ministers,
leaders of the Army and Navy, and fifty members of Eisenhower's own
party, some of them enlisted men.

The address, in the vein of the General's previous and subsequent
public speeches, paid tribute to the contribution made by "America's
fighting men"; by the Allied troops, including those of Great Britain;
by the joint Commanders in Chief, Roosevelt and Churchill; by the
American and British navies and air forces; by the Russians; by the
French, Belgian, Dutch and other resistance forces; and by civilian America. Eloquent was the conclusion.

The General departed from his usual custom of speaking extempo-
raneously. He read rapidly, emphatically, sometimes moved by latent
emotion. Always he was calm, soldierly, confident, optimistic, the kind
of leader and speaker who won rounds of applause from his immediate
hearers and from the millions of others who listened to the broadcast.

Mr. President, Mr. Speaker, Members of Congress, Ladies
and Gentlemen:

There is a message that I should like to bring to you from
the fighting front this morning. There is so much I would like
to say, so many subjects I should like to cover that as the only
way of saving an unconscionable trespass upon your time I have
tried to reduce my thoughts and notes and therefore I ask your
permission for me to break my invariable custom and for once to
use notes in addressing an audience such as this.

[8] Text is from the *New York Times,* June 19, 1945. The War Department
also supplied this compiler with a text. See also *Congressional Record,* Vol. 91,
No. 120, p. 6352-4, June 18, 1945 (daily edition).

[9] For biographical note see Appendix.

My imagination cannot picture a more dramatic moment than this in the life of an American. I stand before the elected Federal lawmakers of our great Republic, the very core of our political life and a symbol of those things we call the American heritage. To preserve that heritage, three million American citizens, at your behest, have faced resolutely every terror the ruthless Nazi could devise. I come before you as the representative of those three million people—their commander—because to them you wish this morning to pay the tribute of a grateful America for military victory. In humble realization that they, who earned your commendation, should properly be here to receive it, I am nevertheless proud and honored to be your agent in conveying it to them.

This does not seem to be the moment in which to describe the great campaigns by which the victory in Europe was won. They will become the substance of history, and great accounts they will be! But I think you would want from me some brief estimate of the quality of the sons, the relatives and friends that you—all America—have sent to war.

I have seen the American proved on battlegrounds of Africa and Europe over which armies have been fighting for more than two thousand years of recorded history. None of those battlefields has seen a more worthy soldier than the trained American.

Willingly, he has suffered hardships; without a whimper he has made heavy sacrifices. He has endured much, but he has never faltered. His aggressiveness—his readiness to close with the enemy—has become a by-word in the embattled armies of Europe. You have read many reports of his individual exploits, but not one tenth of them ever has been or ever will be told. Any one of them is sufficient to fill a true American with emotion —with an intense pride of his countryman.

Never have soldiers been called upon to endure longer sustained periods of contact with a vicious enemy nor greater punishment from weather and terrain. The American has been harassed by fire and automatic weapons, pounded by hand grenades, by artillery and rocket shells, attacked by tanks and airplane bombs! He has faced the hazards of countless mines and booby traps and every form of static obstacle. He has conquered them all!

The tempo of battle has increased tremendously during the span of this conflict. When the Germans launched their blitz-kriegs through Poland, the Low Countries and France, featuring tactical use of airpower with mechanized units on the ground, it seemed to a fearful world that at last there had been achieved the ultimate in destructive force—that nothing could stand against the German armies.

When America entered the war arena the Nazi machine was at the zenith of its power. In 1940 it had overrun practically the whole of western Europe, while, a year later, in the East, it had hammered back the great Red Army into the far reaches of its own territory.

The Allies met this challenge with vision, determination, and a full comprehension of the enormity of the task ahead. America brought forth her effort from every conceivable source. New techniques of war were developed. Of these the most outstanding was the completely coordinated use of ground, air and sea forces. To his dismay the German found that far from having achieved perfection in the combined employment of all types of destructive power, his skills and methods were daily outmoded and surpassed by the Allies.

Through tactical and strategic unification the Allies successfully undertook the greatest amphibious landings yet attempted in warfare. Following each of these, forces were swiftly built up on the beaches, and sustained by our naval strength. The next step was always a speedy advance, applying to the astonished enemy an air-ground teamwork that inflicted upon him defeat after defeat.

The services of supply, by their devotion to duty, performed real miracles in supporting the battle lines. America, and her Allies, sent finally into Europe such an avalanche of aggressive power by land, by sea, by air, as to make the campaigns of 1939 and 1940 seem puny in contrast. The result was the unconditional surrender of an arrogant enemy.

All this America and her Allies have done.

The real beginning, for us, was in December 1941 when our late great war leader, President Roosevelt, met with his friend Prime Minister Churchill and forged a definition of Allied organizational and directional method for the prosecution of this war.

During most of my three years in Europe these two God-given men were my joint Commanders in Chief. Their insistence on making common cause the key to victory established the pattern of the war in Europe.

To those two all of us recognize our lasting obligation. Because no word of mine could add to your appreciation of the man who, until his tragic death, led America in war, I will say nothing other than that from his strength and indomitable spirit I drew constant support and confidence in the solution of my own problems.

In Mr. Churchill he had a worthy partner, who had led his country through the blackest hour, in 1940. The Prime Minister's rugged determination, his fighting spirit and his singleness of purpose were always a spur to action. Never once did he give less than full cooperation in any endeavor necessary to our military objectives. And never did he hesitate to use his magnetic and powerful personality to win cheerful acceptance from his countrymen of the great demands he was forced to make upon them.

It was no small test of the hospitality and generous understanding of the British people to have 2,000,000 strangers moved among their already limited and crowded facilities. The added confusion imposed by the extensive gear of a great army was accepted with a cheerfulness that won the admiration of us Americans.

In critical moments Mr. Churchill did not hesitate to cut Britain's already reduced rations to provide more shipping for war purposes. Their overburdened railways had to absorb additional loads until practically all passenger traffic was suspended and even essential goods could be moved only on an emergency basis. For the hospitality the British offered us, for the discomforts they endured on our behalf, and for the sacrifices they made for the success of operation, every American acquainted with the facts will always carry for them a warm and grateful place deep within his heart.

Under these two great war leaders were the combined British American Chiefs of Staff who were my direct military superiors and the channel through whom I received all my orders. Their unwavering support, their expressed and implied confidence, their wise direction, and their friendliness in contact, were things to which I am happy to bear witness. They devised the machinery by which huge Allied forces were put together as a single unit, and through them were implemented the great military purposes that America and Great Britain agreed upon to further the political objectives of the war.

The spirit of unison that they developed was absorbed by the forces in the field.

In no place was this vital unity more strikingly evidenced than among the individuals that served as my principal commanders and on my staff. British and Americans forgot differences in customs and methods—even national prejudice—in their devotion to a common cause. Often have I thanked a kind Providence for these stanch Allies, from highest commander to the newest recruit, and for their readiness to serve within the team.

From our first battle associations with the British air forces in England, with her navy in the African invasion, and with the British armies in North Africa, we have measured their quality through many months of war. We well know and respect the fighting heart of the British, Canadian and French soldiers and their leaders.

This teamwork was equally strong among the several services, air, ground, navy and supply. The navy's task in gaining our first European footholds was a staggering one. Without wearying you with tactical details I ask you to take my word for the truth that in all the brilliant achievements of the American navy, and of her sister service in Great Britain, there is none to excel the record that was written in the great and successful invasions of Africa, Sicily, Italy and France. With the navy was always the merchant marine, in which Americans have served with a devotion to duty and a disregard for danger and hardship that defies any attempts to describe.

To the air forces, without whose services all else would have been futile, I—all of us—owe similar debts of gratitude. Perhaps it is best for me merely to say that in every ship, on every plane, in every regiment, was a readiness to give life itself for the common good. And in this statement, I must include the men that have been responsible for the tactics of the battle itself.

As an Allied commander, I have tried in London and in Paris, to record something of the debt the United Nations owe to the fighting leaders of the British Empire and of France. Today as an American, I would like to give you the names of our own officers that will always rank high in any list of those noted for service to their country. But any enumeration would necessarily be incomplete, so I must content myself by saying that, in great numbers, these battle leaders of the army, the navy, and the air, have served loyally, devotedly, and brilliantly in my commands in Europe and Africa. Particularly I think you would like to know that without exception, their first concern, their first care, has been the welfare—spiritual and physical—of their men —your sons, relatives and friends. You have as much right to swell with pride in the quality of the battle commanders you have sent to Europe and Africa as you have in the conduct of the millions they have led so skillfully and devotedly.

I have spoken mostly of Americans and British, because troops from this country and the British Empire always formed the bulk of my own command. But the campaigns of the Red Army, crushing all resistance in the East, played a decisive part in the defeat of Germany.

The abilities of the Soviet leaders and the courage and fortitude of their fighting men—and women—stir the emotions of anyone who admires soldierly virtues. The Soviet peoples have been called upon for terrible sacrifices in their own land, ravished by the bestial excesses of the German. Driven back to Stalingrad, their calm refusal to acknowledge the possibility of any other outcome than victory will be honored in history for all time to come. Finally when the Russian armies and ourselves started the great drives that met on the Elbe, the end was merely a matter of days—the Allies, east and west, linked up and Nazi Germany was no more.

Here at home you played a very special part in the Soviet victory. Large quantities of American equipment, sent over the Arctic route to Murmansk and up from the Persian Gulf, furnished vital material of war to assist the Russians in mounting their great drives. The production of our people has won high praise from the Soviet leaders, as it has from other leaders in the Allied nations. There is not a battlefront in Europe where it has not been of decisive importance.

The liberated countries of Europe have played a part in fashioning the victory.

Following upon our invasion of Normandy, the breakthrough last summer permitted the swift liberation of most of France and gave that people an opportunity to begin resumption of normal conduct of their own lives. France's own resistance forces, and some of her own divisions, took a notable part in driving out the enemy.

Every American soldier has seen the toll that war has exacted from France. Towns have been destroyed. Broken bridges make difficult road and river transport. The destruction of rolling stock or its allocation to military needs has denied its use to carry needed civilian goods, particularly food and fuel. Even now, although the guns are silent, the urgent necessities of our redeployment to the Pacific make it impossible to do all that we would wish toward improving the trying conditions in which the French people live.

This feeling extends also to Belgium, Holland and Luxembourg, which endured four years of Germany tyranny, and which supported effective resistance movements. In the Netherlands, during the last few months of conflict, real starvation prevailed in certain sections, where the German garrisons refused assistance. Our sympathy was aroused and tons of food were dropped by parachute to alleviate their suffering. Those countries still need, and deserve, our help.

And now, because this meeting typifies, for me, the spiritual unity of the American home and battlefronts, I address a word to that relationship.

The American fighting man has never failed to recognize his dependence upon you at home. I am grateful for this opportunity to stand before the Congress and express my own and the thanks of every soldier, sailor and airman to the countrymen who have remained devoted to their tasks.

This feeling goes beyond the tangible things—guns, ammunition, tanks and planes, although in these things you have sent us the most and the best. It extends to such intangibles as the confidence and sympathetic understanding which have filled the letters written by families and friends to the men up front. For a few moments, simple words of affection and cheer blot out the danger and loneliness and hardship which are the soldier's life. They send him back with renewed vigor and courage to his inexorable task of crushing the enemy.

I hope you realize that all you have done for the soldier has been truly appreciated. Never have they felt absent from your anxious care and warm affections. The Red Cross—to name just one outstanding organization—stands high in their admiration. The Red Cross, with its clubs for recreation, its coffee and doughnuts in the forward areas, its readiness to meet the needs of the well and help minister to the wounded—even more important, the devotion and warm-hearted sympathy of the Red Cross girl! The Red Cross has often seemed to be the friendly hand of this nation, reaching across the sea to sustain its fighting men.

The battlefront and the home front; together we have found the victory! But even the banners of triumph cannot hide from our sight the sacrifices in which victory has been bought. The hard task of a commander is to send men into battle knowing some of them—often many—must be killed or wounded in order that necessary missions may be achieved.

It is a soul-killing task! My sorrow is not only for the fine young lives lost or broken, but it is equally for the parents, the wives and the friends who have been bereaved. The price they pay is possibly the greatest. The blackness of their grief can be relieved only by the faith that all this shall not happen again! Because I feel this so deeply I hope you will let me attempt to express a thought that I believe is today imbedded deep in the hearts of all fighting men.

It is this. The soldier knows how grim and black was the outlook for the Allies in 1941 and '42. He is fully aware of the magnificent way the United Nations responded to the threat. To his mind the problems of peace can be no more difficult than the one you had to solve more than three years ago, and which, in one battle area, has been brought to a successful conclusion. He knows that in war the threat of separate annihilation tends to hold Allies together; he hopes we can find in peace a nobler incentive to produce the same unity.

He passionately believes that, with the same determination, the same optimistic resolution and the same mutual consideration among Allies that marshalled in Europe forces capable of crushing what had been the greatest war machine of history, the problems of peace can and must be met. He sees the United Nations strong but considerate; humane and understanding leaders in the world to preserve the peace he is winning.

The genius and power of America have, with her Allies, eliminated one menace to our country's freedom—even her very existence. Still another remains to be crushed in the Pacific before peace will be restored. The American men and women I have been so honored to command, would, I know, say this to you today:

In our minds and hearts there is no slightest doubt that our people's spirit of determination which has buoyed us up and driven us forward in Europe, will continue to fire this nation through the ordeals of battle yet to come. Though we dream of return to our loved ones, we are ready, as we have always been, to do our duty to our country, no matter what it may be. In this spirit we renew our pledge of service to Commander in Chief President Truman, under whose strong leadership we know that final victory is certain.

THE FOURTH TERM CAMPAIGN

THE CAMPAIGN AND MEN IN UNIFORM [1]

Quentin Reynolds [2]

Mr. Quentin Reynolds gave this address at the Democratic National Convention at Chicago, on Thursday evening, July 20, 1944. That session, the final one of the second day of the four-day convention, was called to order by the permanent chairman, Samuel D. Jackson, of Indiana. Mr. Reynolds was preceded by Mrs. Helen Gahagan Douglas, a brilliant speaker from California. President Roosevelt's acceptance speech followed immediately.

Said the chairman in introducing Mr. Reynolds:

"Ladies and Gentlemen, back from the field of combat where he faced the enemy fire as an observer and participant in the opening of the Western Front has come one of America's best-known and best-liked writers. We shall hear tonight what the boys over there think about, not from hearsay but as seen, and felt at first hand by one who went side by side with our soldiers into battle. Ladies and Gentlemen, I take great pleasure in introducing to you Quentin Reynolds."

Mr. Reynolds on this occasion adapted his voice and delivery in general unusually well to the loud speaker and to the radio. In the opinion of many observers and listeners his speech was the ablest one, both in substance and in delivery, given before this convention. His delivery was essentially conversational, clear cut, and yet forcible.

The speaker was in sharp contrast to some other "headline" convention speakers who both in tone and emotional approach to their theme and their audience were artificial in expression. His conciliatory attitude and non-polemic spirit were unexpected but effective. Reynolds represented a new style of convention oratory. His radio and public speaking effectiveness was based on considerable experience before audiences. In Brooklyn Technical High School and at Brown University he had engaged in speaking activities. He had obtained a law degree in Brooklyn Law School in 1930. His career as a brilliant writer and journalist had been accompanied by continual speaking. In motion pictures of his own composition, portraying life in London during the blitz, he was his own effective narrator. Said Damon Runyon, the dramatic critic, "Reynolds'

[1] By permission of Mr. Quentin Reynolds. Text is from "The National Political Campaign of 1944, Part II." *United States News*. p. 43-5 July 1944.

[2] For biographical note see Appendix.

voice produces an even greater effect than the film. His tones are low pitched. He uses few adjectives, and attempts no fancy stuff." For a full two weeks, for example, he personally appeared in the Strand Theatre, in New York, to tell audiences about how the British "could take it" under the German blitz.

In this Chicago convention address Mr. Reynolds introduced with much tact and personal proof his thesis of what the G.I. fighter thinks and expects of those back home in their political judgments.

His ideas are simple: (1) This is no "foreign" war. (2) The boys know what they are fighting for. (3) They expect this campaign to be fought without name-calling. (4) They regard the election as an opportunity for a vote of confidence. (5) They have discovered a new America of national unity and they expect to find such an America upon their return. (6) Carping criticism of the war effort and the administration should be condemned.

The talk was written and delivered to hold the attention of a turbulent and expectant visible audience and of a large radio audience, alert for the voice of Roosevelt. The Reynolds ideas were fully illustrated. The idea, for example, "Your sons have learned that this is no foreign war," was vividly amplified. Skilful and original was the extended dialogue, the concrete pictures of the military front, and the psychology of the American fighter. Especially well expressed was the section beginning, "It is dawn in Normandy now."

The conclusion of the speech, expressed and delivered with especial power, was a highly appropriate introduction to President Roosevelt himself, who immediately followed with his speech of acceptance.

The war has done a great many things to us as a people. For one thing, it has changed millions of us who used to be mere spectators into participants. Millions of us who once went meekly to the polls on election day or didn't bother to go at all, now for the first time have become conscious of the fact that we have no right to sit by idly and allow professional politicians to do our thinking for us. We have no right to be mere spectators in any affair which concerns the welfare of our country, and nothing concerns the welfare of our country more than the forthcoming campaign and election. Mr. Justice Oliver Wendell Holmes once said, "Life is action and passion. I think that it is required of a man that he should share the action and passion of his time at peril of being judged not to have lived." That, then, is my excuse for being on this political platform. I am just one of the 55,000,000 voters, and like most of those 55,000,000, a complete amateur in politics. I realize that it is not customary for an amateur to appear on the platform of a political convention—but after all, the Republicans set the precedent last month when they presented many, many amateurs.

Today, more than in any other election year, it is the duty of anyone who has anything to say, to raise his voice. Eight million of your sons are abroad in uniform. Each of them has a larger stake in this election; each of them has a greater right to know everything that there is to be known about the parties, the platforms and policies of both parties—than any of us here at home.

Now I do not propose to speak for your son abroad, and I would never commit the unholy sacrilege of speaking for his dead brother who has been killed in combat. No man—or woman —can speak for him. His grave speaks for him. We can only accept his sacrifice humbly and not presume to speak for him with our unworthy tongues.

Nor can any of us speak politically for the G.I. who fights tonight. But those of us who have lived with him before, during and after combat; those of us who have heard him speak of his hopes and fears; those of us who have shared his life and his laughter—can perhaps tell some of the things he has discovered, since he left the youthful joys of quiet living, to join the ranks of those who fight and die that this country and her kind of civilization shall remain inviolate.

Perhaps the first thing that your sons and the sons of your neighbors learned when they went abroad, was that this was no "foreign war." This was no war that any leader of ours had forced us into. It was a war that was forced upon us. It was, in effect, a world revolution aimed by Germany and Japan, not at any one country, but at all types of society not their own. Germany first went to work on our neighbors and soon their houses were flaming infernos. We tried to help, not only because they were friendly neighbors but because if we didn't help the flames might spread to our own home and destroy us. The long record of arrests and convictions made by the F.B.I., the confessions of hundreds of professed saboteurs and German agents, the fact that thousands of our own honest decent citizens were caught up in the creeping fires of national socialism—are proof enough that the flames were beginning to gnaw at our national institutions, at our way of life. From then on this was our war.

Not everyone knew that the inevitable was going to happen. Even as late as 1940, there were a few who still thought we could isolate ourselves from this inferno. It seems incredible now that such a distinguished statesman as the Honorable Robert A. Taft, in opposing the Selective Service Act, could say on August 4, 1940, "I am opposed to the bill because in my opinion no necessity exists requiring such tragic action." Happily, men of both parties had better vision than the gentleman from Ohio. They realized that Selective Service then was some insurance that when we were engulfed by the inferno we would at last be partly prepared to fight it, not with bare hands, raw recruits and wooden guns, but with trained men and up-to-date weapons.

One voice kept warning us, one man charted us through the dangerous shoals of wartime diplomacy, doing everything in his power to avert the catastrophe.

As far back as 1937, in this very city of Chicago, this man said, "War is a contagion whether it be declared or undeclared. It can engulf states and peoples remote from the original scene of hostilities. We are determined to keep out of war, yet we cannot insure ourselves against the disastrous effects of war."

We could no more escape this war than King Canute could hold back the tides. We could no more escape this war than we could hold back the winds of a hurricane or stop the earth from rotating around the sun.

But millions of our countrymen didn't realize this until December 7, 1941, when that other comfortable world we knew came to an end. And then the Japanese told us in no uncertain terms that this was our war. They convinced millions of Americans, who until then had been using the old ostrich defense of sticking their heads in the sand and hearing nothing, seeing nothing, feeling nothing. They forgot that when you use the ostrich defense, you leave part of yourself in a mighty vulnerable position, and the obvious thing is apt to happen.

By now, your sons know that this is no foreign war. They know it each night back of the lines when they listen to the German radio. Incidentally, they listen to Radio Berlin assiduously. The good Dr. Goebbels gives them half an hour of American swing music every night, and ten minutes of propaganda. They love the music, and get a laugh out of the propaganda. The propaganda is frankly and bluntly aimed at our democracy, at our way of living, and if any of them ever had any doubts as to what they were fighting for—the good Dr. Goebbels, by his propaganda, has taught them what they are fighting against.

They learned that this was no foreign war when they first landed in England. They saw the shrines of England in ruins. They saw the scars on the House of Commons and they saw the precious stained-glass windows of Westminster Abbey lying broken in the dust. The House of Commons has always been the symbol of free speech in Britain. This, indeed, was a logical target for Hitler's bombs. Westminster Abbey has always been the symbol of the Christian way of life in Britain. This, too, was a logical target for Hitler's bombs. Your sons knew then that Hitler was waging war, not against any one country, but against our ideals and our way of life, no matter where they were found —whether it be in Prague, or Olso, or London, or Chicago.

Your sons learned that this was no foreign war when they captured their first prisoners in Northern Africa and heard arrogant, contemptuous voices sneering at our democracy. They knew it was no foreign war when they saw the bestiality of the Hermann Goering Division in Sicily, a division which even booby-trapped its own dead. Then they entered the cities and towns of Sicily and Italy and they saw the incredible ravages the Germans had been guilty of; when they heard the stories of those who had survived, these grim-faced, tight-lipped sons of yours knew then that this was their war and ours.

Yes, your sons know what they're fighting for, even if some of us at home seem a little bit confused. On the way into the Bay of Salerno last September, I was on a ship that had just one chaplain. Three A. M. was to be H-hour at Salerno. We steamed through the Mediterranean, one of a thousand unseen ships, and the quiet and darkness of the night pressed down upon us all. I passed the chaplain's cabin. He had a sign on his door which merely said, "Open All Night," and there was a line of forty men waiting to talk to him. I went on deck and sat with a group of assault troops. They were quiet now, each in his own way trying to overcome his fear. All soldiers are afraid just before battle. They're afraid of the waiting, they're afraid of being afraid at the crucial moment; they're afraid of nameless, unseen ghosts that walk through the night. They're always all right once they swing ashore with their guns in their hands, their grenades in their belts, but it's always bad just before that. You men who were in the last war know you always suffered more during that period of waiting before zero hour than when you were actually going over the top. It was like that approaching Salerno. The boys got to talking. One of them joined us and he said he'd just been in to see the chaplain.

"A nice fellow, the padre," the boy said. "You know, I talked to him and got some things off my mind and he was pretty swell to me. And do you know, he never asked me what my religion was!" One of the other fellows chimed in and said he'd had the same experience with the chaplain. Then the boys squatting there in the quiet of the deck, surrounded by their guns and tin hats and ammunition and rations, started talking about why we were fighting and what we were fighting for. They all knew what we were fighting against but they weren't very articulate in puttting into words just what we were fighting for until a big corporal from Texas, member of the 36th Division, said quietly, "I'll tell you what we're fighting for. We're fighting for things like what happened tonight with the chaplain. Half the ship went in to see him because we were scared. He didn't do any preaching about patriotism or hell-fire. He just soothed us, kind of, and let us talk about home to him and then we left feeling much better. Yeah, and he never asked us what our religion was. Could that happen anywhere but in our kind of country? No, and that's what we're fighting to keep. And we're fighting for another thing, too. We're fighting for the right to bawl out the umpire."

He went on and he said, "I mean when I go home, if I get a job and don't like the boss, I can quit and get another job. If I think the boss is calling the plays wrong, I can just leave. If I go to a movie and I don't like it, why, I can leave and shop around until I find the kind of movie I do like. Nobody is going to tell me what kind of movies I got to like—the way it is in Germany. And, if I don't like what one newspaper says, if I don't like the way it calls the play, well, that newspaper fellow is the umpire and I can bawl him out and find myself a paper I do like. Nobody is going to tell me what paper I got to read. And when I turn on the radio, it isn't like in Germany where there's only one station and you gotta listen to it because the Government controls it and you hear nothing but propaganda. If I don't like what I heard on the radio, I can make with a twist of the wrist and get another station. Sure, that's what we're fighting for."

He said, "Add it all together and it means we're fighting for the right to bawl out the umpire."

Yes, believe me, your sons know what they're fighting for and they're doing a lot of thinking over there on both sides of the world. They think of the world they're coming back to one day. They don't want a world of promises. Their fathers were given that kind of a world in the 1920's, promises that were paid off on bread lines. They don't expect any Utopia when they return but they do expect their country to have jobs ready for them. They are smart enough to know that American industry, great as it is, cannot do this alone. It couldn't twenty-four years ago; it won't be able to this time. They will look to their government for help, not for a dole or a dollar, not for pity or patronage, but for a concrete program that will help them get started quickly on the road to economic security. Such a program is conspicuous in the Republican platform—by its absence.

Our boys abroad know about platforms. A platform is something you build to throw across a river so that you can get to the other side. Soldiers test every plank in a platform before they use it. By now, perahps they have waded through the delightful double-talk of the Republican platform and I doubt if they've found half a dozen planks in it strong enough to bear even the light load of the Republican promises. But as I said, they don't want promises. They don't want anyone saying to them, "I can get it for you wholesale."

Their eyes are on this convention tonight, and their eyes will be on the campaign. Because these sons of yours have been dealing with the fundamentals of life and death, they have become very sensitive to a commodity which they call bunk.

This forthcoming campaign, to them, is strictly an argument "in the family," and if it is conducted in any other manner there will be a sharp reaction from them. They have room in their hearts for only one hatred—the enemy. They've discovered America abroad and they're pretty proud of it and they'd hate to see it tarnished by the sad spectacle of fellow Americans indulging in the childish pastime of name calling. If either party starts anything in the nature of what you men call a smear campaign, I promise you the reaction from the men in uniform will be quick. They think of this as a family argument, in which no one has the right to inflict wounds that can't afterwards be cured with a hearty handshake. We voters, too, I think, feel that way. In this family quarrel, the opposition has seen fit to select as a candidate, a very promising younger brother; we can still maintain in good faith that we do not for a moment believe this young man capable of leading our nation in the trying days to come, and we can say that straight out, without impugning his character or his honesty. Yes, it's going to be a family quarrel and when it's all over, we're still going to live with each other, respect each other and work together for the only sovereign we recognize—our country. Believe me, I know that is how your sons in uniform feel. Yes, they're proud of their country and they're proud that we are the only country at war which not only dares, but insists upon holding a free election even in the midst of an all-out war. Mind you, if our great allies were to hold elections tomorrow, I am sure that the present leaders of Russia, England and China would be returned virtually unanimously to office. Our allies may not know the game of baseball very well, but they know it well enough to follow the cardinal rule of the game which is—never remove a pitcher while's he's pitching a winning game. But we, at least, give the fans (the voters) the opportunity of giving our winning pitcher a vote of confidence. It might give him additional strength, it might put an added zip to his fast ball, so that when the count is 3 and 2 he can throw in that hard one, knowing that even if the batter connects, we, the members of his team, are ready to give him all-out support in the traditional Yankee manner—and I don't mean the New York Yankees.

You know, these 8,000,000 kids of ours have changed a little since they left civilian life. Not much, but a little. For one thing, they've discovered America, a great and glorious America that many of them never knew existed before. They have discovered America in the desert camps of Egypt, and Palestine; in the murderous heat of Iran; in the hearts and minds of men and women who die in Russia; in the friendly atmosphere of the English country pub; and this past month, they have been discovering America in the flowered fields of Normandy. You can see America so much more clearly from the vantage point of distance, so that the minor defects are invisable, and only the magnificent glorious whole can be seen.

When our men realize there on hostile shores that the weapons they carry are by every known test the best in the world, they suddenly recognize the genius of our industrial leaders. When they look upon the lines of countless tanks emerging from landing craft, when they see the clouds above, speckled with darting Thunderbolts and Mustangs and Lightnings and Hellcats and when they see swarms of Fortresses and Liberators winging through the soft Normandy skies, they realize that American hands made these weapons of combat, that American labor bent its back over lathe and rivet, and that honest American sweat fell upon them in the making. When our boys, confident in their young strength, notice the worried looks upon the faces of even their highest-ranking officers and when the realization comes to them that this concern is due to worry over their welfare, over the desire to spare them any needless risk or suffering, they discover yet another segment of America.

You know, war is like poverty or taxes. It's hard to find anything good to say of it. But there is one fine thing that our boys have found out about war—there are no barriers at the front. Kids here at home grow up surrounded by barriers—all man-made. Neighborhood barriers, city barriers, state barriers, social barriers, racial barriers, political barriers, barriers of wealth. You climb over one barrier only to find another ahead of you.

Then you find yourself at the front, thousands of miles from home. And suddenly, perhaps for the first time in your life, you realize that here on foreign soil is an outpost of America where there are no barriers. This was always the dream you'd had of America, a dream that never before had quite come true. This was the America they told you about when you were a school kid studying history.

There are no Democrats, no Republicans at the front; there are no Italian-Americans or Polish-Americans; there are no Jews, Catholics or Protestants at the front; there are no New Yorkers or Californians or Texans or New Englanders—only Americans— that's all: Only Americans purged of the artificial barriers we still make so much of here at home.

Our boys, our sons, are living in the wonder of this new America they are discovering day by day. I saw them in Sicily and in Italy discovering this new and glorious America. I saw them sometimes look puzzled as though they were thinking of the absurd prejudices they had grown up with, and not knowing any better, had accepted. When these boys come home, they'll expect to find the kind of America that they discovered at the front—an America without artificial man-made barriers, the kind of America our forefathers intended should be our heritage. This at least, we owe to the men who will return; and this at least we owe to the memory of the men who will not return.

We are merely holding this country in trust for these sons of yours. The future is theirs, not ours. They are earning it right now in Saipan, in the Marianas and in Normandy. It is dawn in Normandy now. In Normandy the lights are white and still and the stars linger in the Normandy skies. But now the dawn is putting the stars out—one by one. It is dawn and that is the worst time for any soldier. The chill of the dawn enters your heart and you feel alone. They are unconscious of the beauty of Normandy as they prepare for yet another day of battle. They don't notice how the dawn is bathing the dew-tinted hills with melancholy gold; they don't notice that the dawn is unlocking the apple blossoms and the white and purple clusters of the chestnut blossoms which later today will be trod under by the heavy boots of fighting men. The chill is in their hearts and they feel alone.

But they are not alone. Whoever fought and died for freedom is with them. Whoever raised his voice against the harsh voice of tyranny is with them and we, 130,000,000 strong, are with them. They are confident in their strength, these sons of yours.

Here at home, criticism seems to have become our national hobby. The paragraph troopers hurl the dumdum bullets of their phrases against our national war effort. The saboteurs of our national unity do their best to tell us that the war is not being conducted properly. The Ship of State has been torpedoed, depth-bombed, dive-bombed and sabotaged by the armchair commandos, but it still floats.

We criticize, criticize, criticize. Three meals a day are given up to criticism. But the boy in Normany or Saipan doesn't criticize our war effort. Our boys know (and the enemy knows) that we have performed the greatest military and industrial miracle of the ages; and that this miracle was performed here—at home. Your sons know that, great as their generals are, they can't wave magic wands and suddenly produce thousands of guns, aircraft, ships and tanks in a given spot three or six thousand miles away. It would be absurd to say that this party or that was responsible. It would be presumptuous to say that any one man did it alone. Your sons know, and we know, that it was the American people of all parties who have worked this great miracle. It was industry; it was labor; it was the American farmer; it was the banker buying a million dollars' worth of bonds; it was the school boy buying his twenty-five cent war stamps; it was the man in the mine, the man in the factory, the man in the street. It was the voice of America singing loud and strong in a mighty chorus of victory. Your sons know this; they know that all of America has contributed to making the victory possible— but they also know one other thing. They know that this mighty achievement which dwarfs any other in the whole history of our country, was all accomplished under the leadership of their Commander in Chief and ours—Franklin D. Roosevelt.

KEEPING POLITICAL FAITH [3]

Franklin D. Roosevelt [4]

President Roosevelt addressed the International Brotherhood of Teamsters, Chauffeurs, Warehousemen, and Helpers of America, in the opening political speech of his campaign for reelection to a fourth term, in Washington, D.C., on September 23, 1944.

It was a typical political address, widely broadcast. It was reminiscent of his political manner of earlier national campaigns.

His Hotel Statler audience of a thousand, composed largely of members of the Brotherhood of Teamsters, was an intensely friendly one. On his left was Daniel Tobin, the Union's president, who introduced him. On his right was President Green, of the American Federation of Labor. At the outset President Roosevelt departed from his prepared manuscript. The audience interrupted the address at least fifty-six times with applause and laughter. The audience, standing, gave him a five-minute "We want Roosevelt" as he left the hall.

The speaker remained seated. "He appeared to take his time in using his voice to highlight his words and phrases" to bring a maximum reaction from his audience.

The speech is essentially one of rebuttal against the attacks by Dewey and the Republicans. (1) In his opening sentence he referred to the charge that he was old. His method of refutation was *reductio ad absurdum* (ridicule)—all are older than they were ten years ago. (2) He refuted the Republican statement that that party was the friend of labor. His method here was to show the inconsistency between their words and their previous program, and thus proved the Republican's insincerity. (3) He refuted the suggestion that the Republican party is the party of progress. His method was that of showing that his opponents are attempting to take over the opponent's position by imitation. (4) He refuted the proposition of the Republicans that they were better fitted to take charge of the foreign and domestic problems in 1945. His method here was to show by the history of 1940-44 that these Republicans in their record were incompetent. They had been against lend-lease, conscription, maximum preparedness, repeal of neutrality legislation. (5) He refuted the criticism of our conduct of the military end of this war by showing that such critics were ignorant and therefore should remain silent. (6) He defended labor from the charge that it

[3] The text was from a recording. The White House also supplied the editor with the text prepared for release to the press.

[4] For biographical note see Appendix.

had supported strikes and had not been wholeheartedly in support of the war program. His method of refutation was to cite the figures of production, to quote Eisenhower, to show that labor leaders (save Lewis) had gone on record against strikes, and to cite the small percentage of time lost through strikes. (7) He defended labor's right to enter politics, by showing that capital did so and by arguing that the Republicans were unfair in their blocking of the soldier vote. (8) He refuted the charge that the depression was a Democratic one. His method of refutation was to show that this Republican method of indictment was an unfair one—a method typical of Nazi propaganda. (9) He refuted the charge that he would keep the Americans in the army after peace had come; he cited counter-facts and called his opponents unreliable witnesses. His refutatory tactics were thus varied and polemic. He inserted much persuasive material, including humor and personal appeal, with specific illustrations. It was Roosevelt the rough-and-tumble campaign speaker at his best.

What was the effect of the speech? According to the *Des Moines Register* (September 25, 1944), "Then, the whole speech, or practically the whole of it, was so pitched as to be lofty, superior, condescending and amused." According to Ray Tucker, the Washington correspondent and columnist, there was "growing resentment against the tone of the speech, especially its seeming flippancy and arrogance." The *New York Herald Tribune* derided the address. The *New York Times,* on the other hand, praised it. *Time* (October 2, 1944, p. 21) concluded, "The Old Master still had it. Franklin Roosevelt was at his best." Obviously audiences listened to it.

The President did not go to the same lengths of humor, satire, castigation, in his later political addresses. They were more on the plane of statesmanship.

Well, here are are together again—after four years—and what years they have been! I am actually four years older—which seems to annoy some people. In fact, millions of us are more than eleven years older than when we started in to clear up the mess that was dumped in our laps in 1933.

We all know certain people who make it a practice to depreciate the accomplishments of labor—who even attack labor as unpatriotic. They keep this up usually for three years and six months. But then, for some strange reason, they change their tune—every four years—just before election day. When votes are at stake, they suddenly discover that they really love labor, and are eager to protect it from its old friends.

I got quite a laugh, for example—and I am sure that you did—when I read this plank in the Republican platform adopted at their National Convention in Chicago last July:

The Republican party accepts the purposes of the National Labor Relations Act, the Wage and Hour Act, the Social Security Act and all other Federal statutes designed to promote and protect the welfare of American working men and women, and we promise a fair and just administration of these laws.

Many of the Republican leaders and Congressmen and candidates, who shouted enthusiastic approval of that plank in that Convention Hall would not even recognize these progressive laws, if they met them in broad daylight. Indeed, they have personally spent years of effort and energy—and much money—in fighting every one of those laws in the Congress, in the press, and in the courts, ever since this Administration began to advocate them and enact them into legislation. That is a fair example of their insincerity and of their inconsistency.

The whole purpose of Republican oratory these days seems to be to switch labels. The object is to persuade the American people that the Democratic party was responsible for the 1929 crash and depression, and that the Republican party was responsible for all social progress under the New Deal. Imitation may be the sincerest form of flattery—but I am afraid that in this case it is the most obvious common or garden variety of fraud.

There are enlightened, liberal elements in the Republican party, and they have fought hard and honorably to bring the party up to date and to get it in step with the forward march of American progress. But these liberal elements were not able to drive the Old Guard Republicans from their entrenched positions.

Can the Old Guard pass itself off as the New Deal? I think not. We have all seen many marvelous stunts in the circus, but no performing elephant could turn a hand-spring without falling flat on his back.

I need not recount to you the centuries of history which have been crowded into these four years since I saw you last. There were some—in the Congress and out—who raised their voices against our preparations for defense—before and after 1939—as hysterical war mongering, who cried out against our help to the Allies as provocative and dangerous. We remember the voices. They would like to have us forget them now. But in 1940 and 1941 they were loud voices. Happily they were a minority and—fortunately for ourselves, and for the world—they could not stop America.

There are some politicians who kept their heads buried deep in the sand while the storms of Europe and Asia were headed our way, who said that the lend-lease bill "would bring an end to free government in the United States," and who said "only hysteria entertains the idea that Germany, Italy or Japan contemplate war upon us." These very men are now asking the American people to intrust to them the conduct of our foreign policy and our military policy.

What the Republican leaders are now saying in effect is this, "Oh, just forget what we used to say, we have changed our minds now—we have been reading the public opinion polls about these things, and we now know what the American people want. Don't leave the task of making the peace to those old men who first urged it, and who have already laid the foundation for it, and who have had to fight all of us inch by inch during the last five years to do it—just turn it all over to us. We'll do it so skilfully—that we won't lose a single isolationist vote or a single isolationist campaign contribution." There is one thing I am too old for—I cannot talk out of both sides of my mouth at the same time.

This government welcomes all sincere supporters of the cause of effective world collaboration in the making of a lasting peace. Millions of Republicans all over the nation are with us—and have been with us—in our unshakeable determination to build the solid structure of peace. And they too will resent this campaign talk by those who first woke up to the facts of international life a few short months ago—when they began to study the polls of public opinion.

Those who today have the military responsibility for waging this war in all parts of the globe are not helped by the statements of men who, without responsibility and without knowledge of the facts, lecture the Chiefs of Staff of the United States as to the best means of dividing our armed forces and our military resources between the Atlantic and Pacific, between the Army and the Navy, and among the Commanding Generals of the different theaters of war.

When I addressed you four years ago, I said, "I know that America will never be disappointed in its expectation that labor will always continue to do its share of the job we now face, and do it patriotically and effectively and unselfishly."

Today we know that America has not been disappointed. In his Order of the Day when allied armies first landed in Normandy General Eisenhower said, "Our home fronts have given us overwhelming superiority in weapons and munitions of war."

I know that there are those labor baiters among the opposition who, instead of calling attention to the achievements of labor in this war, prefer to pick on the occasional strikes which have occurred—strikes which have been condemned by every responsible national labor leader—every national leader except one. And that one labor leader, incidentally, is certainly not among my supporters.

Labor-baiters forget that, at our peak, American labor and management have turned out airplanes at the rate of 109,000 per year; tanks, 57,000 per year; combat vessels, 573 per year; landing vessels, 31,000 per year; cargo ships, 19 million tons per year; and small arms ammunition, 23 billion rounds per year.

But a strike is news, and generally appears in shrieking headlines—and, of course, they say labor is always to blame. The fact is that, since Pearl Harbor, only one tenth of one per cent of man-hours have been lost by strikes.

But even those candidates who burst out in election-year affection for social legislation and for labor in general still think you ought to be good boys and stay out of politics. And above all, they hate to see any working man or woman contribute a dollar bill to any wicked political party. Of course, it is all right for large financiers and industrialists and monopolists to contribute tens of thousands of dollars—but their solicitude for that dollar which the men and women in the ranks of labor contribute is always very touching.

They are, of course, perfectly willing to let you vote—unless you happen to be a soldier or sailor overseas, or a merchant seamen carrying the muntions of war. In that case they have made it pretty hard for you to vote—for there are some political candidates who think they may have a chance if only the total vote is small enough.

And while I am on the subject of voting let me urge every American citizen—man and woman—to use your sacred privilege of voting, no matter which candidate you expect to support. Our millions of soldiers and sailors and merchant seamen have been handicapped or prevented from voting by those politicians and candidates who think they stand to lose by such votes. You here at home have the freedom of the ballot. Irrespective of party you should register and vote this November. That is a matter of good citizenship.

Words come easily, but they do not change the record. You are old enough to remember what things were like for labor in 1932. You remember the closed banks and the breadlines and the starvation wages; the foreclosures of homes and farms, and the bankruptcies of business; the "Hoovervilles," and the young men and women of the nation facing a hopeless, jobless future; the closed factories and mines and mills; the ruined and abandoned farms; the stalled railroads and the empty docks; the blank despair of a whole nation—and the utter impotence of our Federal Government. You remember the long hard road, with its gains and its setbacks, which we have traveled together since those days. Now there are some politicians, of course, who do not remember that far back, and some who remember but find it convenient to forget. But the record is not to be washed away that easily.

The opposition has already imported into this campaign the propaganda technique invented by the dictators abroad. The technique was all set out in Hitler's book—and it was copied by the aggressors of Italy and Japan. According to that technique, you should never use a small falsehood; always a big one, for its very fantastic nature will make it more credible—if only you keep repeating it over and over again.

For example, although I rubbed my eyes when I read it, we have been told that it was not a Republican depression, but a Democratic depression from which this nation has been saved—that this Administration is responsible for all the suffering and misery that the history books and the American people always thought had been brought about during the twelve ill-fated years when the Republican party was in power.

Now, there is an old and somewhat lugubrious adage which says: "Never speak of rope in the house of one who has been hanged." In the same way, if I were a Republican leader speaking to a mixed audience, the last word in the whole dictionary that I think I would use is that word "depression."

For another example, I learned—much to my amazement—that the policy of this Administration was to keep men in the Army when the war was over, because there might be no jobs for them in civil life. Why, the very day that this fantastic charge was first made, a formal plan for the method of speedy discharge from the Army had already been announced by the War Department—a plan based upon the wishes of the soldiers themselves. This callous and brazen falsehood about demobilization was an effort to stimulate fear among American mothers, wives and sweethearts. And, incidentally, it was hardly calculated to bolster the morale of our soldiers and sailors and airmen fighting our battles all over the world.

Perhaps the most ridiculous of these campaign falsifications is the one that this Administration failed to prepare for the war which was coming. I doubt whether even Goebbels would have tried that one. For even he would never have dared hope that the voters of America had already forgotten that many of the Republican leaders in the Congress and outside the Congress tried to thwart and block nearly every attempt which this Administration made to warn our people and to arm this nation. Some of them called our 50,000 airplane program fantastic. Many of those very same leaders who fought every defense measurse we proposed are still in control of the Republican Party, were in control of its National Convention in Chicago, and would be in control of the machinery of the Congress and of the Republican Party in the event of a Republican victory this fall.

These Republican leaders have not been content with attacks upon me, or my wife, or my sons—they now include my little dog, Fala. Unlike the members of my family, he resents this. Being a Scottie, as soon as he learned that the Republican fiction-writers had concocted a story that I had left him behind on an Aleutian Island and had sent a destroyer back to find him—at a cost to the taxpayers of two or three or twenty million dollars—his Scotch soul was furious. He has not been the same dog since. I am accustomed to hearing malicious falsehoods about myself—such as that old, worm-eaten chestnut that I have represented myself as indispensable. But I think I have a right to object to libelous statements about my dog.

But we all recognize the old technique. The people of this country know the past too well to be deceived into forgetting. Too much is at stake to forget. There are tasks ahead of us which we must now complete with the same will and skill and intelligence and devotion which have already led us so far on the road to victory. There is the task of finishing victoriously this most terrible of all wars as speedily as possible and with the least cost in lives. There is the task of setting up international machinery to assure that the peace, once established, will not again be broken. And there is the task which we face here at home—the task of reconverting our economy from the purposes of war to the purposes of peace. These peace-building tasks were faced once before, nearly a generation ago. They were botched by a Republican Administration. That must not happen this time.

Fortunately, we do not begin from scratch. Much has been done. Much more is under way. The fruits of victory this time will not be apples to be sold on street corners. Many months ago, this Administration set up the necessary machinery for an orderly peacetime demobilization. The Congress has now passed legislation continuing the agencies needed for demobilization—with additional powers to carry out their functions.

I know that the American people—business and labor and agriculture—have the same will to do for peace what they have done for war. And I know that they can sustain a national income which will assure full production and full employment under our democratic system of private enterprise, with government encouragement and aid whenever and wherever it is necessary.

The keynote of all that we propose to do in reconversion can be found in the one word—"jobs." We shall lease or dispose of our government-owned plants and facilities and our surplus war property and land, on the basis of how they can best be operated by private enterprise to give jobs to the greatest number. We shall follow a wage policy which will sustain the purchasing power of labor—for that means more production and more jobs. The present policies on wages and prices were conceived to serve the needs of the great masses of the people. They stopped inflation. They kept prices on a stable level. Through the demobilization period, policies will be carried out with the same objective in mind—to serve the needs of the great masses of the people.

This is not the time in which men can be forgotten as they were in the Republican catastrophe which we inherited. The returning soldiers, the workers by their machines, the farmers in the field, the miners, the men and women in offices and shops, do not intend to be forgotten. They know they are not surplus. Because they know that they are America. We must set targets and objectives for the future which will seem impossible to those who live in and are weighted down by the dead past.

We are even now organizing the logistics of the peace just as Marshall, King, Arnold, MacArthur, Eisenhower and Nimitz are organizing the logistics of this war. The victory of the American people and their Allies in this war will be far more than a victory against fascism and reaction and the dead hand of despotism and of the past. The victory of the American people and their Allies in this war will be a victory for democracy. It will constitute such an affirmation of the strength and power and vitality of government by the people as history has never before witnessed.

With that affirmation of the vitality of democratic government behind us, that demonstration of its resilience and its capacity for decision and for action—with that knowledge of our own strength and power—we move forward with God's help to the greatest epoch of free achievement by free men the world has ever known of imagined possible.

GOVERNMENTAL INTEGRITY [5]

THOMAS E. DEWEY [6]

Thomas E. Dewey, candidate for President on the Republican ticket, gave this speech at Oklahoma City, on September 25, 1944. The address was the final major address in a coast-to-coast campaign trip which began on September 7 and which included important speeches at San Francisco and Los Angeles.

The speech was a direct reply to Roosevelt's political address of September 23 before the Teamsters' Union.[7] Mr. Dewey displayed unusual ingenuity in quickly abandoning his prepared talk to refute the Roosevelt argument of forty-eight hours previously.

After Dewey had decided to make this reply, the Republican campaign committee arranged to double the number of stations carrying the program. One hundred and seventy Blue Network stations were added to the one hundred and forty-one outlets of the N.B.C.

This was an excellent "debating" speech, in that the speaker put down a general proposition and proceeded to prove it. The Republican candidate began this speech by reassuring his audience that his aim and methods had been to strengthen national unity in his campaign speechmaking. His proposition was that his opponent (despite Roosevelt's own implication to the contrary) resorted to arguments and political demagoguery that tended to destroy this unity. Therefore, concluded Dewey, he would attempt to answer Roosevelt—but without stooping to similar tactics. The appeal was thus personal proof: Dewey deserved support because he had lofty aims and because he would not resort to mudslinging.

Note the contrast between Dewey's refutatory technique and that of Roosevelt a few hours before. Dewey refuted Roosevelt's argument that the latter would bring home "speedily" the American armed forces after victory. Dewey quoted Major General Lewis B. Hershey, head of Selective Service, as asserting that it would be as cheap to "keep people in the army." "We can keep people in the army about as cheaply as we could create an agency for them when they are out." Dewey's evidence was widely attacked, on the ground that it was illogical to assume that Hershey spoke for the administration.

Dewey's next argument by way of refutation was that the "administration with its peacetime failure is afraid to bring home men after victory." That argument was obviously assertion that needed proof.

[5] By permission of Governor Thomas E. Dewey. The text was supplied through the courtesy of Mr. Dewey and was corrected from the recording by Robert Ray.

[6] For biographical note see Appendix.

[7] See p. 134-42.

Dewey next refuted the argument that the Republican party was responsible for the "economic depression." Both Roosevelt and Dewey confused the argument by failing to make clear what they meant by the
"depression." Roosevelt was stressing the fact that his party in 1933
inherited a depression that had been under way two or three years.
Dewey was stressing the "depression" as having persisted long after
Roosevelt took office. When Dewey referred to the New Deal depression
it is obvious that he meant the continuance of large-scale unemployment
and economic distress from 1933 to 1941. Dewey's point was that if the
treatment given by the New Deal failed, then the Democratic administration was to blame for not curing it. Roosevelt was attaching the original
economic breakdown to a Republican administration. The two obviously
were stressing different things. Whatever the logic involved, the people
had jobs under Roosevelt and during the war, and it was difficult for any
critic-orator to shake them out of their confidence in September-October,
1944.

Dewey's third point of refutation was that of preparation for the
war. Roosevelt argued that the country was much better prepared for war
than it would have been if the Republicans had been in the saddle.
Dewey stressed the fact of our unpreparedness. Dewey quoted liberally
and was right as far as he went. His citations without consideration of
context may have been misleading. For example, he quoted Barkley as
saying, "When the treachery of Pearl Harbor came, we were not ready."
Dewey did not quote Barkley's later sentence, "And though unready for
it when it came, we have gone further and faster and with more profound
temporary adjustments in our lives than was ever true of any other nation
on earth in all the history of mankind. . . . No democracy is ever ready
for war at the drop of a hat. That is true of Europe and Asia no less
that of America." Dewey's fallacy, his critics alleged, was in his interpretation of the word "ready." He used the term absolutely rather
than relatively.

Dewey's fourth point of refutation was that our unpreparedness was
due to Roosevelt's opposition. Dewey quoted Roosevelt statements which
suggested that the Democratic President was trying to warn us against
preparedness. Again the context needed to be examined. Dewey would
probably have strengthened his attack on Roosevelt at this point if he
(Dewey) had cited Roosevelt's signing of the neutrality act in 1937, the
President's torpedoing of the London Economic Conference, and his opposition to the League of Nations in 1933 and after. Dewey naturally
kept silent on the comparative policy of the Republican party, which included resistance to the arms embargo repeal, selective service, and lend-
lease. Every one of these measures was rejected by a large majority of
the Republican members of both houses of Congress.

Dewey's next contention was that Roosevelt was the "indispensable
man." Again the fallacy was in the use of the word "indispensable."
It obviously did not mean absolute but rather relative indispensability.

The practical question was, were the voters more inclined to continue the leadership of Roosevelt than they were to turn the reins over to somebody else?

Political candidates in the heat of their campaigns argue from unproved premises, and resort to propagandistic techniques, including name-calling, glittering generalities, appeal to custom, unsupported testimony, and slogans. Dewey and Roosevelt were no exceptions. Their campaign speeches were, nevertheless, excellent examples of intelligent and cogent arguments. Both were highly effective speakers. Their efforts before audiences and over the radio helped to stimulate millions of Americans to listen and to vote, almost fifty million strong. These candidates were fit leaders in the demonstration of American democracy, functioning at its best in spite of our huge sacrifices and complete commitment to the winning of the war during those critical months of 1944. The Republican candidate lost, partly because Americans decided to have no break in the war leadership. Dewey, nevertheless, emerged from the campaign as one of this country's outstanding political debaters.

Senator Moore, Governor Schoeppel, My Friend and Next Senator from Oklahoma, Bill Otjen, Fellow Americans everywhere: For two and a half weeks I have been laying before our people the program I believe we must adopt if we are to win here at home the things for which our American men are fighting abroad. In six major speeches I have set forth a part of that program. There is much more to come. In doing this I have been deeply conscious that this campaign is being waged under the most difficult circumstances and at the most trying time in the history of our nation. Our national unity for war and for the cause of lasting peace must be strengthened as a result of this campaign. I believe the conduct of the campaign on our side has greatly strengthened that unity.

I had assumed that every American joined me in hoping that would be the spirit of this campaign. Last July, Franklin Roosevelt, in accepting his party's nomination for a fourth term said, and I quote, "I shall not campaign, in the usual sense . . . in these days of tragic sorrow, I do not consider it fitting." Last Saturday night the man who wants to be President for sixteen years made his first speech of this campaign. Gone was the high-sounding pledge. Forgotten were these days of tragic sorrow. It was a speech of mud-slinging, ridicule and wise-cracks. It plumbed the depths of demogogy by dragging into this campaign the names of Hitler and Goebbels; it descended to quoting from "Mein Kampf" and to reckless charges of "fraud" and "falsehood."

Let me make one thing entirely clear. I shall not join my opponent in his descent to mud-slinging. If he continues in his desire to do so, he will be all alone. I shall not use the tactics of our enemies by quoting from "Mein Kampf." I will never divide America. Those tactics also I leave to my opponent. I shall never make a speech to one group of American people inciting them to hatred and distrust of any other group. In other nations the final product of such discord has been communism or fascism. We must never reap that harvest in America.

The winning of this war and the achievement of a people's peace are too sacred to be cast off with frivolous language. I believe that Americans whose loved ones are dying on the battle-fronts of the world—men and women who are praying daily for the return of their boys—want the issues which vitally affect our future discussed with the utmost earnestness. This I shall continue to do with full consciousness of the solemn obligation placed upon me by my nomination for President of the United States.

My opponent, however, has chosen to wage his campaign on the record of the past and has indulged in charges of fraud and falsehood. I am compelled, therefore, to divert this evening long enough to keep the record straight. He has made the charges. He has asked for it. Here it is.

My opponent describes as, and I quote him, a "fantastic charge" the statement that his Administration plans to keep men in the army when the war is over and that it intends to keep them there because it fears there will be no jobs for them in civil life. Well, who brought that up? Here is the statement of a high official of the Administration as reported on August 23, 1944, in the publication of the United States Army, *The Stars and Stripes*. He said, "We can keep people in the army about as cheaply as we could create an agency for them when they are out." Now, who said that? It was the National Director of Selective Service appointed by Mr. Roosevelt and still in office.

But, says Mr. Roosevelt, the War Department thereafter issued a plan for what he called "speedy discharges." You can read that plan from now until doomsday and you cannot find one word about "speedy discharges." It is, in fact, a statement of the priority in which men will be discharged after the war. It does not say whether they are to be retained in service a month or years after victory. That will be up to the next Administration. The present Administration, with its record of peacetime failure, is afraid to bring men home after victory. That's why it's time for a change. Now why does my opponent first describe what is a matter of record as a "fantastic charge" and then try to laugh off the problem of jobs after the war? He jokes about depressions—about the seven straight years of unemployment of his Administration. But he cannot laugh away the record.

In March 1940, Mr. Roosevelt had been in office seven years. Yet the depression was still with us. We still had ten million Americans unemployed. Those are not my figures—those are the figures of the American Federation of Labor. Is that fraud or falsehood? If so, let Mr. Roosevelt tell it to the American Federation of Labor.

By waging relentless warfare against our job-making machinery, my opponent succeeded in keeping a depression going eleven long years—twice as long as any previous depression in our history, and the somber, tragic thing is that today he still has no better program to offer. That is why the New Deal is afraid of peace, that's why it resorts to wise-cracks and villification—when our people want victory followed by lasting peace in the world—and jobs and opportunity here at home. That's why it's time for a change.

Now I had not intended in this campaign to rake over my opponent's sad record of failing to prepare the defenses of this country for war. It's all in the past—a very tragic past. It has cost countless American lives; it has caused untold misery. But my opponent has now brought that subject up. He seized violently upon the statement that we were not prepared for war when it came. In his speech of Saturday night he called that a falsehood which not even Goebbels would have invented.

Now, were we prepared for war, or were we not? It's a perfectly simple question of fact. In 1940, the year after the war began in Europe, the United States was in such a tragic condition that it couldn't put into the field as a mobile force 75,000 men. The army was only "25 per cent ready." Now, Mr. Roosevelt, did those statements come from Goebbels? Was that fraud or falsification? Those are the words of Gen. George C. Marshall, Chief of Staff of the United States Army, under oath.

I quote again: "December 7, 1941, found the Army Air Forces equipped with plans but not with planes." Did that come from Goebbels? That statement was made in an official report on January 4th of this year by H. H. Arnold, commanding general of the Army Air Forces of the United States of America.

Does my opponent still desire to use the words "falsification" and "Dr. Goebbels"? Does he still claim we were "prepared"? If so, let's go further.

Four months before Pearl Harbor, there was a debate in the United States Senate. The chairman of a Senate committee described on the floor of the Senate the shocking state of our defense program. Senator Vandenberg asked the chairman where the blame should be laid, and the chairman replied, "There is only one place where the responsibility can be put." Then Senator Vandenburg said, "Where is that—the White House?" and the chairman of that committee replied, "Yes, sir." Who was that committee chairman? It was Harry Truman, the New Deal candidate for Vice President of the United States.

Again, in a magazine article in November 1942, this statement appeared, "The reasons for the waste and confusion, the committee found, were everywhere the same: the lack of courageous, unified leadership and centralized direction at the top." Again, on the floor of the Senate in May 1943, these words were uttered, "After Pearl Harbor we found ourselves woefully unprepared for war." Was that Dr. Goebbels on the floor of the Senate? The very words my opponent calls a falsification came from the mouth of his running mate, Harry Truman, the Democratic nominee for Vice President.

Now listen to this: "When the treachery of Pearl Harbor came we were not ready." Mr. Roosevelt, was that from Dr. Goebbels? The man who said that was Alben Barkley, your majority leader of the United States Senate. And where do you suppose Alben Barkley said, "When the treachery of Pearl Harbor came we were not ready"? Right in his speech nominating Mr. Roosevelt for a fourth term.

Now, why is it we were not ready when we were attacked? Let's look at my opponent's own words. In a message to Congress in 1935, he said, "There is no ground for apprehension that our relations with any nation will be otherwise than peaceful." In 1937 he said, and I quote, "How happy we are that the circumstances of the moment permit us to put our money into bridges and boulevards . . . rather than into huge standing armies and vast implements of war."

But war came just two years later. It was in January of 1940 that I publicly called for a two-ocean Navy for the defense of America. It was that statement of mine which Mr. Roosevelt called, and I quote his words, "Just plain dumb." Then as now we got ridicule instead of action.

The war rose in fury. When Hitler's armies were at the gates of Paris, Mr. Roosevelt once again soothed the American people with the jolly comment: "There is no need for the country to be discomboomerated."

The single truth is, of course, that my opponent's record is desperately bad. The price the American people have had to pay for that record is desperately high. This is not a record on which any man should seek the confidence of the American people.

My opponent now announces his desire to be President for sixteen years. Yet in his speech of Saturday night he called it a "malicious falsehood" that he had ever represented himself to be "indispensable." Let's look at these closely supervised words of his hand-picked candidate for Vice President. Mr. Truman said of my opponent, and I am quoting him: "The very future of the peace and prosperity of the world depends upon his re-election in November." Now I have not heard Mr. Truman repudiated by Mr. Roosevelt as yet. He usually waits to shed his vice presidents until they have served at least one term.

Here are the words of Boss Kelly of the Chicago machine, who was the manager of tha fake third-term draft of 1940, you remember? He said, "The salvation of this nation rests in one man." Was that statement ever repudiated by my opponent? No, it was rewarded by increased White House favors. So it was repeated again by the same man in the same city and for the same purpose this year: "The salvation of this nation rests in one man."

Now, was it a malicious falsehood that one of the first acts of my opponent's newly selected National Chairman was to announce last May that he was for a Fourth Term and that he was looking forward to a Fifth Term? Let's get this straight. The man who wants to be President for sixteen years is, indeed, indispensable. He is indispensable to Harry Hopkins, to Mme. Perkins, to Harold Ickes, he's indispensable to a host of other political job holders. He's indispensable to America's leading enemy of civil liberties—the Mayor of Jersey City. He's indispensable to those infamous machines, in Chicago—in the Bronx— and all the others. He's indispensable to Sidney Hillman and the Political Action Committee. He's indispensable to Earl Browder, the ex-convict and pardoned Communist leader.

Shall we, the American people, perpetuate one man in office for sixteen years? Shall we do that to accommodate this motley crew? Shall we expose our country to a return of the seven years of New Deal depression because my opponent is indispensable to the ill-assorted, power-hungry conglomeration of city bosses, Communists and career bureaucrats which now compose the New Deal? Shall we submit to the counsel of despair that in all the great expanse of our nation there is only one man capable of occupying the White House? The American people will answer that question in November. They will see to it that we restore integrity to the White House, so that its spoken word can be trusted once again.

On battlefields and at home the Americans have won the admiration of the world. Under the stress of war, we have thrown off the stupor and despair that seemed in the decade of the Nineteen Thirties to have settled permanently on our land. Today we know our strength and we know our ability. Shall we return to the philosophy my opponent proclaimed when he said our industrial plant is built? Shall we go back to the seven straight years of unemployment? Shall we go back to the corroding misery of leaf-raking and doles? Shall we continue an administration which invokes the language of our enemies and recklessly hurls charges of falsehood concerning things it knows to be the truth?

I say the time has come to put a stop to everything that is summed up in that phrase "the indispensable man." If any man is indispensable, then none of us are free. But America, America hasn't lost its passionate belief in freedom. America has not lost its passionate belief in opportunity. It need never lose those beliefs. For here in this country of ours there is plenty of room for freedom and for opportunity, and we need not sacrifice security to have both freedom and opportunity.

To achieve these objectives we must have intergrity in our government. We need a new high standard of honesty in the government of the United States. We need a singleness of purpose, a devotion to the people of this country and to the gigantic problems we face at home after this war. We need a whole-souled devotion to the building of a people's peace that will last far beyond the lives and friendships of any individuals.

We need humility and courage. With the help of Almighty God we shall achieve the spiritual and physical strength to preserve our freedom in the pursuit of happiness for all.

END OF A REGIME

FOURTH INAUGURAL ADDRESS [1]

FRANKLIN D. ROOSEVELT [2]

Franklin D. Roosevelt continued to make history as on January 21, 1945, he gave his fourth inaugural address as President of the United States, the first man ever to be so inaugurated. Historians on this occasion referred to the inauguration of James Madison in 1813 while the War of 1812 was in progress, and to Abraham Lincoln's second inaugural address in 1865 as the Civil War was ending.

The setting of Roosevelt's fourth inauguration contrasted with those of the three previous occasions. There were no extended parades, no long columns of the military or massed flights of planes overhead, no platforms for notables. The ceremony was held on the South Portico of the White House. Seven thousand spectators, including members of Congress, were admitted to the snow-covered South Lawn to make up the audience.

Although Roosevelt's message contained only 551 words, it had been carefully prepared and would rank among his important state papers. The composition was unmistakably that of Roosevelt himself, although Robert Sherwood, former head of the foreign branch of the Office of War Information, and Judge Samuel Rosenman, the President's legal adviser, had contributed to its labor. (See *New York Times,* January 21, 1945, Section IV., p. 2).

The aim of the President was not so much to recapitulate the achievements and records of the past four, eight, or twelve years, as to look forward (as Lincoln did in 1865) to peace and to a world of co-operation. Behind the restrained and generalized declaration of faith in America's good judgment and policies in solving foreign and domestic problems and in the prayer with which the President closed his brief oration were the implications of the tremendous issues that must be solved in the immediate months of 1945 and after. As he spoke, the Allied coalition was in process of realignment to complete the conquest of Italy and Germany; the Big Three were about to confer again, their last meeting before V-E Day; the war on Japan's inner fortress was about to mount to its climax; the forthcoming conference to frame the Dumbarton Oaks Proposals into a new League of United Nations was in

[1] Text furnished by the White House. See also *Congressional Record,* Vol. 91, No. 12, p. 380, January 22, 1945, (daily edition).

[2] For biographical note see Appendix.

preparation; Washington, too, was active in determining policies and detailed measures for the shifting of the war economy to that of peace to insure maximum peacetime employment, to broaden social security, and to share American skills and production to the end that the economic and political world might move from chaos to order.

Mr. Chief Justice, Mr. Vice President, my friends, you will understand and, I believe, agree with my wish that the form of this inauguration be simple and its words brief.

We Americans of today, together with our allies, are passing through a period of supreme test. It is a test of our courage—of our resolve—of our wisdom—of our essential democracy.

If we meet that test—successfully and honorably—we shall perform a service of historic importance which men and women and children will honor throughout all time.

As I stand here today, having taken the solemn oath of office in the presence of my fellow countrymen—in the presence of our God—I know that it is America's purpose that we shall not fail.

In the days and in the years that are to come we shall work fora just and honorable peace, a durable peace, as today we work and fight for total victory in war.

We can and we will achieve such a peace. We shall strive for perfection. We shall not achieve it immediately—but we still shall strive. We may make mistakes—but they must never be mistakes which result from faintness of heart or abandonment of moral principle.

I remember that my old schoolmaster, Dr. Peabody, said, in days that seemed to us then to be secure and untroubled, "Things in life will not always run smoothly. Sometimes we will be rising toward the heights—then all will seem to reverse itself and start downward. The great fact to remember is that the trend of civilization itself is forever upward; that a line drawn through the middle of the peaks and the valleys of the centuries always has an upward trend."

Our Constitution of 1787 was not a perfect instrument; it is not perfect yet. But it provided a firm base upon which all manner of men, of all races and colors and creeds, could build our solid structure of democracy.

And so today, in this year of war, 1945, we have learned lessons—at a fearful cost—and we shall profit by them. We have learned that we cannot live alone, at peace; that our own well-being is dependent on the well-being of other nations far away. We have learned that we must live as men, not as ostriches, nor as dogs in the manger. We have learned to be citizens of the world, members of the human community. We have learned the simple truth, as Emerson said, that "The only way to have a friend is to be one."

We can gain no lasting peace if we approach it with suspicion and mistrust or with fear. We can gain it only if we proceed with the understanding, the confidence, and the courage which flow from conviction.

The Almighty God has blessed our land in many ways. He has given our people stout hearts and strong arms with which to strike mighty blows for freedom and truth. He has given to our country a faith which has become the hope of all peoples in an anguished world.

So we pray to Him now for the vision to see our way clearly —to see the way that leads to a better life for ourselves and for all our fellow men—to the achievement of His will, to peace on earth.

ADDRESS TO CONGRESS [3]

HARRY S. TRUMAN [4]

Franklin D. Roosevelt, War President and the only Chief Executive to have more than two terms, died suddenly at 4:35 o'clock on Thursday afternoon, April 12, at Warm Springs, Georgia. The President, stricken by a cerebral hemorrhage, died on the eighty-third day of his fourth term and less than thirty days before the ignomious deaths of Mussolini and Hitler, the capture of Berlin, the unconditional surrender of the German armies, the proclamation of V-E Day, and the triumph of the European phase of the war for democracy.

Two hours later Harry S. Truman, of Missouri, was sworn in as President. At noon the next day, April 13, in the midst of national and world-wide grief and mourning, such as the peoples of all nations have never before so spontaneously expressed, the Senate convened in a thirty-five minute executive session, before crowded galleries. After the opening prayer Senator Barkley, majority leader of the Senate, paid tribute to Mr. Roosevelt. His voice was strained. He talked without notes. As the speech proceeded the members bowed. Some wept openly. [5]

"It is given to few men to occupy the Chief Magistracy of this great nation of ours, which was conceived in liberty and dedicated, as Lincoln said, to the proposition that all men are created equal; not equal in physical power, not equal in intellectual endowments, not equal either in moral fiber, but without regard to differences—physical, moral, or intellectual—without regard to differences of race, color, or religion, are born equal in the right and opportunity to enjoy the blessings of freedom under a nation and under laws and under a system which undertakes, so far as human institutions can do so, to guarantee the equal enjoyment of every right which a government ought to guarantee to those who support and defend it. It is, therefore, given to few men to attain this high distinction as the head of a nation so dedicated and so conceived, but it is a rarer thing for fate and destiny to call to supreme leadership in the world any man born of woman. Franklin D. Roosevelt enjoyed that high distinction.

"We do not honor him today merely because the American people allowed him to shatter precedent; we do not honor him merely because he, through the interposition of destiny, became a world leader; we honor him today because also of his personal qualities—of his moral and in-

[3] *Congressional Record*, Vol. 91, No. 74, p. 3440-1, April 16, 1945, (daily
[4] For biographical note see Appendix.
[5] See the *New York Herald Tribune*, April 14, 1945. Compare this speech with Senator Barkley's address nominating President Roosevelt at Chicago.

tellectual stature; we honor him as an American; we honor him in that capacity because wherever men long for liberty, wherever they fight for the enjoyment of human rights, wherever they shed their blood today or tomorrow, or lay down their lives in order that a great ideal may be attained, his name is and will be cherished and revered around the world and throughout all the ages." [6]

At the conclusion, the Senator introduced resolutions expressing the sentiment of the Senate. Other addresses followed. Senator Vandenberg of Michigan, representing the "loyal opposition," said that Roosevelt "belongs now to history, where he leaves a mark which not even the rushing centuries can erase . . . an amazing genius in behalf of his always vigorous ideas, a valiant knight in the armor of his commandership as he waged global war." Senator White, Republican leader of Maine, said, "His genius in leadership was unmatched in the political life of our nation." Senator Wagner, of New York, concluded, "Like our very greatest Americans in stature, he will become more and more heroic with the passing years." Mr. Connally concluded, "He died with the armor upon him which he had won so gallantly, and with a sword in his hand, fighting for the triumph in this war and for the establishment of an instrumentality for peace."

President Harry S. Truman, who took the oath of office on April 12, two hours after the death of Roosevelt, gave his first address to a joint session of Congress, on Monday, April 16, 1945.

The President, as he walked down the center aisle of the house, received a strong ovation from Congress, the members of the Supreme Court, the cabinet and foreign diplomatic corps. He began, harking back to his Senate days, "Mr. Speaker," and then paused while the Speaker, Sam Rayburn, introduced him.

At least thirteen times applause interrupted him. Especially strong audience approval came when the speaker asserted that "America will continue to fight for freedom until no vestige of resistance remains; I want the entire world to know that this direction must and will remain unchanged and unhampered. The responsibility of the great states is to serve and not dominate the peoples of the world."

The President, as he read before the fourteen microphones, spoke clearly and earnestly. Twice only he gestured, once to raise his right hand and bring it down palm outstretched persuasively, and once when he held up both hands and brought them down in emphatic enforcement of his point. His reading of the address was on the whole accompanied by a lively sense of communication. Here and there he obviously followed the mansucript and lapsed into routine reading, for example, in the passage beginning, "Fortunately people have retained hope of a durable peace." He omitted one passage of the prepared manuscript, "The breaking of the peace anywhere is the concern of peace-loving nations everywhere."

[6] *Congressional Record*, Vol. 91, No. 72, p. 3401-2, April 13, 1945, (daily edition).

Comparison between Truman and Roosevelt as radio speakers was inevitable, since the former President was clearly the foremost political radio speaker of America. Truman came off with a most respectable performance under most trying conditions. His voice was unduly high, at times tense. Harshness was apparent. He attempted no oratorical inflections, although both his voice and his printed manuscript (by capital sentences) stressed key ideas. His enunciation and pronunciation were Midwestern. His inflection and vocal intensity were comparatively unchanged, but he projected his voice and his ideas with success. Although no great orator, he promised to be fully acceptable as the vocal spokesman for the executive branch of American government. Sincerity and directness were especially evident in his platform manner.

What of Mr. Truman's development as a speaker? As a school boy and high school pupil in Missouri, he declaimed and debated. He gained much background for his speeches through wide reading, study, and observation of various speakers. His first serious public speech came when he ran for county judge. His experience in the Senate was of material help to him in developing his ability as a speaker. His give-and-take in committee sessions increased his vocal skill and gave him more confidence. For his more formal talks he follows a manuscript. He is not a powerful extempore speaker or a dominating senatorial debater. He did, however, give a good account of himself in ready reply to more than three hundred reporters in his first press conference—no small test of vocal and mental readiness.

What was the immediate impression of Truman's speech? Senator Connally said, "I have only commendation." Andre Tromysko, the Russian Ambassador to this country, remarked, "It was wonderful." Senator Arthur Clapper, of Kansas, concluded, "I've been listening to speeches of Presidents for twenty-six years, and it's the first time I've heard no comment or criticism by Congressmen." Senator Robert A. Taft of Ohio, one of the Republican leaders of the Senate, said the speech was "a simple, direct statement of American ideals." He added, "I particularly liked his emphasis on the necessity that law and justice be the foundations for international organization."

Senator Johnson of California, said, "I have just heard a fine American speech. I am confident President Truman will give to the people of this country the same high idealistic service he rendered as United States Senator." Representative John Rankin, of Mississippi, a bitterly outspoken foe of President Roosevelt and the New Deal, said, "A great speech—one worthy of the man, the subject and the occasion. Everyone who knows Mr. Truman as I do realizes that the affairs of the nation are in safe hands."

America was assured that the new President would faithfully execute the principles and programs of Roosevelt, both in the conduct of the war and in the administration of domestic affairs. Further Congressional comment indicated that a new era of cooperation between the executive and legislative branches of Congress had opened.

Mr. Speaker, Mr. President, Members of the Congress: It is with a heavy heart that I stand before you, my friends and colleagues in the Congress of the United States.

Only yesterday, we laid to rest the mortal remains of our beloved President, Franklin Delano Roosevelt. At a time like this, words are inadequate. The most eloquent tribute would be a reverent silence.

Yet, in this decisive hour, when world events are moving so rapidly, our silence might be misunderstood and might give comfort to our enemies.

In His infinite wisdom, Almighty God has seen fit to take from us a great man who loved, and was loved by, all humanity.

No man could possibly fill the tremendous void left by the passing of that noble soul. No words can ease the aching hearts of untold millions of every race, creed, and color. The world knows it has lost a heroic champion of justice and freedom.

Tragic fate has thrust upon us grave responsibilities. We must carry on. Our departed leader never looked backward. He looked forward and moved forward. That is what he would want us to do. That is what America will do.

So much blood has already been shed for the ideals which we cherish, and for which Franklin Delano Roosevelt lived and died, that we dare not permit even a momentary pause in the hard fight for victory.

Today, the entire world is looking to America for enlightened leadership to peace and progress. Such a leadership requires vision, courage, and tolerance. It can be provided only by a united nation deeply devoted to the highest ideals.

I call upon all Americans to help me keep our nation united in defense of those ideals which have been so eloquently proclaimed by Franklin Roosevelt.

I want, in turn, to assure my fellow Americans and all of those who love peace and liberty throughout the world that I will support and defend those ideals with all my strength and with all my heart. That is my duty, and I shall not shirk it.

So that there can be no possible misunderstanding, both Germany and Japan can be certain, beyond any shadow of doubt, America will continue the fight for freedom until no vestige of resistance remains. We are deeply conscious of the fact that much hard fighting is still ahead of us. Having to pay such a heavy price to make complete victory certain, America will never become a party to any plan for partial victory. To settle for merely another temporary respite would surely jeopardize the future security of all the world. Our demand has been, and it remains, unconditional surrender. We will not traffic with the breakers of the peace on the terms of the peace.

The responsibility for the making of the peace—and it is a very grave responsibility—must rest with the defenders of the peace, the United Nations. We are not unconscious of the dictates of humanity. We do not wish to see unnecessary or unjustified suffering. But the laws of God and of man have been violated and the guilty must not go unpunished. Nothing shall shake our determination to punish the war criminals even though we must pursue them to the ends of the earth.

Lasting peace can never be secured if we permit our dangerous opponents to plot future wars with impunity at any mountain retreat, however distant. In this shrinking world, it is futile to seek safety behind geographical barriers. Real security will be found only in law and in justice.

Here in America we have labored long and hard to achieve a social order worthy of our great heritage. In our time tremendous progress has been made toward a really democratic way of life. Let me assure the forward-looking people of America that there will be no relaxation in our efforts to improve the lot of the common people. In the difficult days ahead, unquestionably we shall face problems of staggering proportions. However, with the faith of our fathers in our hearts, we fear no future. On the battlefields, we have frequently faced overwhelming odds—and won. At home, Americans will not be less resolute. We shall never cease our struggle to preserve and maintain our American way of life.

At this very moment America, along with her brave allies, is paying again a heavy price for the defense of our freedom. With characteristic energy, we are assisting in the liberation of entire nations. Gradually, the shackles of slavery are being broken by the forces of freedom. All of us are praying for a speedy victory. Every day peace is delayed costs a terrible toll. The armies of liberation today are bringing to an end Hitler's ghastly threat to dominate the world. Tokyo rocks under the weight of our bombs.

The grand strategy of a United Nations' war has been determined—due in no small measure to the vision of our departed Commander in Chief. We are now carrying out our part of that strategy under the able direction of Admiral Leahy, General Marshall, Admiral King, General Arnold, General Eisenhower, Admiral Nimitz, and General MacArthur. I want the entire world to know that this direction must and will remain unchanged and unhampered.

Our debt to the heroic men and valiant women in the service of our country can never be repaid. They have earned our undying gratitude. America will never forget their sacrifiecs. Because of these sacrifices, the dawn of justice and freedom throughout the world slowly casts its gleam across the horizon.

Our forefathers came to our rugged shores in search of religious tolerance, political freedom, and economic opportunity. For those fundamental rights, they risked their lives. We well know today that such rights can be preserved only by constant vigilance, the eternal price of liberty.

Within an hour after I took the oath of office, I announced that the San Francisco Conference would proceed. We will face the problems of peace with the same courage that we have faced and mastered the problems of war. In the memory of those who have made the supreme sacrifice, in the memory of our fallen President, we shall not fail.

It is not enough to yearn for peace. We must work, and if necessary, fight for it. The task of creating a sound international organization is complicated and difficult. Yet, without such organization, the rights of man on earth cannot be protected. Machinery for the just settlement of international differences must be found. Without such machinery, the entire world will have to remain an armed camp. The world will be doomed to deadly conflict, devoid of hope for real peace.

Fortunately, people have retained hope for a durable peace. Thoughtful people have always had faith that ultimately justice must triumph. Past experience surely indicates that, without justice, an enduring peace becomes impossible.

In bitter despair, some people have come to believe that wars are inevitable. With tragic fatalism, they insist that as wars have always been, of necessity, wars will always be. To such defeatism, men and women of good will must not and cannot yield. The outlook for humanity is not so hopeless.

During the darkest hours of this horrible war, entire nations were kept going by something intangible—hope. When warned that abject submission offered the only salvation against overwhelming power, hope showed the way to victory. Hope has become the secret weapon of the forces of liberation. Aggressors could not dominate the human mind. As long as hope remains the spirit of man will never be crushed.

But hope alone was not and is not sufficient to avert war. We must not only have hope but we must have faith enough to work with other peace-loving nations to maintain the peace. Hope was not enough to beat back the aggressors as long as the peace-loving nations were unwilling to come to each other's defense. The aggressors were beaten back only when the peace-loving nations united to defend themselves.

If wars in the future are to be prevented, the peace-loving nations must be united in their determination to keep the peace under law. The breaking of the peace anywhere is the concern of peace-loving nations everywhere. Nothing is more essential to the future peace of the world than continued cooperation of the nations which had to muster the force necessary to defeat the conspiracy of the Fascist powers to dominate the world.

While these great states have a special responsibility to enforce the peace, their responsibility is based upon the obligations resting upon all states, large and small, not to use force in international relations except in the defense of law. The responsibility of the great states is to serve and not dominate the peoples of the world. To build the foundation of enduring peace we must not only work in harmony with our friends abroad but we must have the united support of our own people. Even the most experienced pilot cannot bring a ship safely into harbor, unless he has the full cooperation of the crew. For the benefit of all, every individual must do his duty. I appeal to every American, regardless of party, race, creed, or color, to support our efforts to build a strong and lasting United Nations organization.

You, the Members of Congress, surely know how I feel. Only with your help can I hope to complete one of the greatest tasks ever assigned to a public servant. With divine guidance, and your help, we will find the new passage to a far better world, a kindly and friendly world, with just and lasting peace. With confidence, I am depending upon all of you.

To destroy greedy tyrants with plans of world domination, we cannot continue in successive generations to sacrifice our finest youth. In the name of human decency and civilization, a more rational method of deciding national differences must and will be found. America must assist suffering humanity back along the path of peaceful progress. This will require time and tolerance. We shall need also an abiding faith in the people, the kind of faith and courage which Franklin Delano Roosevelt always had.

Today, America has become one of the most powerful forces for good on earth. We must keep it so. We have achieved a world leadership which does not depend solely upon our military and naval might. We have learned to fight with other nations in common defense of our freedom. We must now learn to live with other nations for our mutual good. We must learn to trade more with other nations so that there may be—for our mutual advantage—increased production, increased employment and better standards of living throughout the world. In that way, America may well lead the world to peace and prosperity.

At this moment, I have in my heart a prayer. As I assume my heavy duties, I humbly pray to Almighty God, in the words of Solomon:

Give therefore thy servant an understanding heart to judge thy people, that I may discern between good and bad: for who is able to judge this thy so great a people?

I ask only to be a good and faithful servant of my Lord and my people.

TRIBUTES TO ROOSEVELT [7]

Bernard J. Sheil and Hilmar R. Baukhage [8]

From the moment President Roosevelt's death was announced on Thursday afternoon, April 12, until the following Sunday midnight, hours after the burial at Hyde Park, the radio reflected with taste and credit the national mourning. The news was announced at the White House at 5:48 E.W.T. Immediately the networks began the announcements. Radio "probably had more attentive listeners on the day of his death than it had ever had before." (*Time,* April 25, 1945, p. 68) Commercial radio was abandoned for four days. Commentators at home and throughout the world, leaders, prominent speakers representing every race, religion, political creed, contributed their testimony to Roosevelt's power as man and President. Soap operas, gay music, lurid dramas, comedy shows were omitted. In their place were tributes, prayers, sermons, reminiscences, and appropriate music, including selections from Gounod and Tchaikowsky. At four o'clock on Saturday the radio was silent for one minute.

Typical of these radio broadcasts was the tribute by the Most Reverend Bernard J. Sheil, D.D., auxiliary Bishop of Chicago, over stations WIND and WBBM, on April 14. Bishop Sheil has a pleasing radio voice, well pitched, sonorous. He is a religious philosopher and a poet with imagination. He possesses literary power, skill in analysis, spiritual insight.

Congressman John M. Coffee characterized him as possessing, "one of the great minds of America," and referred to one of the Bishop's addresses at Catholic University, Washington, D.C., as "one of the most outstanding contributions made by any thinker in America." [9]

On Sunday morning, April 15, the burial rites of Roosevelt were held in the Rose Garden at Hyde Park. Hilmar R. Baukhage, of the American Broadcasting Company, later broadcast the brief ceremonies. His talk, widely listened to, was generally recognized as a masterpiece of its type. Inserting the Baukhage talk in the *Congressional Record,* Representative Clifton A. Woodrum, of Virginia, said,

[7] For the text of Bishop Sheil's broadcast, see *Congressional Record,* Vol. 91, No. 82, p. A 2102-3, April 26, 1945, (daily edition). See *Congressional Record,* Vol. 91, No. 75, p. A 1915-16, April 17, 1945, (daily edition) for speech of Hilmar Baukhage.

[8] For biographical notes see Appendix.

[9] For Congressman Coffee's comments and the text of Bishop Sheil's address at that time see *Congressional Record,* Vol. 89, No. 93, p. A 5802-5, December 10, 1943, (daily edition).

"I think one of the splendid things that has happened in the last few days in the way of an expression of great esteem and appreciation of the President was the very fine way in which American radio responded. The several broadcasting chains, as well as the individual stations, laid all commercial activities aside and brought only appropriate news and information in the hour of mourning. In my judgment, one of the classics of the several programs was the description of the ceremony at Hyde Park made immediately thereafter by Baukhage, a distinguished analyst and commentator of the American Broadcasting Company. I believe this description should be preserved and, under leave granted me, I herewith include the same."

Bernard Sheil

The great friend of the common man is gone. The defender and protector of the "little people" is dead. He who knew their thoughts and their aspirations, who voiced their hopes and dreams, has laid down his burdens and gone to rest. Across his record can be written in lines of burnished gold, "Died in the line of duty."

"For greater love than this hath no man . . . that he lay down his life for his friends." And he laid it down with a will, fully conscious of the fact that he had carried forward a little farther mankind's eternal quest for freedom.

> Freedom is not to limit—but to share,
> And freedom here . . . means freedom everywhere.

But his memory shall live on. His brave words and braver deeds will become as shining beacons beckoning onward a tired and flagging humanity. There can never be rest for those of us who hold dear his memory. As he did, so must we do.

We must spend lavishly our coin of life to purchase for our fellowman those ideals he fought and died for. We must pour out, with generous measure, the very breath of existence in an unceasing struggle for the dreams he dreamed, but did not live to see accomplished.

Yes, his memory shall live on. It will spring into being in the smile of a little child yet unborn, who will know a richer, fuller life because he lived.

It will shine in the face of a tired, benumbed laborer, crouched in front of a mammoth machine, overwhelmed by the mechanics of industry, yet conscious of his dignity as a human being because of the goal President Roosevelt had pointed out.

It will burn in the hungry breast of a war-weary European peasant who will again know of hope—and faith—and charity because these were gifts of which he gave freely.

It will blaze as an unquenchable fire in the minds and hearts of all men, everywhere, who yearn for freedom.

It will gleam in the dark nights of human despair, and men will warm themselves in its glow and return renewed and revitalized to the struggle for human rights.

His memory will stand as a mighty bulwark, an impregnable fortress against those enemies of democracy who would encompass and destroy it. And his name alone will be sufficient to rally free men to the standard of humanity.

Dry your tears. Lift up your hearts. Let not the hours be wasted in unavailing grief.

His work remains to be finished and it needs the willing hands of all those who marched beneath his banner. He cannot rest in peace while one human being wears the chains of slavery. He cannot rest if one mouth goes unfed, one body unclothed. He will not rest if the fires of victory turn into the dead ashes of forgotten promises—broken pledges and battered hopes.

But he shall rest, aye, and endlessly—if the dreams he dreamed become the reality of a bright tomorrow. He shall rest, and his gallant spirit will at last go winging home, if mankind can find in the unity of grief over his death that unity of life to which he dedicated his entire being.

The stage is empty. The great, brave voice is stilled. And from the wings the soft-murmured lamentations, eddy and swell. The people are taking him to his last resting place. "The long journey" is over. The tired and strained ship has anchored in the harbor. And on the shore the watchers stand mute, each man alone. The people are taking him to his last resting place. To deep solitudes and quiet moments. To silent hours and noise-

hushed thoughts. To that small castle in which few may enter.
The people are taking him to his final resting place.

> Beat softly drums,
> Blow gently bugles.
> This moment is sacred.

The people are enshrining him in their hearts.

> Eternal rest grant unto him, O Lord:
> And may perpetual light shine upon him.

HILMAR BAUKHAGE

Baukhage, talking from a little house down the Boston Post
Road a bit from Hyde Park where I've come, following the
President's funeral—a little way from the rolling farmland, the
woodland and hedgerows, and stone fences, and plowed fields,
the old home behind the trees where Franklin Roosevelt first
saw the light over the hills of the Hudson, and where I've just
left him in the midst of his own acres, taking his last long rest.

I'm not going to talk about the death of the President today
because I'm thinking of something else. I'm thinking about an
American—like others who fell at Lexington, Appomattox, at
San Juan Hill, and Chateau-Thierry, on the Normandy beaches,
on Guadalcanal, at Aachen, and now at the very gates of Berlin.
I am thinking of Franklin Roosevelt that way because of the
last broadcast I made from Hyde Park on September 8, four
years ago on a mellow autumn day. On that day thousands in
America were not thinking of the most thought-about man in
the country then in terms of politics or policies or rank or title
or achievements or failures. But they were thinking of him
humanly and vainly trying to share the grief that a son alone
must bear when he repays with the anguish of parting, the debt
in travail of her who bore him. That was the day when Sara
Delano Roosevelt passed away. And that is what I saw then—
then, not a President but a man mourning for his mother.

And today a nation mourns not for a President but for a
loss made the more poignant by the sorrow of the mothers all

over the nation whose sons have been lost on the wide battle-fields of the world. To me there is no question whatever but that Franklin Roosevelt died in the service of his country, a service grown too great for any single man to bear, just as other mother's sons have died for their country, the ones who gave their lives in action. To me, this ceremony that I have just witnessed is part of the great panoply of sacrifice that men since time began have made, giving their lives to preserve an ideal which lived on because they were willing to exchange their own lives for it. A part of the eternal miracle of nature when earth takes back her seed only to return it in the rich harvest, and flower and stalk should be the nourishment of others that mourn.

I have come, as I say, from Hyde Park where in an ancient old-fashioned garden, protected by the high walls of a hemlock hedge, another American has gone to rest on the acres where he was born, the acres he loved. He chose this spot among the old-fashioned blooms—now only brown shoots, I noticed before me, brown and unobstrusive compared to the mountains of riot-ous color heaped above the grave. But those were plucked flowers—they will fade. The others, they will bloom again in this eternal miracle of spring. Over the boxwood hedge the old red barn looks down. Thousands of those red barns are on America's farms. Beyond and hidden by the great trees is the old home, and beyond—the Hudson River flowing gently to the sea.

And now as I have taken the notes down I'll give them to you:

First there was the roar of planes overhead and then the sharp order, "Attention," the salute, and then echoing over those deep hills of the Hudson, like Henry Hudson's bowling balls, came the salute of forty-eight guns. And between those shots all was so silent that you could hear bird songs everywhere. And then, "Present arms," and then the planes coming back. And then last, in the distance, the low tap of the muffled drums from the West Point band and then the sound of the slow rhythm of the Death March which grew louder and louder as they entered the grounds. And now they come in before us, and the West Pointers follow at that strange slow march, and finally the caisson is outside the hedge, you can hear it. It halts just beyond the little entrance where I am standing. The bombers soar over and now the colors are advanced—the Stars and Stripes, the gold of the Presidential Flag. And now, "Order arms," "Present arms," and the bugles sound off, the Star-Spangled Banner, and at that moment the cool wind from the Hudson River blew and whipped out the flags. "Order arms," "Parade rest," and now softly the band began "Lead, Kindly Light." And now a choir boy with the crucifix comes in, behind, in white surplice, the white-haired minister, and then the coffin with the pall bearers, soldiers and sailors and marines, and next the wife and the daughter and the son, Elliott, and then President Truman. The coffin rests, a flag upon it—the flag is raised and held above it. And now the minister speaks, then comes a prayer, and then the poem that he reads with this refrain: "Father in Thy gracious keeping leave we now Thy servant sleeping." And then after the silence, bird songs again. And then the sharp order to the firing party, "Fire three volleys," "Ready," "Aim," "Fire." The shots ring out—three times the volleys are shot over the grave—and after each the bark of a little lonely dog. And then that sweetest and saddest of all music—the bugle sounds Taps. There is a pause as the echoes die and the coffin is lowered into the earth. The sergeant, with military precision, marches over and lays the flag that decked the coffin in the hands of Mrs. Roosevelt. And so, an American has gone to rest in the green of the garden, in the shadow of the old red barn, and his spirit, like that of all his fallen comrades on the battlefield, rolls on like the eternal river flowing softly to the sea.

HUMANITY'S LOSS [10]

WINSTON CHURCHILL [10]

Winston Churchill, Prime Minister of Great Britain, paid tribute to the late President Roosevelt, in the House of Commons, London, on April 17, 1945. The address was later broadcast to America and the world. Mr. Churchill's remarks were peculiarly well adapted to his subject, his audience, and the occasion. They were brief, without rhetorical expansion, reminiscent, reverent. The expression was unhackneyed, sincere, Churchillian. The greatest orator of his day had again given his theme profound and inspiring treatment. To Britishers and the Anglo-Saxon world would long echo the simple finale of the eulogy, "In Franklin Roosevelt there died the greatest American friend we have ever known and the greatest champion of freedom who has ever brought help and comfort from the New World to the Old." [12]

My friendship with the great man to whose work and fame we pay our tribute today began and ripened during this war. I had met him, but only for a few minutes, after the close of the last war and as soon as I went to the admiralty in September, 1939, he telegraphed, inviting me to correspond with him direct on naval or other matters if at any time I felt inclined. Having obtained permission of the Prime Minister, I did so. Knowing President Roosevelt's keen interest in sea warfare, I furnished him with a stream of information about our naval affairs and about various actions, including especially the action of the Plate River which lighted the first gloomy window of the war.

[10] Reprinted by permission from *Vital Speeches of the Day.* 11:421. May 1, 1945.

[11] For biographical note see Appendix.

[12] For comments on Churchill as speaker, for his speeches, and for references to Churchill in his relations with Roosevelt see *Representative American Speeches: 1939-40,* Roosevelt, F. D., "Message to Congress," p. 26-37; *Representative American Speeches: 1940-41,* Roosevelt, F. D., "The Preservation of American Independence," p. 19-32; Roosevelt, F. D., "A State of Emergency Exists," p. 57-74; *Representative American Speeches: 1941-42,* Roosevelt, F. D., "War Address," p. 15-19; Churchill, Winston, "Address to Congress," p. 19-29; Roosevelt, F.D., "America Accepts the Challenge," p. 30-39; Roosevelt, F. D., "Eight Common Principles for a Better World," p. 247-50; *Representative American Speeches: 1942-43,* Roosevelt, F. D., "Message to Congress," p. 16-29; Churchill, Winston, "Address to Congress," p. 30-46; *Representative American Speeches: 1943-44,* Roosevelt, F. D., "Message to Coongress," p. 15-26; Churchill Winston, "British-American Cooperation," p. 27-36. See also, Roosevelt, F. D., "The Yalta Conference," *supra,* p. 19-36.

When I became Prime Minister and war broke out in all its hideous fury and when our own life and survival hung in the balance, I was already in position to telegraph to the President on terms of association which had become most intimate and to me most agreeable. This continued through all the years of the world struggle until Thursday last, when I received my last message from him. These messages showed no falling off in his accustomed clear vision and vigor on perplexing and complicated matters. This correspondence, which greatly increased after the United States entry into the war, comprises to and fro between us over 1,700 messages. Many of these were lengthy messages. To this correspondence there must be added our nine meetings, comprising in all about 120 days of close, personal contact.

I conceived an admiration for him as a statesman, as a man of affairs and as a war leader. I felt the utmost confidence in his upright and inspiring character and his outlook and personal regard—affection, I must say, beyond my power to express today. It is a loss, indeed a bitter loss to humanity, that those heartbeats are stilled forever. President Roosevelt's physical affliction lay heavily upon him. It was a marvel that he bore up against it through all the many years of tumult and storm. Not one man in ten million, stricken and crippled as he was, would have attempted to have plunged into a life of physical and mental exertion and of hard and ceaseless political controversy.

Not one in a generation would have succeeded. There was never a moment's doubt in this war upon which side his sympathy lay. He never lost faith in Britain. The bearing of the British nation, when we were all alone, filled him and vast numbers of his countrymen with the warmest sentiments toward our people. He and they felt the blitz of the stern winter of 1940-41 when Hitler set himself to rub out the cities of our country. There is no doubt that he felt the blitz as much as any of us did and perhaps more, indeed, for imagination is often more torturing than reality.

There's no doubt that the bearing of the British and above all the Londoners kindled fire in American bosoms far harder to quench than the conflagrations from which we suffered. There was also at that time an apprehension widespread in the United States that we should be invaded by Germany after the most full preparation in the spring of 1941. It was in February that the President sent to England the late Mr. Wendell Willkie, who, although a political rival and opposing candidate, felt as the President did on many important points.

Mr. Willkie brought a letter from Mr. Roosevelt which the President had written in his own hand. This letter contained the famous lines of Longfellow:

> Sail on, O ship of state!
> Sail on, O union, strong and great!
> Humanity with all its fears,
> With all the hopes of future years,
> Is hanging breathless on thy fate!

At about that time he devised the extraordinary measure of assistance called lend-lease which will stand forth as the most unselfish, unsordid financial act of any country in all history. The effect of this was greatly to increase British fighting power and for all purposes of the war effort to make us, as it were, a much more numerous community.

In the autumn I met the President, for the first time during the war, in Newfoundland and together we drew up the declaration which has since been called the Atlantic Charter and which will, I trust, long remain the guide for both our peoples and other peoples of the world.

All this time and in dark and deadly secrecy the Japanese were preparing their act of treachery and greed. When next we met in Washington Japan had declared war on the United States and both our countries were in arms, shoulder to shoulder. Since then we have advanced over land and over sea, through many difficulties and disappointments, but always with a broadening measure of success.

At Yalta I noticed that the President was ailing. His captivating smile, his gay, charming manner had not deserted him. But his face had a transparency and an air of purification and often there was a faraway look in his eyes. When I took leave of him at Alexandria I must confess that I had an indefinable sense of fear that his strength and health were on the ebb. But nothing altered his inflexible sense of duty. To the very end he faced his task unfailing. Only one of the tasks of the President is to sign maybe a hundred or two hundred state papers every day. All this he continued to carry out with utmost strictness and when death came suddenly upon him he had finished his mail—that portion of his day's work was done.

As the saying goes, he died in harness and we may well say in battle harness like his soldiers, sailors, and airmen who died side by side with ours and are carrying out their tasks to the end all over the world. What an enviable death was his.

He has brought his country through the worst of its perils and, happiest of all, its trials. Victory had cast its sure and steady beam upon him. He had broadened and stabilized in days of peace the foundations of American life and union. In war he had raised the strength, might and glory of a great republic to a height never attained by any nation in history. On her left hand she was leading the advance of our conquering Allied Armies into the heart of Germany. On her right, on the other side of the globe, she was irresistibly and swiftly breaking the power of Japan.

And all the time ships, munitions, food and supplies of every kind were on every side aiding on a gigantic scale her allies in the course of the struggle. But all this was no more than worldly power and grandeur had it not been that the causes of human freedom and social justice, to which so much of his life had been given, had added a luster quite of its own which will long be discernible among men.

He has left behind him a band of resolute, able men handling numerous interrelated parts of the vast American war machine. He has left a successor who comes forward with firm steps and sure conviction to carry on the task to its appointed end. For us it remains only to say that in Franklin Roosevelt there died the greatest American friend we have ever known and the greatest champion of freedom who has ever brought help and comfort from the New World to the Old.

AMERICAN IDEALS

INTOLERANCE [1]

ERIC A. JOHNSTON [2]

Mr. Eric A. Johnston, president of the United States Chamber of Commerce, gave this address before the Writers' War Board, in New York City, on January 11, 1945.

The Writers' War Board was a private organization, formed originally in December 1941, at the request of the Treasury Department to enlist the aid of professional writers in the sale of war bonds. The Board soon expanded its operations to include the preparation of articles, scripts, stories, poems, slogans, pamphlets, and books on all aspects of the war. The Group also arranged for writers to speak on war subjects on the radio and lecture platform. It cooperated with such government agencies as the Office of Civilian Defense, Office of Price Administration, and Office of War Information, as well as the Navy and War Departments. Other private agencies it served included the American Red Cross, National War Fund, United Nations Information Office, Russian War Relief. Rex Stout was chairman, Franklin P. Adams, Clifton Fadiman, Paul Gallico, John P. Marquand, William L. Shirer and eight or ten others comprised the Board proper. The Advisory Council was made up of an impressive list of well-known writers, William Rose Benét, Van Wyck Brooks, Mary Ellen Chase, Carl Van Doren, Thornton Wilder, and some fifty others. The members served without compensation.

Throughout 1944 Mr. Johnston continued to give speeches of exceptional interest and timeliness.[3] The theme of national unity was, as he said in New York, "the most challenging" of all social problems. Social historians of the period since 1941 will trace the increase of racial, religious, and economic prejudice in this country. World War II carried in its path latent or ill-concealed conflicts, such as those against the Negroes and the Jews, or the more open and violent discriminations against alien races, notably the Japanese on the West Coast. The political campaign of 1944 also contributed to the "spree of intolerance," stimulated by the attacks upon the C.I.O. and other labor groups and upon the American "communists."

---

[1] Text furnished by Mr. Eric Johnston and the Chamber of Commerce of the United States. Permission to reprint the speech through the courtesy of Mr. Johnston. For copy of the text see also the *Congressional Record*, Vol. 91, No. 26, p. A 611-12, February 12, 1945, (daily edition), proceedings and debates of the 79th Congress, first session.

[2] For biographical note see Appendix.

[3] See *Representative American Speeches: 1943-44*, p. 200 ff.

When Johnston spoke, the "propagandas and whispering campaigns directed against foreigners, against Jews, against Catholics, against Negroes," were evident throughout the land. The issue was sharpened by the continual reminder that this was a "war for the Four Freedoms and for liberty."

The speaker, as usual, had a simple but well-knit series of ideas: (1) We need unity. (2) This unity depends on the protection of individual freedom. (3) The threats against individual freedom are now rising; there is intolerance against foreigners, Jews, Catholics, Negroes, and other "minority" groups. (4) These tensions strike at the roots of our American system. (5) Our remedies must be to (a) face the realities of such friction, (b) denounce such intolerance, (c) analyze the bad economic effects of the conflict, (d) recognize that we are a polyglot of nations, (e) recognize that our progress in solving these things must be gradual, (f) develop moral and ethical idealism.

The oral style, characteristic of Johnston, is informal, highly concrete, attention-getting. There are hidden humor, personal reference, epigrams ("You can't legislate the golden rule as you can the gold standard") and quotable statements.

The address was widely reprinted; it enhanced the reputation of Johnston as speaker and national leader, and no doubt strengthened the case against intolerance.

I like to look on my presence here as a sign that the Hatfields of business and the McCoys of the writing world have ended their old-time feud. Maybe business is beginning to see more clearly that art has its practical aspects; and maybe the artist is beginning to realize that industry has its artistic values. More importantly, maybe both are beginning to understand that each is part of America and that neither has a right to pluck the mote out of the other's eye until he has first extracted the beam from his own.

Your subject tonight is "The Myth That Threatens America." Surely, the business man and the artist share responsibility in eradicating the myth of group or class superiority. Those who pretend that it does not exist are kidding themselves.

Of all the social problems that face our great country in this era of crisis, that of national unity seems to me the most challenging. Most other problems will not be solved if the American people are divided into mutually hostile and suspicious groups, sections and classes. More than that; even if solutions were possible under such conditions, they would hardly be worth achieving. They would be empty victories, utterly meaningless, if the character of our American civilization were changed in the process.

And the core of that civilization, it seems to me, is in the sacred dignity of the human being, regardless of race or class or place of birth. Individual freedom—liberty within a framework of law—is essential to the America we know and love. Without these elements it would no longer be *our* America, except in the geographical sense. In the deeper moral sense it would be an alien country, where those of us who cherish ideals of freedom would be exiles in our own homes.

We are all of us, in our several ways, seeking to preserve America. Millions of our sons are doing it on battlefields with bombs and bayonets. You who write and inspire and propagandize do it with the weapon of words. Those of us who build and manufacture do it with machines and goods. But what all of us have in mind is not simply the physical preservation of our country. It is the preservation of those human values which are implicit in the word America—the freedom, the opportunities, the equalities, the democratic ideals celebrated in our national songs and poetry and books and holiday speeches.

I know there are the clichés of American patriotism and after-dinner oratory. But we do not discount them for that reason. On the contrary, we accept them and cherish them as proof positive that the American Dream is a dream of free men living together in a spirit of harmony and trust.

I regard as profoundly significant the fact that the average American, whether he be a blasé business man or a cynical writer, looks on these so-called clichés as desirable even when he doesn't live up to them. Equally significant is the fact that even the salesmen of dissension must disguise their sales talks in the phraseology of American freedom.

Race hatreds and group intolerance simply do not jibe with any of the formulas of freedom so dear to the American heart. To the extent they are allowed to flourish, they threaten to change the American Dream into another European nightmare.

Let's not underestimate the threat. There is a tendency to soft-pedal the spread of alien doctrines of intolerance. The theory, I suppose, is that the best way to treat a disease is to pretend that it doesn't exist. That is a cowardly theory and worse, a futile one. It seems to me that honest diagnosis is the first and indispensable measure in meeting the challenge of propagandas and whispering campaigns directed against foreigners, against Jews, against Catholics, against Negroes.

Equally dangerous, but not so dramatic, and therefore not so well understood, are the campaigns of intolerance and vilification that are directed against economic groups such as business, labor and agriculture—sometimes by one another, and sometimes by the enemies of one or all. To the extent that business has been guilty of such intolerance in any direction I deplore it. I have set my face against it, and I shall continue to denounce it. To the extent that you, as writers have been guilty of this same type of intolerance with respect to any of these groups, including business, I invite you to have another look to see if the beam in your eye has gotten you off the beam of tolerance.

I have been privileged to travel widely in our country, and I do not hesitate to offer my personal testimony that the tremendous tension of race and group animosities is warping the very foundations of American democratic life. Men and women who should know better—who do know better—allow themselves to mouth the catch phrases of anti-Semitism and anti-foreignism, of anti-business, or anti-labor, anti-farm. Most of them are not themselves aware that they have been infected by the virus of intolerance which already has the whole world writhing in the fatal fever of war.

When there's a riot in Detroit or Harlem, when racial antagonisms break into the open in Boston or Brooklyn, it's more comfortable to shrug them off as local incidents. But the truth must be faced. These episodes of violence are symptoms of pressures and emotions and maladjustments which are nation-wide.

The first thing we must do, it seems to me, is to confront the reality. Obviously the most violent and deep seated of our antipathies are racial and religious. Widespread though these expressions of group hatred are, it is a hopeful fact that they still afflict only a small minority of the American population. That minority can be curbed and re-educated if conscious and organized efforts are undertaken.

At the very worst, that minority can be frightened into desisting. Not by legal threats—you can't legislate the golden rule as you can the gold standard. I mean that Americans can be made sharply aware that intolerance endangers not merely the small groups against whom it is directed but the country as a whole. The obstreperous hate-mongers and their foolish or frivolous fellow travelers who think it is smart to rock the American boat may drown with the other passengers.

If they achieve the calamity of race persecutions, they will drag our beloved America down to the barbarian level of Nazi Germany and we will pay for it in death and suffering and national degeneration, precisely as the Germans are doing today. We need to emphasize, day in and day out, that the spread of intolerance is not primarily a threat to the intended victims but to the whole country. Once the poison enters a nation's bloodstream, the entire population is doomed. Only six hundred thousand German Jews suffered through the triumph of Nazi barbarism—but the non-Jews who suffered from it include the more than eighty million Germans!

If the day ever comes in this country when tolerance gives way to internal enmities and persecutions and discriminations, it will be the end of American civilization. Remember this: The dictates of intolerance cannot be enforced finally without the connivance of government. Should intolerance triumph, it will mean, as a matter of course, that free government is stamped out. Racial persecutions—whether in the old Russia or the present day Germany—have always been conducted under the protection of a tyrannical governmental regime.

Viewed from the narrowest vantage point of the nation's well-being, quite aside from human and moral considerations, the growth of doctrines of race and group hatreds represents a major economic threat. America has prospered because it has provided avenues of economic expression to all men who had the urge and the capacity to advance themselves. Wherever we erect barriers on the grounds of race or religion, or of occupational or professional status, we hamper the fullest expansion of our economic society. Intolerance is destructive. Prejudice produces no wealth. Discrimination is a fool's economy.

Freedom of the individual is the most vital condition for creative life in economy as in every other department of human existence. Such freedom is impossible where men are restricted by reason of race or origin, on the one hand, or on the other, paralyzed by fears and hatreds of their neighbors.

There are some in our country—industrialists, white collar workers, laboring people—who hold to the myth that economic progress can be attained on the principle of an unbalanced seesaw. They think that if some groups can be forever held *down*, the others will forever enjoy economic privileges and prosperity at the end which is up.

Fortunately it does not work that way. Any advantage thus gained must be paid for out of the fruits of the productive plant. The withholding of jobs and business opportunities from some people does not make more jobs and business opportunities for others. Such a policy merely tends to drag down the whole economic level. You can't sell an electric refrigerator to a family that can't afford electricity. Perpetuating poverty for some merely guarantees stagnation for all. True economic progress demands that the whole nation move forward at the same time. It demands that all artificial barriers erected by ignorance and intolerance be removed. To put it in the simplest terms, we are all in business together. Intolerance is a species of boycott and any business or job boycott is a cancer in the economic body of the nation. I repeat: Intolerance is destructive. Prejudice produces no wealth. Discrimination is a fool's economy.

These are things that should be made manifest to the American people if we are to counteract the pestiferous labors of race and group hate-mongers. The job lies to a large extent in the hands of you writers, in your colleagues in the movies, the theater, radio, the press. You are the people with direct access to the mind—and what is more important, to the heart and emotions—of the American people.

You must somehow take words like freedom and democracy and unity and lift them to the level of religious fervor. We require more than a broad acceptance of these American concepts.

We need an eager enthusiasm. And you, in particular, have the power to arouse it and to keep it alive. I want to emphasize that.

If eternal vigilance is the price of liberty, the writer and the artist generally have a prime duty in keeping the vigil. It is for them to dramatize the strength and beauty that resides in America's multiplicity of races, religions, national origins and social backgrounds. The totalitarians who looked on us as "mongrels," as a chaos of clashing cultures, have learned their mistake. We always must remember that America is a nation made up of the peoples of all lands.

Any metallurgist will tell you that the toughest, most resistant metals are not "pure" ores but alloys that blend the most valuable qualities of many ores. It is thus with the American, who fuses in his blood and his spirit the virtues and vitalities of many races, creeds, and cultures—giving us an amalgam that is new, unique, and immeasurably strong.

That is why tolerance is necessarily and rightly a supreme American characteristic. In truth, we must continue to cultivate our native American tolerance for everything except intolerance.

Our enemies have learned in this war the toughness of our fiber. It not remains for the American people, likewise, to absorb that lesson. It was Walt Whitman who celebrated the diversity that is America's strength. "This is not a nation," he proclaimed, "but a teaming of nations." In some measure every poet sensitive to the nature of our still young American experiment has felt and expressed that diversity. Russell Davenport has just done it in "My Country." Perhaps the poet, more than the economist or historian, senses the absurdity in attempts to hammer all Americans into a single national type and discriminate against the minorities who do not conform to an arbitrary creation.

Let's not apologize for the amazing variety of our human material here in America. Let us rather glory in it as the source of our robust spirit and opulent achievements. Let's not deny that there are differences in race and that our country has all the fifty-seven varieties of God's humanity. Let us merely make clear that these differences cannot be measured on any scale of good, better and best. They are all equally valid and all must continue to contribute to the magnificent mosaic of American life.

Subtract from the grand total of America the contributions of our racial and religious and economic minorities—and what remains? Subtract foreign-born Andrew Carnegie from our metallurgical industry; or David Sarnoff from American radio; or George Gershwin and the Negro composers from our native music; or Norwegian-born Knute Rockne from our football; or Dutch-born Edward William Bok from publishing; or Danish-born William S. Knudsen from the automotive industry; or Russian-born Major de Seversky from American aviation; or Belgian-born Leo H. Baekeland from American chemical achievements; or slave-born Dr. George Washington Carver from biological developments. The temptation is to list hundreds and thousands who have thrown their particular genius into the American melting pot.

And behind those whose names we know are the nameless legions of immigrants, generation after generation, whose labor and lives went into every bridge, and tunnel, every mine and factory in these United States.

Too many Americans—indeed, too many of the immigrants themselves, whatever their race or land of birth—behave as if America only *gave* things to newcomers. We need to be reminded that America *received* more than it gave. After all, our country let the strangers in because it needed their muscle power, their purchasing power, their fecundity and their brains.

It is this vision of a society wonderfully rounded by reason of its many racial contributions—of an *inter*nation within the borders of a vast nation—that should be brought home to every American child and adult. The cooperation of these multiple elements—the unity of a powerful amalgam—has given a peculiar destiny and genius to our country. In pointing out our achievements to our preachers of division and distrust we are protecting that part of our history that still lies in the future.

But it seems to me that all of us who fight against intolerance can hurt our own cause by expecting too much too soon. The simple human fact is that prejudice is latent in all of us. The average Protestant, Catholic, Jew is normally prejudiced in favor of his own kind and against the others. The underprivileged are prejudiced against the well-to-do. The strong are prejudiced against the weak and vice versa. Men are prejudiced against women and women, alas, are even more prejudiced against men. The saintly soul who goes through life devoid of all prejudices is rare indeed.

These attitudes cannot be wished away or talked away or smothered with fine phrases. They are the products of centuries of history which must be taken into account in any functioning society. Those who would eliminate such things overnight may deserve good marks for their intentions, but they do not rate high in commonsense. Let me say frankly that the bigotry and impatience of the right-minded can do as much harm as good. There is always the danger that their unrestrained zeal may sharpen animosities and stimulate unrealistic demands. I for one would caution such people that in clamoring for what is impossible they are sacrificing what is possible. A counter-propaganda that is divorced from living usually creates more tension than its cures.

On the whole, America, through the generations, has shown itself capable of preventing natural prejudices from spilling over into unnatural intolerance. On the whole the trend has been towards greater equality. Even the worst manifestations of prejudice have been gradually tempered.

The danger today comes because the normal prejudices are being stimulated by deliberate propaganda. Watered by hate they flourish in more and more places as outright intolerance and discrimination. What is a mild and natural disaffection is being turned into a malignant disease. It is that which we are called upon to combat with all the skills, with all the energies that we possess.

Ill abused and unjustly treated are the victims of intolerant hate, but the dupes who follow the intolerant leader are unmercifully betrayed. Look at Nazi Germany. Intolerance is a hideous beast with an insatiable appetite. When it has devoured its unhappy victims, it turns upon its guilty followers. The strong Nazies liquidated the weak Nazis.

The inevitable cycle of organized intolerance is that it destroys the individual, the family, the community, and finally the state. In contrast, tolerance is constructive. It creates, builds, unifies. It gives strength and nobility to the individual, to the family, the community, the state. The fight against intolerance is not merely our duty as decent human beings, it is the indispensable condition of our survival as free individuals and as a prosperous nation.

More than all this, it is a condition of happiness and a guarantee of spiritual enlargement. The very word tolerance itself derives from the same Latin stem as the words to lift up and to bear.

"Bear ye one another's burdens," said a clear voice long ago. This counsel should have been remembered by us during the past generation.

We all recognize that the two decades between the two world wars was a period of cynicism and little faith. In the enslaved and dictated countries, this cynicism found its most complete and ugliest expression.

But this degradation was not confined within the borders of totalitarian countries alone. Even among us in America there were symptoms of moral decay. During these two decades it was smart to question moral values, to debunk traditional virtues, to rationalize brutalities, to make excuses for moral indignities. During this period we heard men sneer at freedom and make light of democracy. A lot of us forgot that our code of morals, respect for truth and fair dealing are not arbitrary laws imposed upon us from without. They are the products of thousands of years of human experience—the quintessence of the wisdom of the ages. To violate these codes brings disaster as surely as the violation of physical laws of nature brings disease and death.

To the extent that we yielded to this wave of cynicism, we have contributed to the greatest crisis of our epoch which came to a head in the most destructive war of all time. It has not been merely a political or economic crisis. It has been a spiritual and moral crisis. An evil wind has swept throughout the world and its havoc is all about us.

and is the author of many books, including *Science and the Idea of God*, 1944. He, like Niebuhr, has been in wide demand as a lecturer. He also participated in the Town Meeting of the Air, "What price victory?" September 6, 1942, and in other University of Chicago Round Table Discussions, e.g., "The Near East," June 28, 1942.

Robert Redfield, a member of the anthropology department at the University of Chicago, has been dean of the Division of Social Sciences at the University since 1934. Like the others on this program he is an effective extempore speaker. He has done important research and publication in his field, especially his studies concerning Central America. He has served as participant in various University of Chicago Round Tables, including "What should the churches do in war?" February 15, 1942, and "Peace as a world race problem," August 20, 1944.

President Hutchins concluded the symposium. He spoke as an educator. His remarks, as is obvious from the reading, were much more concrete and more interesting to the lay listener than were the three preceding talks. He revealed his lively reaction to ideas and his own educational philosophy and outlook.[10] He is an extempore speaker of superior effectiveness.

REINHOLD NIEBUHR

The Christmas song and the Christmas hope of peace on earth and good will toward men stand once more in tragic incongruity with the experience of our generation. We are involved in a world-wide war in which mighty nations are locked in a conflict which is costing millions of lives and reducing whole continents to destruction. This is obviously one of the great crises of world history.

If we seek to understand the meaning of this crisis, the most obvious explanation for it is that modern man has not been able to adjust himself quickly enough to the new demands of a technical age, so that he could create a tolerably just community within the conditions established by technical power. Technical power still tends toward injustice rather than justice, even within national communities.

But, in the world of nations, our failure is even more obvious and tragic. Technical instruments have made the nations

[10] For other speeches by Hutchins, comments on those speeches, and their speech background, see *Representative American Speeches*: *1937-38*, p. 184-9; *1938-39*, p. 199-209; *1940-41*, p. 33-8; *1942-43*, p. 235-45.

dependent upon each other in global terms, but we have not had
the moral or political resources to use this world-wide dependence upon each other for the creation of world community. The
Nazis gave us a false answer to this problem. They intended to
unite the world tyrannically. We have proved that we have the
moral and the other resources to prevent this false answer.

But the now certain, though increasingly costly, defeat of
the Nazis does not give us the right answer to our unsolved problem. We still face the necessity of organizing the world in such
a way that both international tyranny and international anarchy
are overcome and so that a just world order is established. We
must solve that problem or perish, for the technical instruments
which have made a world community necessary also aggravate
the anarchy of nations and make the conflicts between them ever
more deadly.

The achievement of world community requires religious,
moral, and political resources of a very high order. Since the
world community is composed of many races, peoples, cultures,
languages, and laws, we are forced, for the first time in history,
to create a community which does not have a core of common
tradition, culture, or experience. This demands a very profound
religious and moral humility and tolerance.

The pride of race and the arrogance of culture have proved
themselves great hazards to justice and peace, even in our national communities. The most perfect constitutional international instruments will not guarantee peace if the pride of nation
and race is not mitigated in the international community. White
peoples particularly, so greatly outnumbered and yet today holding such strategic positions of power in the international community, have a special responsibility. Unless the white man's
arrogance is moderated, no world-wide community can be established. Religious humility and moral tolerance are thus the first
conditions of a stable peace.

In addition to these more purely religious and moral requirements, the world community waits upon a statesmanship imagin-
ative enough to combine two strategies: First, it must suppress
national self-interest for the sake of the general welfare; and,
secondly, it must harness self-interest to the cause of the gen-

eral welfare. We need a political order which will implement the sense of moral obligation beyond the limits of the nation—long since acknowledged in all high religions and philosophies but never actualized in political constitutions.

For centuries, men have known that our obligation to our fellowmen does not stop at the national boundary. Yet we have expressed that obligation in only minimal terms; and, therefore, the international community continues in anarchy. Now the new intimacy of a technically united world gives a new urgency to this obligation.

Modern machines have added the fear of destruction to the gentler suasion of conscience to prompt us to our task. Our political instruments must, however, not merely suppress but also harness, deflect, and beguile the residual self-interest of the nations for the sake of the general welfare. A pure morality merely condemns the self-interest which endangers the harmony of the whole, but a wise political program, based upon the certain knowledge that collective and national self-interest cannot be completely eliminated, seeks ways of so relating it to the needs of the whole community that it will serve rather than imperil the total community.

It is now apparent that the statesmanship which fashioned the old League of Nations was too idealistic to understand this aspect of politics. It seemed, for a moment, that the kind of statesmanship which is embodied in the Dumbarton Oaks agreement, while probably erring too far on the other side, was, nevertheless, set in the right direction. But the sorry events of recent weeks now make it quite apparent that we are definitely in danger of making too many concessions to the self-interest of the nations—particularly of the great nations—to allow a general system of mutual security to emerge. Each of the great powers seems so intent upon establishing its own security in the eventuality of another war that all of them are gradually undermining the possibility of achieving a genuine world-wide order which would give all of us security against war itself.

The revelation of this growing tendency among the great powers is in some respects more tragic than the war itself. It proves how slow mankind is to learn even the most obvious and the most dearly bought lessons of history. Even as this tendency among the nations is checked, it is now quite apparent that our generation lacks the resources for complete solution of our global problem. This means that we may spend weary years in the wilderness before entering the promised land.

In this situation the final moral and spiritual resources which our generation needs are the kind of patience and courage which will enable us to work toward the solution of a problem, even though we may not live to see the fruition of our labors and the fulfilment of our hopes.

We have been given a task too great for any generation to solve. Yet we have our special responsibility in the fulfilment of that task.

WILLIAM ERNEST HOCKING

Any collapse of civilization is a moral collapse, because civilization is a moral fabric. The principle of order among men lies in the mind and the will, not in our animal inheritance. Man can build great societies, because he can restrain his impulses in order to allow scope for the impulses of others; he can learn to settle his quarrels by appeal to reason and common good. War can begin only when the human relationship of persuasion ends; when arguments fitted to move minds are replaced by blasting powder fitted to move rocks and hills.

The birthday we celebrate tomorrow is the birthday of a person and also, inseparably, of an idea. This idea was first defined in two words—peace and good will—as principles of order for the human world. Today we are again occupied with two words, slightly different—peace and security. The difference between "peace and good will" and "peace through security" may fairly represent the moral crisis of modern man. In a world of good will, preoccuption with security would be unnecessary. In so far as we are compelled to seek peace through security, we are removed from the original hope of Christendom.

This is not for us now a matter of choice—we must attend to security, because we do not know how to command good will.

The ancient formula, we say, is "too simple" for the modern world; in truth, it is too difficult! The modern formula is "realistic"—a necessity of prudence—but also a counsel of despair. For, in this present world, apart from good will, there is not sufficient security for any nation.

Hence we moderns live uneasily in two worlds—the world of hard fact and the world of apologetic and baffled hope. How did this inner conflict and frustration arise?

Like us, the early Christians were also living in two worlds. Their religion did not allow them to escape into a sphere of mystic rapture; it required them to bring about the Kingdom of God *in this earth*. They must live in the world of facts, but they must live for the world of their ideas. They had a single allegiance.

Now, modern man made a discovery. He discovered a value in the world of facts which had been disparaged by that earlier single-minded allegiance. He rediscovered the world of facts. He felt that his primary allegiance was there. He must do the work we call "science"; he must learn nature's laws as a way to his own power and control. This became for him a way of high moral purpose. It took a new dimension of honesty to report the facts precisely, whatever they might be. It took a new type of genius and sympathy to discern nature's laws through skilled hypothesis.

But the time had to come when the new methods of science were turned upon man himself. Man must see himself as a part of physical nature—which he is—and therefore not as a free spirit but as a thing of natural law—his very ideas and ideals varying with the chemistry of his blood and, therefore, devoid of authority. The full consequences of this new view of himself were slowly drawn. Conscience became, not an announcement of unyielding principle, but an effect—an echo of custom, a residue of ancient taboos. As a fact among the facts of his nature, man too must be, like them, free from praise and blame, from morality and purpose. Here is surely one source of the moral confusion and impotence of the modern mind.

For these results it would be absurd and ungrateful to berate the sciences of psychology and sociology. It is their duty to report what they find; and what they find is an important part of the truth.

It is only when the physical facts about man are presented as the whole truth that these sciences, by implication, convey falsehood. For it is still true that man lives in two worlds—the world of fact and the world of ideas. An idea may also be a fact, but it is a strange and wonderful kind of fact—one which reaches beyond itself. An idea is a way man has of grasping the vein of meaning that runs through the world—that which some call God; the Chinese, Tao; the Hindu, Brahman. Through his ideas, man, the limited creature of a million past events, finds his way something not relative but absolute and eternal, in whose service he recovers his lost dignity, his duty, and his happiness.

On what a physical psychology can discover in human nature no democracy can be built. For democracy is creative; it makes man something more than it finds in him. It exists because of what men ought to be rather than because of what they are. Of all political forms, it has the greatest possibility. But it is also the most difficult, the most demanding, the most vulnerable. When the word "ought" has lost its meaning democracy cannot survive.

Modern man is not wrong in his distrust of ancient rigidities of moral codes and standards; he is only wrong when he denies the existence of standard itself. The modern philosopher, seeking a principle valid in all cases, does not lie if he reports that he cannot formulate one; he lies only if he asserts that there is no such principle. The modern psychologist does not lie if he says he cannot find a soul; he lies only if he says no soul exists.

The modern university, spreading to its students the half-truths about the animal nature of men, does not necessarily deceive them. It deceives only if it fails to announce, at the same time, that these are half-truths and that, as a university, it is under obligation to declare the rest of the truth. The moral crisis of our time lies in its loss of integrity; the task is to recover it.

Gandhi has said that his god is Truth. If anyone thinks that this is an abstract and easy god to serve, let him try. Let modern man try it. For it is still the truth which alone is able to beget good-will and bring men together in social and political life. And truth in its nature is whole and holy.

Robert Redfield

The moral problem of our times is to make the material means of living the servants of great ends. The task of our times is to fashion new principles to take the place of our worship of practical and material success. The world community of which Niebuhr has spoken must rest on examined convictions as to justice, morality, and truth.

Today the material means of living are not the servants of great ends. I should say that they are rather the masters of mankind. Man has often been described as the maker of tools, but now it may also be said that man's tools are making him. We know how to make weapons for destroying us. We increase the world's wealth, but we cannot distribute it wisely and justly. We take pride in what we have, but we cannot take corresponding pride in what we are. So there has come about a distortion of means and ends in human living. What we live with is immense, ever increasing, and overwhelmingly powerful. But what we live for is unclear, uncertain, and unwise. The making of things and the getting of things are our successes; and our successes shape such character as we have. We understand efficiency, and we applaud it. But piety makes us feel uneasy. If a man offers himself to us as able to do things, we choose him, and it appears of no great importance what he does—provided he promises to do it efficiently. Indeed, if he has principles and speaks of them, our practical men reject him. So it seems to me that man has built himself the instruments for living and has become an instrument himself.

Like Hocking, I think that science played a part in the loss of moral standard. But I think that what science tells us about the world is a help rather than a hindrance to morality. The error seems to me to lie rather in the fact that the people value science only for its material successes. The practical results of science are great goods, of course; no sensible person would regret the achievements in medicine and manufacture. But science is conceived, I say, only as a man in a laboratory about to invent ten thousand new ways to use rubber or steel. The people use science, but they do not listen to it. Yet science could be the great interpreter of our world that it is. What it tells us of our place in the universe enriches our lives. What it tells us of our own unique moral nature and the events by which we came to have certain moral values, or to lose others, could be a source of strength for us in the building of a new moral world. But science is conceived only as a sort of workman.

As an anthropologist—a scientist whose subject of study is mankind—I see these times as a turning in the road of history. The societies of ready-made morals are at an end. In primitive society (which I know a little something about) there were few tools and little wealth, but there were ordered convictions as to the good. Customs and institutions formed a self-consistent whole. The customs expressed values fitted to local circumstances and impressed themselves with conviction on everyone. The means of living, poor as they were, served principles of conduct.

But civilization, as it has meant the accumulation of tools and techniques, has brought about disintegration of convictions as to the good. For a time, even after the appearance of cities and the development of industry, a religious feeling held in check materialism and the surrender to expediency. But that surrender is now complete in the totalitarian state, where all moral values are denied and where man is but a means to the power of the state or the race. And within our own community such principles as we have are confused and weakened by our practice of approving either what works or what is widely known. So we have many successful technicians, and we set about making more of them. We have radios and magazines and moving pictures that make songs and personalities and commodities popular, and so we set high values on these songs and personalities and commodities. The measure of worth has become a production record or a circulation figure or a Crossley rating.

The principles of primitive man may not have been very good principles, but at least he lived up to them. We do not live up to ours. For the fact is that, beneath this yielding to the expedient and the successful which so perverts us, we have principles—principles which are not hardheaded and utilitarian—in which we do believe. But we do not live up to them, and so we fail to understand them.

Freedom is one of these. But in our confusion with material success, freedom is often understood to mean somebody's freedom from interference to make a personal profit. Freedom can yet be understood to mean freedom to make a good society for all. Equality is another principle. Some of us deny to other men of another class or race equal opportunity to work, to be educated, or to find a dwelling. Yet we are still, somehow, dedicated to the proposition that all men are created equal.

The way is forward—not backward to a past time or a dead society. Because some primitive people had ordered convictions that cannibalism was a good, we do not have to become cannibals. What we have to do is to bring to clarity and to supremacy over our actions those principles in which our people, in their confused way, do believe. The effort that is required is to prevent the technical and material success which we have from determining our values. We cannot, as could early men, allow our principles of living to grow out of the lines of conduct that we find ourselves following. We shall not yield to the automatic authority of material success. We have come to a time when just principles of living must be made by the deliberate effort of free men. The opportunity is still before us to make the tools and possessions which have mastered us into the servants of great ends.

ROBERT MAYNARD HUTCHINS

A theologian, a philosopher, and a scientist have shown that the crisis of our time is a moral crisis. They have shown that, unless we can surmount this crisis, such civilization as we have will fall apart, for civilization is a moral fabric. They have shown that the defeat of our enemies in this war, though it may be an indispensable means to the preservation of our civilization, in no sense guarantees its preservation. Peace without good will cannot be durable, because it cannot be just. And technology is not a substitute for justice. Our machines seem, in fact, on the point of wiping us off the face of the earth. They are, moreover, so expensive that we cannot afford to let them stand idle. We must fight for the oil to feed them. We must die that our machines may live. So a distinguished educator said before Pearl Harbor that we should have to go to war with Japan to get rubber for our tires.

The speakers who have preceded me on this program have emphasized that the underlying problem is one of ends, goals, and ideals. With the tremendous resources which science has placed in our hands we should be able to reach almost any conceivable human goal. But if we have the wrong ideals, or if we fail to live up to good ones, the great scientific accomplishments of modern man will end in suicide.

The testimony of the educator is the same as that of the theologian, the philosopher, and the scientist. The educational system of a country is a reflection of what the country thinks it wants. What is honored in a country will be cultivated there. If we look at the educational system of the United States, we get the same impression we got from the speeches in the last campaign—what the American people want is not peace and goodwill, but peace and a good job. The ideal of the full dinner pail and a chicken in every pot and two cars in every garage has been attenuated to the mere possession of a job, any kind of job that will sustain life. It is not surprising, therefore, that although it has never been possible to obtain federal appropriations for education for citizenship, a representative of the United States Office of Education has lately advocated a federal appropriation of three hundred million dollars for vocational training. It is not surprising that every suggestion affecting our youth is considered in terms of the labor market. It has been proposed in high quarters that men ought to be kept in the army if jobs cannot be found for them after the war. One of the current arguments for universal military training is that it would give at least a million young men a year something to do.

Now certainly there is no use talking about the aims of life to those who are starving to death. Mass unemployment is a menace to any society. But are we to work merely to exist? Is a job a good thing just because it is a job, no matter how trivial and degrading the occupation? Jobs are means, not ends; and our problem is: What are we working for and what are we living for? If the answer is that we are living merely to live, the whole process loses its meaning. We are in search of values, and there are no values here.

Insofar as we have a definite goal, then, it appears to be a goal of success interpreted in material terms. Though material goods are goods, there are other goods beyond them; for, in the order of goods, material goods do not stand high. The passionate pursuit of material goods disrupts human relations—as when a prominent labor leader was asked whether, now that China was our ally, we should not repeal the Chinese Exclusion Act, and he replied, "A Chinaman is still a Chinaman."

The passionate pursuit of material goods disrupts the common good, for our government is now the sport of pressure groups—each seeking its material advantage. The passionate pursuit of material goods impairs the hope of world organization and necessarily substitutes security for good-will. For each country, even if it does not want territory for itself, must grab territory in order to keep other nations from grabbing it.

America is the strongest and richest nation on earth. Since we are not under the material pressure to which other nations are subject, since we are not in danger of starvation or invasion, we have no excuse for failing to offer the world what it needs most —moral leadership and a moral example. For the sake of suffering humanity everywhere the people of this country must rediscover the ends of human life and of organized society; they must base their own lives and their own society upon these foundations. As Santayana said of the United States long ago, "This soil is propitious to every seed, and tares must needs grow in it. But why should it not also breed clear thinking, honest judgment, and rational happiness? These things are indeed not necessary to existence, and without them America might long remain rich and populous, like many a barbarous land in the past. But in that case its existence will be hounded, like theirs, by falsity and remorse. May Heaven avert the omen, and make the new world a better world than the old."

There is a slight trace of selfishness in Santayana's prayer. Let us change it to read, "May the new world help to make the whole world new."

SOCIAL AND ECONOMIC PRINCIPLES

CHARTER FOR POSTWAR PROSPERITY [1]

HENRY A. WALLACE [2]

Henry Wallace appeared before the Senate Commerce Committee on January 25, 1945. President Roosevelt had nominated him to the post of Secretary of Commerce to succeed Jesse H. Jones, who had resigned at the President's request.

Wallace, since his appointment as Secretary of Agriculture in 1933, had been an active exponent of the New Deal philosophy. He had advocated tight control of agricultural production (e.g., "plowing under the pigs"), the rights of the "common man," the need for "global thinking," and restraints upon big business.

The issue of his appointment as Secretary of Commerce involved the question of how far the enormous spending power of the Federal Loan Agency, administered under the Commerce Department, should be used in postwar America. On the same day that Mr. Wallace's nomination reached the Senate, Senator Walter F. George introduced a bill to separate the Federal Loan Agency from the Commerce Department. The Senate Committee then summoned the two men to testify.

The hearings were held in the "spacious, white marble walled" Senate caucus room, which seats about three hundred people. Into this chamber crowded some five hundred persons on January 24 to hear the testimony of Mr. Jones and on the following day, that of Mr. Wallace. The hearings "were among the most dramatic ever held in Washington." (*New York Times,* January 28, 1944).

Jesse Jones reported that the Reconstruction Finance Corporation and its subsidiaries conducted the "most gigantic business enterprise the world has ever known. . . . The lending agencies of the government could be used to destroy what we have built up in 170 years." He re-

[1] Text is reprinted from the *Philadelphia Record,* January 26, 1945. According to an editorial in that newspaper (January 27), "Of all the metropolitan morning newspapers in this country only the *New York Times, Boston Globe,* and the *Philadelphia Record* ran the complete text. The *Washington Star,* a Republican evening newspaper, printed the text yesterday. Apparently it was the only evening newspaper in America which recognized its importance." The *Philadelphia Record* reprinted a million copies in the hope that each would be read by "at least five American voters." Because of the length of this speech and the cross examination, only one section has been included here.

[2] For biographical note see Appendix. For other speeches and accompanying comments see *Representative American Speeches*: 1937-38, p. 142-62; 1941-42, p. 45-55; 1942-43, p. 98-104, 276-86.

ported that some $45 billion had been authorized for lending and invest-
ment, and the F.L.A. owned some 950 war plants costing $6 billion, some
twenty of which cost about $100 million each.

Wallace, the next day, stated that the issue was whether the American people "want these enormous financial powers utilized and invested
in a free America which also is a prosperous America."

The questions were: Was Henry Wallace qualified for the Commerce secretaryship? In addition, was he also qualified to direct the
huge Federal Loan Agency? Jones flatly stated that Wallace was not
able to handle these two jobs. Mr. Wallace used the occasion to present
his liberal economic philosophy.

The Senate Commerce Committee, on Friday, January 26, voted
fifteen to four to separate the federal lending agencies from the Commerce Department; it also rejected fourteen to five, the President's nomination of Wallace. The issue was thus transferred to the Senate and to
the House. Backing Wallace were the C.I.O. and the A.F.L. and the
New Deal wing of the Democratic party. Precedent was also on his
side, for only once in seventy-five years (in 1925 when Charles B. Warren was rejected as Attorney General) did the Senate defy a Presidential
cabinet nomination. On February 1, the Senate passed the George Bill
fourteen to twelve, separating Commerce and F.L.A. authorities, but postponed Senate action on the nomination of Wallace until March 1. In
the House action on the George Bill, more heated debate over the merits
and demerits of Wallace developed. The Rules Committee of the House
tried to hold back floor action, in the hope that Wallace would be rejected by the Senate if his case were passed upon before consideration of
the George Bill. Finally, however, the House passed the bill, on February 16, three hundred ninety-nine to two. On March 1, the Senate, by
a vote of fifty-six to thirty-two, confirmed the appointment of Henry
Wallace as Secretary of Commerce.

The Wallace address is an excellent example of a prepared statement for presentation at a committee hearing. Extensive questioning of
Mr. Wallace followed the formal address. This cross-examination was
an integral part of the speaking program, and threw much light both on
the ideas and speaking techniques of the witness. Wallace emerged from
the two days' performance with enhanced reputation as a speaker.

We now must establish an economic bill of rights, not only
out of common decency, but also to insure the preservation of our
political freedoms. We must accord to this economic bill of
rights the same dignity—the same stature—in our American
tradition as that we have accorded to the original Bill of Rights.

Let us therefore affirm this economic bill of rights—and keep
affirming it—until it is as familiar and real to us as our political
bill of rights. . . .

The first economic right is "the right to a useful and remunerative job in the industries, or shops, or farms, or mines of the nation."

To assure the full realization of this right to a useful and remunerative job, an adequate program must provide America with sixty million productive jobs. We must have more jobs than workers; not more workers than jobs. Only with more jobs than workers can every man be guaranteed a job with good wages and decent working conditions. This requires private enterprise working at expanded capacity.

This necessary expansion of our peacetime productive capacity will require new facilities, new plants and new equipment. It will require large outlays of money which should be raised through normal investment channels. But while private capital should finance this expansion program, the government should recognize its responsibility for sharing part of any special or abnormal risk of loss attached to such financing.

Therefore I propose that the government guarantee the lender against the special and abnormal risks which may be involved in achieving our objective. This will provide new and expanding industry with plenty of private credit at reasonable interest rates. Through this program we shall merely be extending to the financing of old and new business the principles which have proved so successful in our experience with the V loans, T loans and the Federal Housing Administration loans.

A comprehensive investment program dedicated to expanding the peacetime productive capacity of America is the very essence of the American way of raising our standard of living. We build the plants for greater production so that all of us may share in their greater output. But greater output is not our only benefit from this plant expansion.

In fact, our benefits also include the wages paid to the labor employed in building these plants, in constructing the machinery to be used in the plants and in operating the plants after they are erected. These payments as wages all contribute to the nation's buying power, so that as a nation we shall have more money with which to buy the goods produced by these expanded plants.

As a matter of fact, a comprehensive investment program of this character could make possible $20 billion of new private investment each year. Why, just the job of building these plants and the machinery for them would give America five million more jobs a year than we had in this work before the war. And this does not include the workers who would be needed to operate these plants after they are built.

In a nutshell, then, if we are going to have remunerative jobs for all, we must have an expanded private industry capable of hiring millions more men. I propose that the government do its part in helping private enterprise finance this expansion of our industrial plant. It will be privately owned, privately operated and privately financed, but the government will share with the private investor, the unusual and abnormal financial risks which may be involved in getting started.

But, in providing jobs for everyone, we shall not only have to increase demand for our industrial and agricultural production here at home but also abroad. Some parts of our industrial and agricultural production demand a high level of foreign trade to be efficient and prosperous.

This is particularly true in our heavy equipment industries whose output will be needed. The foreign demand for such farm commodities as cotton, tobacco and wheat will also be great if other countries have the opportunity to buy. We, therefore, must take steps, in cooperation with other countries, to see that international trade and investment is resumed promptly on a sound basis.

This Administration has pioneered in the direction of international economic collaboration with its reciprocal trade program and the establishment of the export-import bank. It has again taken the lead in suggesting international monetary stabilization and sound international investment measures—measures that are a fundamental prerequisite to healthy foreign trade and commerce.

It was for the purpose of working out concrete measures of this character that the President convened the United Nations monetary and financial conference at Bretton Woods last summer. At the Bretton Woods conference forty-four countries agreed upon plans for an international monetary fund and an international bank for reconstruction and development.

The international monetary fund, when approved by Congress, will aid the nations of the world in establishing sound currencies. It will clear the channels of foreign trade of discriminatory restrictions and controls so that there can be a genuine expansion of world trade.

With the help of the international bank, American capital can play a great constructive role—and a profitable role—in the development of the economies of other countries. It will provide us with enormous postwar foreign markets. For our greatest markets are in prosperous, industrialized countries.

But America will not be merely a seller of goods abroad. A truly prosperous America—an America with jobs for all—will be a tremendous buyer of raw materials and products abroad. It will be an America constantly enlarging the scope of our reciprocal trade agreements. It will be an America with the time and money to spend on tourist travel, abroad as well as at home. It will be an America from which other countries can afford to buy more because they are selling more.

With Congressional approval of this program and with our program of jobs for all in this country—the foreign trade of the United States can be trebled after the war. This increase in our foreign trade should mean three million more jobs after the war than we had before the war.

Nor are the benefits of increased foreign trade and investment confined to increasing our prosperity. I want to emphasize that such cooperative measures for expanding international trade and investment are at the same time the economic foundation for a lasting peace. A prosperous world will be a world free of both economic and political aggression.

There is one further phase of this program of providing jobs for all which must be made an integral part of any long-range program. That is the task of seeing to it that there are not just jobs for all next year—or for the year after that. No, we are talking about jobs for all as a permanent part of our American way of life.

But it is inevitable, however, that an economy of free enterprise like ours will have some fluctuation in the number of jobs it can provide. Adjustments in employment are an essential part of an expanding free economy, and for these minor fluctuations, we provide unemployment insurance. But we must not allow such fluctuations ever to deteriorate into panic or depression. We cannot again be caught in that vicious downward spiral of unemployment, wage cuts and stagnated business.

Whenever the number of gainfully employed in this country falls below fifty-seven million our government should take prompt steps to see that new jobs are made available to keep the total from falling significantly below that figure. This is the floor below which we must not allow employment to fall.

The basic function of your government in taking care of any such slack in jobs is to see to it that private enterprise is assisted until it can absorb this slack. This is entirely possible. During the war the federal, state and local government have found it necessary to put aside the construction of roads, buildings and public facilities to the value of many billions of dollars. We have a need, too, for vast programs of the type exemplified by T.V.A.

Some of this construction will have to be undertaken immediately after the war. A good deal of it, however, can be postponed so that its construction could be timed with periods when the volume of unemployment that industry, commerce and agriculture can offer begins to fall. We must have a reservoir of planned and approved federal, state and local projects ready to be tapped. And when employment falls below this floor of fifty-seven million jobs, this reservoir of planned and approved public works should be opened up to provide more jobs and take up the slack.

Such useful and essential public works should not produce government or "relief" jobs, however. No, they should produce private jobs. This is possible if we insist that this construction be done by private firms under contract with the government; private firms employing labor at the prevailing rate of wages and under standard labor conditions.

This assurance of a reserve of private jobs, through constructive public works when needed to take up the slack, will have a profound effect on the whole direction of our economy. In fact, the knowledge that government accepts this responsibility of maintaining a floor under jobs will act as an immense stabilizing force on the whole economy.

The second economic right is "the right to earn enough to provide food and clothing and recreation." America must remain pre-eminently the land of high wages and efficient production. Every job in America must provide enough for a decent living.

During the war we have been compelled to hold down wage increases that might have provoked runaway inflation. With all the arms and war materials we were producing, there was only a limited amount of consumption goods available. Increasing wages without increasing the amount of goods available to the consumer would have been an open invitation to inflation.

However, the end of the war, even the end of the war in Europe, will change this picture. Then there will be more goods available for America to buy, and it is only good common sense to see that the workman is paid enough to buy these goods.

The gains made by labor during the war must be retained in full. After the last war, as part of the process of returning to "normalcy," the slogan "Labor must be deflated" was adopted. This must not happen again. This time we must make sure that wage rates are not reduced when the wartime demand for labor is diverted into peacetime channels. We must make sure that the labor market is not broken by unemployment and wage slashes.

American labor should be assured that there are not going to be any wage cuts after this war. What is even more important—when the worker's hours are cut back to peacetime levels a real attempt must be made to adjust wage rates upward.

And wages should be constantly increased as the productivity of industry is increased. An expanding American economy can continue to expand only if the increased productivity is divided equitably between business and the worker. In fact—you know, and I know, that unless the worker does get his share of America's increased production in the form of increased wages and unless business gets its share in the form of increased profits—neither will prosper and all, businessmen, wage-earners and farmers, will lose.

But an increase in wages is not the only benefit the American worker should secure from increased productivity. He should also benefit in the form of shorter hours of work, in the form of increased leisure and opportunities for healthful recreation. Thus increased wages and shorter hours go hand-in-hand in solving the prosperity problem the American way.

There is one further aspect of the wage-earner's problem that I would like to comment on. That is his aspiration for an annual wage or guaranteed annual income from his job. It is a terribly important part of any real attempt to implement America's economic bill of rights. The size of the wage-earner's pay envelope is important—vitally important to American prosperity. But we all know that it is equally important to know how many pay envelopes he gets during a year. I would like to see him get a guaranteed minimum annual wage and I think the time has come for America to begin tackling this most difficult problem.

Now this goal cannot be attained overnight. It cannot be achieved in a manner to harm business. Nor can it be achieved with the same speed in every business.

But we can start on the job of giving labor an annual wage. We can do a lot if we all will only agree that it is a problem business and labor must solve and if we all approach the problem with a genuine desire to succeed. And government must do its part too. It must aid business in stabilizing its labor needs so that the burden of an annual wage will not be uneconomical. This, in my opinion, is the American way to bring about the annual wage, and I have confidence in the American way of doing things.

The third economic right is "the right of every farmer to raise and sell his products at a rate which will give him and his family a decent living."

American farmers now have by far the largest farm income in history. This is their due reward for the greatest agricultural production in history. We must assure the farmers that there will always be a market for all their output at good prices.

Concretely we should maintain an adequate floor on farm prices and thereby assure the farmer against the dangers of falling prices for his products. Our farm program must be one of expansion rather than curtailment. With jobs for all at good wages and with foreign markets greatly expanded, the farmer will be able to sell at good prices all that he can raise.

But this is not all. The farmer's income must have stability. To that end there should be established a comprehensive federal crop insurance program which will secure the farmer against the hazards of crop failure.

To this must be added concrete steps to raise the standards of living on the farm and in the rural areas. We need a complete program of new and modernized homes and farm buildings. We must press forward with rural electrification and improvement. Only in this way can we bring to the rural communities modern facilities for decent and healthful living.

The fourth economic right is "the right of every business man, large and small, to trade in an atmosphere of freedom from unfair competition and domination by monopolies at home and abroad."

Our economic bill of rights, like our political Bill of Rights, is based on freedom of enterprise—freedom of enterprise not merely and exclusively for the few, but broadly and inclusively for the many.

The political Bill of Rights insured the destruction of special prerogatives and privileges. The economic bill of rights will insure the destruction of special economic prerogatives and privileges.

No special class of business deserves to be the spoiled darling of government. The American people have no interest in preserving the vested interests and monopolistic privileges of greedy big business. The interest of the American people lies in using the resources of the country to achieve a prosperous America, prosperous for all business, large and small, and for all the people.

We must break through the barriers of monopoly and international cartels that stand in the way of a healthy expansion of free enterprise. We must overcome the monopolistic frame of mind which thinks of business in terms of restricted output at high prices per unit. We must pass on to workers and consumers the benefits of technological progress and large-scale production. Free enterprise in the American tradition can flourish only by doing a large volume of business at a small profit per unit.

We must protect free enterprise against monopolies and cartels through continued vigorous enforcement of the anti-trust laws. Private enterprise yields its full advantage to the consuming public and to other business only when it is genuinely free and competitive. He is a sinister enemy of free enterprise who pays lip-service to competition but also labels every anti-trust prosecution a "persecution."

Our economy has important new expanding sectors in air transport, frequency modulation, television, and fibers, plastics and many other fields. These new expanding business areas in particular must be kept free of the constricting hand of monopoly. There must be a place in these new business areas—as everywhere in our economy—for enterprising small firms. It is from these new and small firms that the great industries of the future will grow. We need new industries and new firms to have industrial progress and we must not permit them to be stifled by monopoly.

The fifth economic right is "the right of every family to a decent home."

Concretely, we should adopt a housing program looking toward the construction, through private enterprise of two million housing units a year and ridding this country of its urban and rural slums. We need to build at least fifteen million new housing units if we are to eliminate all our slums and substandard dwellings. The right to a home is meaningless when that home is a hovel. We cannot afford slums.

A well-housed America must have modern homes—homes with all the latest electrical and mechanical equipment which will eliminate the drudgery of household work. To the fullest extent possible we must be a land of home owners, and to that end we must assure every family an opportunity for home ownership by making certain that there is available private credit on terms which will reduce the down payment and cut by one third the monthly cost of buying homes.

New residential construction and the modernization of America's homes alone can provide jobs for four million people a year. This is two million more than the maximum amount engaged in such work prior to the war.

The sixth economic right is "the right to adequate medical care and the opportunity to achieve and enjoy good health."

As Selective Service has revealed, too large a proportion of our younger men now fall below reasonable health standards. This is a warning signal to America with respect to the state of health of all segments of our population. This condition calls for immediate and drastic action.

We cannot permit the health of our people to be impaired by poverty or lack of medical and hospital facilities. I say to you that your federal and state governments have just as much responsibility for the health of their people as they have for providing them with education and police and fire protection. Health and adequate medical and hospital care are not luxuries. They are basic necessities to which all are entitled.

We must see that medical attention is available to all the people. But this health program must be achieved in the American way. Every person should have the right to go to the doctor and hospital of his own choosing. The federal and state governments should work hand in hand in making health insurance an integral part of our Social Security program just as old age and unemployment benefits are today.

We need more hospitals and doctors. We should make sure that such facilities are available and that we build hospitals in every community, rural and urban, that does not now have such facilities for all of its people.

Never again can we afford the waste of poor health in America because of poverty or inadequate facilities. And I say to you now that this program will prove in the long run to be a saving to America.

We must not be content to provide medical attention for people after they become sick. We must implement and extend our knowledge of maximum health as well as preventions of sickness. The government should appropriate needed funds to finance a greatly expanded program of medical research in private and public institutions.

The seventh economic right is "the right to adequate protection from the economic fears of old age, sickness, accident and unemployment."

We must assure people who are disabled and temporarily unemployed that they will be taken care of adequately. We must assure them that they will not be in want because of loss of income during this period of compulsory unemployment. We cannot neglect these groups without incurring serious dangers to the stability of our whole economy.

A broader social security program will be needed after the war. Old age insurance should be adequate to provide all of our older men and women with the means for decent living. Our present old age benefits are definitely inadequate. A decent, self-respecting old age social security program should be deemed to be a right, not a charity, a right springing from the years of service each person delivers to the sum total of a better America.

An adequate social security program will, of itself, by adding to the spendable purchasing power available to the people and by placing a floor on consumption, add more than two million jobs a year.

The eighth economic right is "the right to a good education." We must have an educated and informed America. Even now most of our rural areas and some of our urban areas are poorly provided with schools. Our teachers are underpaid. Our schools are badly understaffed. We need more schools and at least five hundred thousand more teachers.

Through federal aid to poorer communities for the development of locally controlled educational programs we propose to equalize and extend educational opportunities through the land. We propose to provide facilities for technical and higher education for all qualified young men and women without regard to their financial means. In this America, the pioneer of free education, the right to technical and higher education should be as universal as the right to a secondary school education.

This is the kind of program that can provide jobs, economic security and rising standards of living for all Americans—regardless of race, color or creed. Our democracy can be a living force only if it means the good life for all the people.

The millions of productive jobs that this program will bring are jobs in private enterprise. They are jobs based on the expanded demand for the output of our economy for consumption and investment. And this program need place no real burden on the federal budget, notwithstanding the reduction in taxes which must come after the war.

On the contrary, a program of this character can provide America with a national income of such a size that it will be possible to reduce the tax rates still further on personal incomes, on business profits and on consumption, and still collect enough tax revenues to meet the needs of the government, including orderly retirement of the national debt. These should be our immediate goals, once final victory over our enemies has been achieved.

Now there are those who say that these goals are the dream of a "man willing to jeopardize the country's future with untried ideas and idealistic schemes." These people think they are the realists.

Actually, these are the persons of limited vision and stunted imagination. These people are of the same breed as these "sound business men" who haggled over pennies in the purchase of strategic stockpiles before the war, only to leave the materials for the Japs to use against us. These are people who will fight against enemies, waging total war, by pinching pennies. These people think the same as those who said the President was dreaming when he declared in 1940 that the American people would produce fifty thousand planes in one year. Do these Monday-morning quarterbacks have that great faith in the American people, and in their way of life, which is required in order to understand the meaning of America?

I am confident, however, that the great majority of the American people share the same great faith in America and in the American way of doing things which I have expressed here. We know our way and the road ahead is straight and broad, although there are many hills which we must climb. The program which I have set forth is only the first milestone, for the capacity of the American way of life in the years to come is beyond the vision of man. The American system of free enterprise is the best the world has ever known, and through it we can obtain, God willing, the best that this world has to offer.

COMPETITIVE ENTERPRISE VERSUS PLANNED ECONOMY [3]

HENNING WEBB PRENTIS, JR. [4]

Mr. H. W. Prentis, President of the Armstrong Cork Company of Lancaster, Pennsylvania, and past President of the National Association of Manufacturers, delivered this address at the fiftieth anniversary celebration of the National Association of Manufacturers, held at the University of Cincinnati, on January 24, 1945.

The issue, one of the two or three outstanding problems demanding early solution in America, was contained in the title of the address: Competitive enterprise vs. planned economy. That is, to what degree would government regulation of our economic system be necessary to ensure a healthy functioning of that system and at the same time to preserve our individual liberty? Would it be advisable and necessary to abandon all or practically all wartime economic controls and to substitute competitive enterprise? Or should a policy of fairly complete "planned economy" be supported? Or would it be practicable and feasible to pursue a middle course between full regulation of our economic life and a minimum of governmental restraints? [5]

Mr. Prentis in this address follows a framework of thinking, logic, and organization, which he adhered to in previous speeches. (1) Individual and competitive free enterprise has "brought more blessings to the average man than any economic system the human race has yet devised." (This point the speaker establishes by concrete illustrations and statistics.) (2) National economic planning (although necessary and comparatively simple in total war) to be effective would involve complete control over our economic system. (3) Such control would be practically impossible ("The planners would have to be supermen"). (4) If the plan should "succeed" it would doom personal and political liberty. Mr. Prentis' argument represented the antithesis of the economic philosophy of Mr. Wallace.[6] Critics of Mr. Prentis' address asked whether he had oversimplified the issue of planning and regimentation as against unfettered enterprise. In the United States under government regulation,

---

[3] By permission of the author. Text furnished through the courtesy of Mr. Prentis and reprinted from the pamphlet published by the National Association of Manufacturers.

[4] For biographical note see Appendix.

[5] For discussion of the issue and accompanying notes see *Representative American Speeches*: 1943-44, p. 209-29, "What of Free Enterprise?" William G. Carleton; and p. 230-41, "Free Enterprise," Henry M. Wriston. Also *Representative American Speeches*: 1942-43, p. 203-15, "Private Agencies and Public Goals in the Postwar World," L. H. Brown.

[6] See p. 203.

have we not had a "mixed economy" that aims to preserve the maximum amount of free enterprise in a capitalist system?

Prentis had given well organized, thoughtful, and highly persuasive addresses on similar themes during the preceding four years. In Kansas City, October 27, 1941, he discussed "Reaping What We Sow" (need for Americans to be educated concerning our governmental philosophy); in Des Moines, Iowa, October 29, 1941, "Faith of Our Fathers" (a plea for an understanding of our democratic traditions and an active demonstration of them in business); in New York City, December 5, 1941, "The Bill of Rights today" (an argument for an understanding of these principles and conformity to them by members of Congress); in New York City, December 9, 1943, "Management's Job" (a concise economic program for industry in the postwar era); in New York City, December 6, 1944, "If I Were a Labor Leader" (suggestions for cooperation between labor and management). He is a superior speaker.

Other representative business speakers during the period of 1944-45 included Ira Mosher, President of the National Association of Manufacturers, James A. Farley, Chairman of the Board of the Coca-Cola Export Corporation, Virgil Jordan, President of the National Industrial Conference Board, Walter B. Weisenburger, Executive Vice President of the National Association of Manufacturers, Eric Johnston, President of the United States Chamber of Commerce, Winthrop W. Aldrich, Chairman of the Board of Directors of the Chase National Bank of the City of New York, Kent Cooper, Executive Director of the Associated Press, Fred G. Clark, General Chairman of the American Economic Foundation, and C. F. Kettering, Vice President of General Motors.

Like the other speakers this evening, I am glad to have the honor of participating in this joint celebration of the fiftieth anniversary of the founding of the National Association of Manufacturers. For me, however, it is a special privilege because two years of my early life were spent on this campus. And when I remember what was here forty years ago and see what is here now, I feel that Competitive Enterprise, recalling Sir Christopher Wren in the crypt of St. Paul's, might well rouse itself from the catacombs of oblivion to which the proponents of Planned Economy have consigned it, and give voice to his famous epitaph, "Si monumentum requiris, circumspice." Yes, if you seek a monument to Competitive Enterprise, look about you at this great University—not the product of a system of national planned economy in education, but a fine and fair example of the American competitive spirit of local responsibility for local affairs. No group of bureaucrats in Washington tell this educational enterprise what it can or must do. The income from private endowments, coupled with public funds from local sources, is here administered by local citizens to serve the educational needs of this particular community as its own people see and define those requirements. Can anyone envisage the creation by local enterprise of such an institution as this in any dictator-ridden city of the planned economies of Germany, Italy or Russia? Why the difference? One does not have to seek far to find it.

In 1840 Henry Reeves, an Englishman, was translating a book by a young Frenchman, Count de Tocqueville, who had just returned from America where he had been studying how "liberty was regulated and reconciled with the social order." In this book, "De la Democracie en Amerique," Reeves found a word that was new to him: Individualism. After duly pondering how he should translate it, he wrote: "I adopt the expression of the original, however strange it may sound to the English ear, for I know no English word exactly equivalent to the expression." To quote De Tocqueville himself: "Individualism is a novel expression to which a novel idea has given birth. . . . Individualists acquire the habit of always considering themselves as standing alone, and they are apt to imagine that their whole destiny is in their own hands. Individualism is of democratic origin."

Individualism, in fact, was the priceless ingredient of the political, personal and economic freedom for which our forefathers fought and died at Bunker Hill, Valley Forge and Yorktown. Under its urge the epic of America has been written. The creation of our unparalleled national wealth has been accompanied by the most sweeping advances in education and philanthropy, the highest standards of living for the common man, the nearest approximation—though still a long way from the ideal—of the Christian concept of human brotherhood, that the world has ever seen. Its philosophical foundation is recognition of the infinite worth of every human soul in the eyes of a Sovereign God.

Why has individualism produced such notable results in America? The men who settled this country were not extraordinary people. They had a vast continent to develop, yet its natural resources were no greater than those of Asia. They had little capital to start with; in fact, they had to seek it abroad. They were not, as a rule, as skilled artisans as the workers in European industries. They believed in education but such facilities were not generally available. How then did they differ from their contemporaries in the old world? They were free. They set up a government that was legally estopped from interfering with their legitimate personal activities. They enjoyed what Justice Brandeis says is the right most highly prized by civilized men—"the right to be let alone." They had known what tyranny was in actual practice. They had been insecure so long under despots—insecure spiritually, intellectually, politically and economically—that when they found they could have freedom in the new world, they did not worry about security. They gladly took a chance on that, for they valued a free mind and a free soul more than a full stomach. The spirit of competitive enterprise possessed them and the results of its driving power are around us on every hand. The industrial machine which it brought into being is now sealing the doom of Hitler and Hirohito. Russia's industrial planned economy is merely a struggling imitation of the production techniques that competitive enterprise long ago developed in America.

Those of us who have never been abroad do not realize how much we Americans owe to our competitive enterprise system. A year or so before the war broke out the National Association of Manufacturers sent an economist to Europe to find out how much the earnings of the average American factory worked would buy in comparison with the earnings of workers abroad. Certain articles were selected that are used by practically all civilized peoples. In each country the economist visited, he showed the store clerks his American articles and asked for similar ones. If there were no goods of comparable quality available, as was frequently the case, he bought the nearest equivalent. He ascertained from the best available official sources the average wages paid factory workers. For his food comparison, he used as his measuring stick a basket containing a selection of twenty-four different foods in ordinary use. The average American family of two adults and three children uses four of these baskets, or the equivalent, every day. To earn these four baskets of food the investigator found that the average American worker had to work about 1.6 hours; the British or French worker 3.2 hours; the Belgian 3.6 hours; the German 3.9 hours; the Italian 6.2 hours and the Russian 10 hours.

The radio that an American factory worker could earn with 59 hours of work cost the German 134 hours; the Swede 262 hours; the Italian 333 hours. Thus it is not hard to see why there was one radio receiving set for every 2.3 persons in the United States against one to 5.2 persons in Great Britain; one to 7.5 persons in Germany and one to 45.2 persons in Russia. While the United States had one automobile in use for every four persons, the proportion was one to eight persons in France; one to 29 in Sweden; one to 252 in Russia and one to 1344 in Bulgaria.

Under our competitive enterprise system in America, a provident worker does not have to spend every cent he earns to support his standard of living. This is evidenced by the amount of life insurance in force.   In the United States life insurance averaged $842 for every man, woman and child in the country at the time this survey was made. In England the average was $353; in Germany $117 and in Italy $36. Never has any country had so many mechanical slaves at its disposal. To be specific, American industry used 2.1 horsepower in 1899 for each worker; in 1939, 6.5 horsepower.   Along with our industrial progress has come a remarkable expansion of general social welfare. Our hospitals, museums, libraries and schools are the envy of the civilized world.

There is no need for me to bombard you with further statistics. With all its shortcomings—and there are many because it is operated by fallible human beings—competitive enterprise in America has undoubtedly brought more blessings to the average man than any economic system the human race has yet devised. The men of our far-flung military forces are discovering that with their own eyes. Just a few weeks ago a young soldier friend of mine in France, who had probably never before been more than a hundred miles from his birthplace in Lancaster, Pennsylvania, wrote me that after seeing the way people lived in Europe he thanked God that he had a country like America to come home to. As a matter of fact, he never will come home because he lies tonight in some lonely grave on the German front where he was killed in action in November.

Thousands like him are pouring out their blood to prevent National Socialism, Fascism and absolutism in any form from overrunning the earth and tyrannizing over the bodies, minds and souls of mankind. And yet even as they fight these evils, many misguided Americans here at home are advocating—paradoxically enough—the self-same economic principles on which the governmental systems of our enemies are based. This seems incomprehensible until one discovers that today only three in ten Americans understand the difference between state socialism and our republican form of government, and that only one in four knows what the Bill of Rights is! A still smaller fraction realize that competitive enterprise, civil and religious freedom, and political freedom are inseparably bound up together and that when any one of the three is undermined, all the liberty they now so smugly enjoy will soon be devoured in the maw of dictatorship. Yet the danger is imminent and real. As Professor Hayek says in his recent book, *The Road to Serfdom,* "We have progressively abandoned that freedom in economic affairs without which personal and political freedom has never existed in the past."

The phrase "planned economy" is very alluring. We have all been taught since childhood to plan ahead, to anticipate the vicissitudes of illness, unemployment and old age, to plan for the education of our children, and the future of our businesses and social institutions. Such individual and voluntary group planning is highly desirable and should be encouraged in every possible fashion. However, over-all planning and control by government is quite a different thing. As Peter Drucker said in one of his recent books, planning in the sense in which it is now employed "is not a preparation for future events and contingencies. It is the abolition of all limitations on governmental power." Yet many short-sighted people seek to impose just that type of planning on America today.

National economic planning in time of war is comparatively simple because military requirements are relatively standardized and uniform. Despite that fact, we can see right now how enormously difficult it is even to plan intelligently for war production. Yet the problems of planning to meet the demands of a free economy in times of peace would be infinitely more complicated, since peacetime demands are subject to consumer preference, personal tastes, the whims of style and the dynamics of advancing technology. They are literally unpredictable. There were eight thousand automobiles in America in 1900. It took eighty thousand barrels of gasoline a year to operate them—enough to keep the cars that we had on the road in 1942 running an hour and a half. Can one imagine any government planning board having the vision and temerity to do what the petroleum industry did at the risk of billions of dollars of private capital; namely, to provide sufficient gasoline for thirty-six million cars in that same year, 1942?

As a matter of fact, there are not enough brains and vision in any group of men in government or elsewhere, to plan and provide—from a central point—a progressively rising standard of living for a great nation like the United States. Just consider for a moment what a national planning board would be expected to do in times of peace. It would have to know what and how much of everything everbody would want, when they would buy, and the approximate prices they would be willing to pay for all sorts of goods and services. Without such information the objectives of a planned economy could not be attained; namely, to keep everybody employed at satisfactory wages, and to eliminate waste by producing neither more nor less than was actually required. The national planning board would also be expected constantly to increase production and develop all sorts of new and improved articles at lower and lower prices so as to raise the standard of living and give everybody more leisure for recreation. Simultaneously the labor unions would be bargaining for higher wages and shorter hours, and naturally, the individual citizen would not relish any interference with his freedom to work or not to work when or where he pleased. The investment of all capital would have to be completely controlled by the planners because otherwise the whole national productive and distributive machine would soon get out of kilter.

The planners themselves would thus have to be supermen—all-wise and utterly beneficent. The advocates of planned economy gloss over that fact. Even though the members of the planning board knew that a change in the complexion of Congress every two years would completely disrupt their long-range economic plans, they would, of course, never, never seek to maintain themselves in power by political alliances, or concessions to friendly pressure groups, or withdrawal of favors from hostile critics, or use of public resources for propaganda purposes. They would always, of course, be models of magnanimity! They would never dream of retaliating even if they did see their cherished dreams—all for the good of the people—vanshing under criticism.

The proponents of planned economy claim, of course, that the press would not be muzzled, even though the planning board did control absolutely the production and allocation of paper and presses; that the producer of motion pictures would also feel free to oppose such portions of the national planning program as the motion picture industry might consider unwise, even though the producers' film supplies were at the mercy of the board. As for radio stations—well, the limited licensing system already has them pretty well in hand. As for businessmen in general, what the fear of the tax collector, the factory inspector, the labor board investigator, the wage and hour auditor, the S.E.C. inquisitor, the O.P.A. checker, the Department of Justice file searcher, et al., have not already accomplished in curtailing their willingness to speak out in opposition to unwise governmental policies, would be finally and completely achieved under the throttling power of an economic planning board. Ways and means of inducing teachers and preachers to fall in line or keep silent would not be lacking. Germany, Italy and Russia all devised effective methods of dealing with intellectual and spiritual recalcitrants in their government planned economies long before the war broke out. The power of labor unions would simply evaporate. The Federalist Papers, 155 years ago, summed it all up in one terse sentence: "Power over a man's support is power over his will."

Gustav Cassel—the great Swedish economist—who died a week or so ago, said, "Planned economy will always tend to develop into dictatorship. . . . Once authoritative controls has been established it will not always be possible to limit it to the economic domain. . . . Without people ever realizing what is actually going on, such fundamental values as personal liberty, freedom of thought and speech and independence of science are exposed to imminent danger." Professor Jacob Viner—a proponent of planning—admits in a recent book, "It is unfortunately . . . difficult to see how . . . central economic planning . . . can withstand the activities of a freely elected, freely legislating Congress." Sidney and Beatrice Webb—the British socialists—writing about the Russian system, concede that "Whilst the work is in progress any public expression of doubt is an act of disloyalty and even treachery."

From past experience a middle-of-the-road course in respect to planned economy is out of the question. Competitive enterprise can be subjected to regulation—as it should be—and survive, but it cannot be combined with government control and still function as competitive enterprise. At the end of the First World War, Walter Rathenau, a conservative leader in Germany, wrote, "From the ruins will arise neither a communistic state nor a system allowing free play to the economic forces." The present holocaust tells how effectively that compromise policy worked out in Germany. It led directly to the destruction of both political and personal freedom. Over-all planning in small doses simply cannot produce results. As Professor Hayek observes, "Planning and competition can be combined only by planning for competition but not by planning against competition."

It is often claimed that a planned economy in the United States would be different from that of Germany, Italy or Russia because here the planning would be done by men who were not actuated by the desire to oppress their fellow citizens. Unfortunately they would simply have to have power to do the job assigned them, and as Lord Acton said, "Power tends to corrupt, and absolute power corrupts absolutely." Without power to enforce their decrees, economic planners would find their efforts nullified at every turn. Even a truly democratic statesman planning a nation's economic life would have either to assume dictatorial powers or abandon his program. And as dictator he would soon have to choose between disregard of ordinary humanitarian morals or failure. That is why unscrupulous men are always likely to be most successful as dictators. Sixty years ago in his famous essay, "Man Versus the State," Herbert Spencer said, "The machinery of communism (planned economy) like existing social machinery, has to be framed out of existing human nature and the defects of existing human nature will generate in the one the same evils as in the other. . . . There is no political alchemy by which you can get golden conduct out of leaden instincts." Those who would substitute governmental control in the economic field for the power exercised by private individuals under competitive enterprise should never forget that they are substituting power from which there is no escape for power which is always limited.

If we ever do lose our freedom in America, I predict that it will be due to planned economy coming as a wolf in sheep's clothing. Sad to relate, we are far closer to it than most of us realize. The shape of things to come over here is often anticipated by what happens in Great Britain. Every thinking American should read the British White Paper entitled "Employment Policy," which was issued last year, and ponder the program there outlined with real concern. For only a short time ago— with little or no publicity in our newspapers in the United States —the policy advocated in that document was enacted into law by the British Parliament under the frank title of "Planned Economy for Great Britain."

The first repercussion in Washington apparently is the bill for a so-called National Job Budget which has the backing of the radical farm and labor groups. This proposal would compel the Federal Government to guarantee a job to every able-bodied citizen at all times. Despite its protestations in favor of private enterprise, it would soon make planned economy and state socialism an accomplished fact in the United States. For do not forget that Lenin pointed out years ago that the surest way to destroy our type of self-government would be to lead the people to believe that public authority could permanently supply them with jobs, for in that event, he said, the demands of the populace would become so insatiable that no free government could possibly withstand them financially. This National Job Budget measure, which is proposed by Senator Murray, should be studied by every citizen. It appears to be the opening gun in an over-all program which is allegedly shaping up in Washington under which:

1. There will be established a National Production Council which would control our entire economy, working in conjunction with committees for each industry composed of representatives of labor, management and government.

2. The volume of production would be set by these bodies and a quota given to each producer, the total being fixed at a level that would insure so-called full employment.

3. The government would guarantee to protect producers against loss by buying any surplus that could not be sold through the regular channels of trade.

4. No new producer could enter any field without the approval of the industry committee concerned.

5. Prices and wages would be fixed and permanently controlled by the planning agency.

This, in essence, is the economic system that was in operation in Germany, Italy and Russia long before the war broke out. It seems well-nigh unbelievable that after we have seen what has happened to civil and religious freedom and political liberty in those countries, we should even contemplate adopting the economic principles of the absolutism we are now fighting to destroy.

A man named Adolf Hitler said this eight or ten years ago about his planned economy, "We shall banish want; we shall banish fear. The essence of National Socialism is human welfare. . . . National Socialism is the revolution of the common man. Rooted in a fuller life for every German from childhood to old age, National Socialism means a new day of abundance at home and a better world order abroad." I repeat, those were Adolf Hitler's beguiling assurances to the German people. I am confident no thinking American would want to follow the economic principles of the Pied Piper of Berchtesgaden! Nevertheless, strangely similar utterances are now falling from the lips of highly placed crusaders for a planned economy in the United States.

Competitive Enterprise versus Planned Economy—the American system versus the Hitlerian system. America stands at the crossroads. Which shall it be? Competitive enterprise with freedom of speech and the press, freedom of worship and assemblage, freedom to choose who shall rule over us; the state the servant of the people? Or, planned economy with the ultimate loss of every freedom our forefathers held dear; the people the servants of the state? Pray God we may have the wisdom and courage to keep faith with those who are giving their lives tonight to preserve the tripod of American freedom—political liberty, civil and religious liberty and competitive enterprise. They stand or fall together.

EDUCATION AND THE WAR

THE CHALLENGE OF THE CRISIS [1]

ANDREW THOMAS WEAVER [2]

Andrew T. Weaver gave this address at the first general session of the annual conference of the National Association of Teachers of Speech, at the La Salle Hotel, Chicago, December 27, 1944. The meeting was a joint one with the American Speech Correction Association. The theme of the session was "Social Responsibility of Teachers of Speech." Bower Aly, of the University of Missouri, President of the National Association of Teachers of Speech, presided. On the program also were Bryng Bryngelson, of the University of Minnesota, President of the American Speech Correction Association, and Congressman Karl Mundt, of South Dakota. Several hundred teachers of speech, research specialists, and graduate students of speech composed the audience.

Professor Weaver had been head of the Department of Speech at the University of Wisconsin since 1927, is a former president of the National Association of Teachers of Speech, former editor of the *Quarterly Journal of Speech,* director of graduate research in the field of speech science and pedagogy, author or co-author of well-known texts on speech, a frequent lecturer at educational gatherings, and recognized as a highly effective and popular public speaker.

This address was an excellent example of speech composition. The organic structure was clearly outlined. The introduction began with a personal anecdote, defined the "crisis," stated the issue as a question, and announced the "partition" of the subject. The discussion proper was an unfolding of each of the three points enumerated. The conclusion contained a brief reinforcement of the preceding theses, especially the proposition that speech teachers "must labor unceasingly to strengthen our claims to academic recognition and respect."

The underlying thinking was based upon a progressive educational philosophy, summarized under the first of the three main propositions and amplified in the remainder of the discourse. The main ideas were illustrated with sufficient copiousness to clarify the meaning and to add interest. The language was oral and sufficiently informal to establish full rapport between speaker and listeners. Professor Weaver followed

[1] Permission to reprint this address through the courtesy of Andrew Weaver and Karl Wallace, editor of the *Quarterly Journal of Speech.* Text furnished by the author. See also *Quarterly Journal of Speech.* 31:128-34. April 1945.

[2] For biographical note see Appendix.

his manuscript but adapted his voice effectively to the loud speaker; he articulated clearly but without over-precision, and projected his ideas with force and persuasiveness.

The audience, teachers of speech, had carried on an important war-time service in instructing armed forces assigned to college campuses, in providing guidance to war casualties whose speech was affected, and in organizing speakers' bureaus for the Office of War Information, Red Cross, and Office of Civilian Defense, and other government or private agencies engaged in war services. Professor Weaver furnished principles for the continuation and development of speech activities in postwar America. The address was a highly successful demonstration of the synthesis of speaker, speech, audience and occasion.

Some weeks ago, at the witching hour of 2 A.M., I was roused from slumber by the insistent ringing of my telephone. The call was from our First Vice President and program-planner extraordinary in Salt Lake City. After neatly anesthetizing me with honeyed words of flattery, he urgently invited me to appear here this morning. Hovering between sleep and waking, I was not in full possession of my faculties and, therefore, not able to protect myself—and you! Thus, in that weak moment, my fate was sealed. In the gray dawn of the next morning I awoke with a sickening realization of the task to which I had committed myself.

My predicament recalls the experience of the farmer who was driving his team up from the back pasture one evening. As he came to the fence, he wrapped the reins about his waist that he might have his hands free to open the gate. Just at this critical juncture a train came along on the nearby railroad, frightening the horses. Off they went across the field, dragging the unfortunate wight behind them. Finally, the reins wore out and he was left lying on the ground in pretty bad condition. A neighbor, hearing his cries for help, arrived, picked him up, and took him home. As he was regaining consciousness, he was asked by his friend why he had ever done such a foolish thing. "Well," he said weakly, "we hadn't gone more than ten rods before I seen my mistake." It did not take me longer than from 2:05 to 7:30 A.M. to see my mistake! But then it was too late.

Perhaps I should plead one extenuating circumstance. It was exactly six years ago that I committed my last offense on the program of a general session at a National Convention. A six-year silence isn't bad for a teacher of speech!

But what of the crisis of which my title speaks? And what of the challenge which confronts us? There are many among us who seem persuaded that after the world conflict there will come hard days of reappraisal of all educational procedures and that, in some very special way, speech will be singled out, haled before the assizes, and summarily ordered to say why sentence should not be passed upon it. Nevertheless, despite these apprehensions of my good friends, the portents of the times do not fill me with foreboding. I agree that we shall be called upon to render an accounting. However, the day of judgment will be the common lot of all who toil in the vineyard of education. I see no reason for supposing that it is especially to be feared by good and faithful servants who happen to wear our professional insignia. This crisis is not unique; rather it is one of those recurring times of testing in which everything and everyone are called upon to justify their existence.

The Scripture says, "It was good for me that I was afflicted." Probably no one in his right mind deliberately elects to suffer affliction. Yet it comes to all. Certainly it should not be a new experience for us. We have passed through periods of trial before. How shall the gold be separated from the dross save by fire?

It was Thomas Paine who wrote:

These are the times that try men's souls. The summer soldier and the sunshine patriot will in this crisis shrink from the service of his country; but he that stands it now deserves the love and thanks of man and woman.

We cannot escape the scales of revaluation even if we should wish to do so. We should not pray that we be not weighed but only that we be not found wanting.

What then, shall we as a profession do to be saved? I wish to suggest today three courses which I think we may follow with some assurance that we will be helped thereby to meet the challenge of the coming crisis:

First: We must demonstrate to educators the nature and the extent of the contributions which we are making to the educational process.

Second: We must cherish a high faith in our own professional enterprise.

Third: We must labor unceasingly to strengthen our claims to academic recognition and respect.

Fourth: We must demonstrate the nature and extent of the contribution which we are making to the educational process. In doing this we should start from the basic assumption that all education is one and that departmentalization exists for reasons of efficiency and convenience only. Every subject-matter field must be integrated with the master purposes of education.

Not long ago a National Educational Policies Commission formulated four basic objectives of education, as follows: 1. Self-realization; 2. Economic Efficiency; 3. Satisfactory Social Relationships; 4. Good Citizenship. Although there is considerable overlapping among these purposes, they do indicate major points of emphasis and establish controlling criteria. As we take them up one by one, we shall attempt to show just why speech training is an indispensable means for achieving them.

What do we mean by self-realization as a goal of education? A man's first obligation is to make maximum use of his natural endowments. The most fundamental objective of education is to help students make the most and the best of themselves. How does speech training contribute to self-realization? Can any individual grow up emotionally and intellectually without learning to speak well? As we refine speech, we build personality, intellect, and emotional balance and control. If man is "the speaking animal," how shall he rise to his full stature without developing his most distinctive capacity? Therefore, we stand ready to demonstrate to all comers that speech training does advance the student along his way toward self-realization.

Now, what of the goal of economic efficiency? The history of our educational system might be written in terms of the emerging idea that one of its chief concerns should be the teaching of vocational techniques. The older point of view was that we should merely draw out the inborn abilities of the individual and then leave him to use his sharpened wits in earning his living. Now we do our best to unfold and furbish those technical skills to be used in acquiring the economic goods without which life must be cramped and handicapped.

In one of our popular magazines recently I saw the picture of a salesman who had undergone surgical removal of his larynx. One day he had called to consult his physician about a chronic laryngitis. The doctor had urged an immediate operation—an operation which would deprive him of his larynx. It had to be that or a particularly horrible form of death. How would we feel in the face of a diagnosis like that? If we had the option, which would we choose to surrender first: our eyes, our ears, or our speech? And how would we earn our living if we should lose our speech? Well, this man now had recovered from the operation and was being taught esophageal speech. He was emerging triumphantly from the dreadful sense of isolation into which he had been plunged and soon he would be back on his job.

Every man is perforce a "business man." And every business man has need of speech. Good speech is vital in the workaday world; it is the lubricant which reduces friction in the economic machine.

The third objective of education is the development of satisfactory social relationships. Those who spend their lives in unhappy tensions with those about them never really live at all. Lotze spoke a deep truth when the observed that "to be is to stand in relation." Our social contacts are the matrix of all our finest experiences. Personality itself is the by-product of social living. Now, speech is the very warp and woof of the social fabric; without it society could not exist. Everything which we can do to improve speech should result in more adequate social adjustments.

And, fourth, there is the high function of preparing boys and girls for citizenship in a democracy. It is not enough that a man should bring his latent capacities to full flower, earn his bread and butter efficiently, and live happily with his fellows. He must carry the obligations of civic living. He is indispensable not only to the body social but to the body politic as well.

Not long ago a "liberal" group on our campus distributed a mimeographed statement of their creed concerning the rights of citizens. With amazement I read that the old formula of life, liberty, and the pursuit of happiness had been amended to include "the right to peace," "the right to free speech," "the right to economic security," and "the right to health"—just to mention a few of the long list! Sometimes its seems to me that we have gone so berserk over our alleged rights that we have ignored our responsibilities. We must help to train a generation who will seek first their civic duties, in the faith that all their rights will then be added unto them.

How shall government derive its just powers from the consent of the governed if the people be inarticulate? Free speech produces the only climate in which free government can flourish. And speech is really free only in proportion to its own excellence.

It is not our proper function as teachers to increase the amount of speech, rather it is to raise the quality. We are charged with a very special responsibility to see to it that freedom of speech is used wisely. As we teach our students the techniques of public discussion, we should warn them that if they deposit nothing but ignorance and prejudice in the crucible of conference, they cannot hope to distill therefrom the precious precipitates of wisdom. We should show them that speech becomes an instrument of the common welfare only when it succeeds in fitting the fragmentary contributions of individuals into the large mosaic of social and civic thought and action.

We cannnot shift onto the shoulders of other teachers accountability for *what* our students say and concern ourselves exclusively with *how* they say it. The *how* must always be evaluated in the light of the *what*. Speech is an indissoluble composite of purposes, attitudes, feelings, ideas, language, voice and visible action, and we neglect any of these at our peril.

In these latter days some of us seem to have forgotten that it is more important to speak true than it is to speak skilfully. Civilization has been dragged down to hell by skilled speakers whose purposes are demoniac. We must look more to the motives and the characters of our students. We must seek to educate good citizens who can speak clearly and with power. No lesser aim will do if we are to make our maximum contribution to this good-citizenship objective.

When we have done what we can to line speech training up with the master aims of education, we are ready to proceed with the second step in meeting the challenge of the crisis; we must have faith in ourselves and in our cause. We should be slow to accept the low appraisal which some uninformed persons in other fields make of us. If we ourselves do not believe in our mission, how can we ask others to believe? And we do have grounds for faith.

Sometimes, those who have not borne the heat and burden of the day come into the field in the cool of the evening and express disappointment with the harvest. To those who have cultivated the soil, sown the seed, and reaped the grain, they complain, saying,

Lo, we have less reward than do those that labor yonder on fairer acres. We are cast down. Shall we not withdraw ourselves and sit apart lest the Lord of the Harvest come and dispossess us utterly?

To such discouraged brethren I would say: In the life of an organization like ours, those who have the perspective of the years should be best able to estimate the progress which has been made and to prophesy the future. A generation has come and gone since our professional sires seceded from the English Council and established the National Association of Academic Teachers of Public Speaking. Six of the seventeen founding fathers since have passed from our sight and the snows lie heavy on the heads of most of those yet among us. As we contemplate what we were and what we have become, we see that much of their great dream already has been realized.

Those of us who remember conditions in 1915 know that it took courage and vision to organize this Association. "We were not many, we who stood before the iron sleet that day." Shall we falter now when less than a dozen and a half have been multiplied miraculously into five thousand? Before the date of our birth only five Master's degrees had been granted in speech. A year ago 4,215 Master's degrees had been recorded, 80 per cent of them conferred within the past decade. In 1915, the first Doctor's degree in speech was six years in the future. Today, well over 300 have been awarded, 85 per cent of them in the last ten years. Then, there were two institutions granting the Master's degree in speech, and none the Doctor's degree. Now, there are 43 institutions offering the Master's, and 13 the Doctor's degree in our field.

Four years ago, speaking at the Washington Convention, Professor O'Neill said:

> The question of whether we have reached professional maturity cannot be answered by certifying that we are twenty-five years old nor that we have so many thousand members in the Association. It can only be answered in terms of our development for our appropriate function, our ability to discharge our professional obligations. . . . Do we function not simply as a large organism, but as a powerful, properly motivated, properly directed organism?

> We have changed from a group of disorganized outposts on an educational frontier to an integrated and cohesive professional group with programs, standards, and facilities comparable to those of the other great fields in education.

On the basis of such facts I feel justified in refusing to be thrown into a panic by pessimistic predictions about our future. If there be those who still would came seeking the young child's life, they are likely to find that he has grown into a strong young man able to defend himself.

But after we have demonstrated our worth in education, and after we have developed a serene confidence in the strength of our present position, we must go yet a third step forward. We must be ever conscious of the weaknesses which do so easily beset us and we must labor without ceasing to remove them.

If the house which we have built should collapse, the causes will be within the structure itself—not in the winds which play about it. If we fail, the fault will be not in our stars but in ourselves. Our future can never be taken from us by outside forces. Right still makes might—even in the educational world!

In the days of our infancy as an Association, Professor Winans spoke a warning word on which we might meditate with profit occasionally in the night watches. He said:

> We complain of prejudice and unjust discrimination, and we have grounds; but we had best face the truth. In the long run men pass for what they are.

We well may recall the plight of the prisoner in the courtroom. As the prosecuting attorney released a particularly poisonous blast of eloquence, counsel for the defense leaned over to his nervous client and whispered, "Don't worrry. I'll see that you get justice." The accused retorted, "That's just what I am beginning to be afraid of." Distressing as it may be to admit the fact, I am convinced that sometimes when we hear wails arising from certain sectors of our line, some brother is getting justice and not enjoying it!

It seems to me that as a profession there are two major mistakes which we are prone to make. First, we dissipate our strength in divisive organizations. And second, we yield too readily to the alluring notion that our security can be achieved by some form of academic P.A.C.

Speaking at Cleveland in 1938, I counseled against the growing menace of sects and schisms among us. I drew attention to the fact that when our Association was founded, we perceived the necessity for submerging our differences and exalting our agreements. I concluded by saying:

> If, and when, workers in the different branches of our subject, having perfected their own organizations, decide that their interests may be served best by separate meetings and that what goes on at the general sessions of the National Association Convention is of little or no concern to them, the process of disintegration will have begun.

I now believe that it has begun and that, unless we meet the threat with a constructive and statesmanlike appreciation of its seriousness, our whole enterprise may suffer a major disaster. I still believe that the prime function of this Association is to unite us all into one army and to provide us with a single high command.

I do not hold with those who seem to believe that the security of an educational program can be guaranteed by the War Department, the Navy Department, or the U.S. Veterans' Administration. Our security must come—if it comes at all—out of relationships of mutual respect between our departments and other departments within our respective colleges and universities, and between our several institutions and the local governmental agencies concerned with educational problems. A good-neighbor policy in those areas will pay large dividends in the days that lie just ahead.

As a people we have been passing through—and I devoutly hope that through is the right word—an era in which everybody has been looking to the Great White Father for the solution of all their problems. When the tensions of war are relaxed, a swing away from that point of view would seem inevitable. Local governments are sure to reassert themselves.

I have talked with a number of men who should know what is likely to happen in the administration of educational programs for veterans. It seems to be their considered opinion that there will be no attempt by authorities in the nation's Capitol to dictate the details of educational policy. The president of a great university not far from here, writing in the December 30, 1944 issue of a well-known weekly, under the title, "The Threat to Education," deplores the failure of the "G. I. Bill of Rights" to provide for any supervision of postwar education for servicemen. He says:

> The only area in which the government shows no interest in protecting its investment is education. It asks no questions about the ability and experience of the veteran. It asks no questions about the reasonableness of the tuition nor about the likelihood that the education it is financing can be turned to successful account.

As a matter of fact, most of the difficulties which plagued us in dealing with the A.S.T.P. originated less in the ignorance and hostility of military administrators than in the coolness and prejudice of our own academic colleagues. Two or three of the foremost universities of the land never have had departments of speech, and unfortunately for us, the administration of some of the army programs was entrusted to professors from those very institutions. If, in the prewar years, we had won our way into those citadels of academic prestige which managed to resist all our efforts at peaceful penetration, the whole story of these "communciations courses" might have been vastly more satisfactory to us. Where speech did get into the programs on favorable terms, it did so because teachers of the subject had succeeded long before in creating around themselves a climate of respect and confidence.

Two examples may help to make the point. The committee in charge of one of the Army programs was composed of the president of a small Midwestern college, a professor of English in an Eastern university, and a professor of physics in a Midwestern university. None of these men had the slightest notion of what the term speech means and, since those who are not "up on" a subject are likely to be "down on" it, they had no intention of having it taught in the program for which they had assumed responsibility. Happily for us, these three men called in a professor of mathematics from another Midwestern university and turned over to him the details of curriculum-making. This man said to me, "I understand what speech is. We have an excellent department of speech on our campus. As an undergraduate, I took courses in speech myself and I know what it can do for these boys. I propose to see that they get it."

The other day I received a letter from a professor of English in one of the best of our state universities. He had just witnessed a demonstration presented by the university speech clinic before the Rotary Club—an organization, in this instance, divided about fifty-fifty between town and gown. He wrote me:

> The Director of the Clinic brought in twelve patients who have formed themselves into a "Slow But Sure Club"—more slow than sure perhaps—but gallant. They began the program by singing their song "Buckle Down"—and they were applauded to the echo. Then a stutterer spoke on "Conquer Fear by Living with it Gracefully." Next a stone-deaf patient spoke; and finally, a returned soldier who had lost his memory. I tell you that I was moved and so were the other men in our group. That clinician is releasing those poor handicapped people from a dark and ghoulish room into the sweet sunlight. All of us should be doing that. I take that to be my job as a teacher, too, but I don't often get such definite and measurable results.

That clinic demonstration was a triumph not for that one department of speech alone but also for our entire profession.

Instead of worrying about whether or not we are going to get our fair share of the teaching in the postwar period, we would do better to expend our time and energy in preparations for rendering real service to the young men and women who will return to the campus when this war is over.

I need hardly say that I do not mean to oppose any proper effort to make our professional voice heard wherever and whenever educational policies are being formulated. My point simply is that, in the last analysis, we hold in our own hands the keys to our future. Each of us working humbly in his own little sphere wins or loses the battle for our common cause. There is no substitute for the honest and intelligent devotion of individuals to their duty. We owe a solemn obligation to each other to hold the line where we are and to move forward where we can. When one of us is slipshod in his work or unwilling to play his full part in the larger life of his community, he injures all of his colleagues everywhere. A break-through at any point may imperil our whole line and force us to surrender ground which has been taken at high cost. When one of us on some lonely outpost stands firm against misunderstanding and prejudice and, at the end of a hard-fought day, drives forward a little, he makes the position of all of us stronger and safer. In the words of Stephen Vincent Benét:

We can call upon the great men, the great words of our own past— and that we should do—for in looking back at our past we can see at what a price, by what endurance and fortitude, the freedom we have inherited was bought. But that is only part of the task. We need new words also—and great ones—to match the present, to build for the future that must be.

If we can continue to subordinate our petty differences to our common welfare, if we can abandon all hope of getting back as speedily as possible to the worn old patterns and the easy old ways, if we can allow the coming crisis to stimulate us into pioneering thought and action, if we can minister to the needs of humanity, we shall achieve that true greatness which is promised to those who become the servants of all. And if we do these things, no matter how searching and prolonged the sifting and winnowing of the war years may be, we shall move irresistibly onward and upward to our high destiny. Sursum corda!

THE RESPONSIBILITY OF YOUTH [3]

Nicholas Murray Butler [4]

President Nicholas Murray Butler gave this address at the 190th commencement exercises of Columbia University, on June 6, 1944. Degrees were conferred on 3,075, the smallest graduating class since 1923. Because many were in service or in essential industry, fewer than one third of the graduates were on hand for the ceremonies. Among the recipients of honorary degrees were Senator Charles Warren, of Vermont, Charles Merz, editor of the *New York Times,* Charles A. Beard, and Archbishop Francis Joseph Spellman.

President Butler's address was given at a most critical hour in our World War II. While he was speaking, the allied invasion of France was in full development. The Four-Power Moscow Declaration had been promulgated, and Senator Warren, in his brief talk at the graduation ceremonies, called for the immediate institution of an international organization based on that Declaration. Such action, he urged, would be a guarantee that those who during this hour were invading fortress Europe would not be required to do it again.

President Butler's brief message, although couched in general language and confining itself to well-known historical instances, nevertheless was an argument for these Columbia graduates and Americans everywhere to support internationalism in the impending Senate struggle concerning cooperation vs. isolationism.

The speaker's political and educational outlook in this critical summer of 1944 was more fully developed in his argument "The Hope of the World," in the September 1944 issue of *International Conciliation,* where he expounded his familiar principles of internationalism, and advocated an amendment to the Federal Constitution to provide for a ratification of treaties by a simple majority of both houses of Congress.

On April 23, 1945, Mr. Butler resigned as President of Columbia, after forty-four years as the acting and titular head of Columbia. He has been an outstanding scholar and educator, a prolific writer on educational and political subjects, and a speaker of force and originality, who through the many years impressed representative audiences in this country, in Great Britain, and in Europe.

The rebuilding of this broken world will be neither easy nor short. As the years pass, it will fall to the youth of today to

[3] Text furnished by the Secretary of Columbia University. Permission to reprint through the courtesy of President Butler.

[4] For biographical note see Appendix.

take the leading part in the far-reaching reconstruction which must follow the war. This is why the education which is now being given to youth is of such vital importance. It is particularly true of that liberal education which leads the way to knowledge and to understanding as nothing else can possibly do.

In order to understand what is now happening or to foresee what is likely to happen, one must know first of all thoroughly and well what has happened. The record of human ambition and accomplishment in the past is the key to open the door of that epoch-marking future which lies just ahead of us.

The center of civilization has been moving steadily westward for more than twenty-five hundred years. It is, therefore, the history of that civilization as it was recorded in Greece, in Rome and in Europe during the Middle Ages which is so essential to an appreciation of the forces, tendencies and aims which rule the world of today. It is liberal education as given in the best type of American college which alone will provide the training and the knowledge that youth must have in order to play its vital part in the world of tomorrow. Given that liberal education, then with open mind, with vision and with courage youth may go forward to constructive leadership. Youth must be optimistic. Optimism is essential to achievement and it is also the foundation of courage and of true progress.

One of the misfortunes of a democratic system of government is the difficulty of finding representatives of the people in executive or in legislative office who will be guided in their thought and official action solely by sound principles, with little or no regard to the possibility of their not being reelected to that public office which they may hold. It is the duty of the chosen representatives of the people in a democracy, truly to represent the fullest knowledge and the highest ideals of their time and not merely the selfish ambitions and preferences of specialized pressure groups. The history of democracy in the United States offers many illustrations of the fact that even though a representative in government who is of the highest type may differ at the moment from what appears to be the opinion of his constituents, he can, nevertheless, carry them with him by persuasive argument and clearness of vision. The task of a representative of the people in a democracy is not to bow down to the lower and more selfish forms of what is called public opinion, but to guide and inspire that public opinion so that it may rise to constantly higher levels. Our own history abounds in illustrations of the great effectiveness of this course of conduct. In particular, Alexander Hamilton, Henry Clay and Abraham Lincoln reflected in their lives and public service this fundamental fact. Properly to represent the people, one must represent them on the highest level to which they can rise instead of descending to the lowest level which the happenings of the moment may record. Reelection to public office may be without special significance, while accomplishment of high purposes and sound principles is of vital importance.

We Americans are indeed fortunate in having possessed in our relatively short history an exceptional number of outstanding captains of the political mind. (Students of today who will read the history of the personality and accomplishment of Samuel Adams, of Benjamin Franklin, of George Washington, of Alexander Hamilton, of Thomas Jefferson, of James Madison, of Henry Clay, of Daniel Webster and of Abraham Lincoln will gain both guidance and stimulus toward effective public service) A chosen representative of the people whether in the executive or the legislative branch of government should and, if he is to be truly efficient, must keep in close personal relationship with his constituents. He must ascertain from them what acts and policies they wish him to support. He should also explain to them the acts and policies which he, himself, advocates and give his reasons for so doing. It is a grave weakening of democratic organization when there is a breach between the people and their chosen representatives, or when those chosen representatives fail to inform and to guide and truly to serve their constituents. (It is these lessons which the youth of today must learn, since—and it cannot be repeated too often—they will in the very near future be called upon to take a controlling part in the conduct of the government of the American people, local, state and federal. They cannot take this great responsibility too seriously and they cannot begin too soon to prepare themselves to discharge it)

It must be remembered that to participate in a democratic government it is by no means necessary that one hold public office. One should always take active part in the work of selecting candidates for legislative and executive office—local, state and federal—as well as in framing the declarations of policy and principle which are to guide these public officers when they shall have been elected. Public office is a public trust, but participation in the choice of public officers and in the formulation of public policy is also a personal obligation which rests upon every citizen.

The government of our people has been built upon the foundation of sound and easily understood principles. It has been protected and developed in amazing fashion for more than a century and a half. What will be its story during the next century? Only the youth of today and tomorrow can give the answer to that question. May they give it with fullness of knowledge, clearness of vision and outstanding courage.

A DESIGN FOR FIGHTING [5]

HARLOW SHAPLEY [6]

Harlow Shapley, Director of the Harvard Observatory, gave this address before the American Association for the Advancement of Science, in Cleveland, Ohio, on September 13, 1944. The lecture was one in an annual series sponsored by Phi Beta Kappa.

Professor Shapley is perhaps the best known astronomer in the United States. "He has almost as many awards and medals as the stars he discovered." [7] He is an authority of photometry, spectroscopy and galaxies. In his public talks Dr. Shapley has the rare scientific gift of explaining in simple, popular language the complexities of scientific research. In addition he is a lively speaker, of excellent voice and platform personality. He holds attention, has a habit of inserting abundant concrete material, of stating his facts with whimsical pleasantry, but of maintaining scientific restraint. He is popular as a radio lecturer; much favorable comment followed his discussion of "Has Twentieth Century Civilization Improved Mankind?" in February 1939, in America's Town Meeting of the Air at Town Hall, New York. He has spoken at many scientific congresses and at universities, including lectures at Cambridge, England, 1925; Belgian universities, 1926; Oxford, England, 1938; Mexico City, 1933, as well as at many higher institutions and before learned societies in the United States. He has a reputation of sociability and for "pungent talk." This friendliness he carries into his formal addresses.

Begging your tolerance, I should like to make a talk on wars. It may not be too tedious, for wars are never dull. I am planning to deal mostly with fights that are outside the history books. To get into our subject, we shall need to examine honestly our attitudes toward war. Subsequently, we shall identify some new enemies, make blueprints (very provisional ones) of new battlefields, take stock of our mobile fighting equipment, and then sketch the preliminary patterns in our Design for Fighting.

First I shall recount a sad folk tale. Once upon a time recently there was a great nation in a mess. When it struggled to disentangle itself from the condition that had been brought on

[5] Reprinted through the courtesy of Dr. Harlow Shapley and of the *American Scholar*. Text from *American Scholar*. 14, no. 1:19-32. Winter 1944-45.

[6] For biographical note see Appendix.

[7] *Current Biography*: 1941. p. 776.

by this and also by that, the situation seemed to grow messier, and no less than twenty-two millions of its adults voted to change horses in the middle of the bog, and to try getting out on the other bank. The nation's ills were everywhere obvious. A great many poor people were hungry, while other citizens destroyed their surpluses; more than ten million were unemployed; the desires of the laborers for greater pay and prestige were doing badly; the women without higher education were submerged by custom and lack of opportunity; the people had no thrifty desires to accumulate savings, and indeed, they had nothing much to save; the young men and women had little systematic training in health or in patriotism; they had little opportunity to travel.

In this economically and spiritually confused country (so continues the tale), diseases like measles, pneumonia, and syphilis were badly controlled, if at all; mosquitoes and flies were destined to be eternal pests and carriers of disease; practically no one in all that nation could use radar, or anti-radar, or anti-anti-radar; social reforms were progressing with difficulty, and educational policy was static.

The airplanes were relatively slow and weak (we continue to list the nation's ills); the researches in the physical sciences throughout the country were listless; the art of ship-building and ship-sailing had practically disappeared; and worst of all, there was little zest for life and liberty, no driving principle or policy to make the citizens from all the corners of the country proud to be citizens of that nation and brothers under a sun that might illuminate a hopeful future.

It was a somber epoch in the history of that great nation, and the prospects for recovery and progress, and for the cure of the enumerated evils, were dim indeed.

If I had, at that time, ventured to offer a remedy for all these ills, every one of them, by advising the afflicted nation to take active part in the greatest and bloodiest human war ever conceived, a war that destroys more property and brutally butchers more innocent people than the worst human butchers have ever enjoyed in their most gorgeous dreams—if I had recommended that mad procedure, guaranteeing the almost complete cure of such ills within ten years, and the practical attainment of all the high goals I have implied, it is quite likely that both my advice and I would have been (to understate it) deplored. It is possible that someone might have written a letter to the Harvard authorities about fanatics, and recommended my transfer to an institution even more suitable than a university.

Naturally, I did not make such a recommendation. Nevertheless, this nation did get into just such a war, and all of those happy desiderata and many more have come about.

Probably never in the history of this country have its people, as a whole, eaten so well as during the past three years. There's practically no unemployment. The soldiers and sailors are the best paid and fed in the world. The thrill, and even the joy of living, has much increased. The nation is healthier. (The death toll in the current war and the number maimed by the war are of the same order of magnitude as the automobile casualties before the war.) The people have rather willingly adopted healthy restraints, constructive collaboration, unified determination, a national spirit of worthy sacrifice. Sensational advances in the treatment of certain diseases, new knowledge of food, new accomplishment in a million new home gardens, new and widespread instruction in world geography—all of these have come also. Without the war, most of them would yet have been totally missing, and the others of slow maturing. The women in the offices, factories, and armed services have discovered abilities and self-assurance heretofore unrealized. Elementary applied sciences have been taught to about a million young men who would otherwise have been deprived of a practical training that is important in a civilization highly dependent on applied science. The political and social prestige of labor has increased remarkably in three years of war; and millions of citizens have billions in savings—establishing a policy heretofore unknown, unpracticed, or impossible.

With such manifold blessings to the majority of individuals and groups in America, and with such apparent social gain for the nation as a whole, who could sincerely regret this world war and who would take steps to prevent another one? Should we not praise those who precipitated it, or should we not? Is there a counteracting Design for Not Fighting—some substitute for Beneficent War?

The problem must be examined further, or some strange conclusions will be reached and astonishing national policies advocated. War was long ago recognized as a good tribal business by certain savage and primitive people, but they fought for food, women, loot, and the joy of personal combat. These are not our American motives. We have food; we have, if anything, too many women; our individual property averages to be the most and best in the world; and the lust for personal combat has been pretty well bred out of us (even if it has not, the modern war provides little opportunity for personal blood-letting, since it is about nine tenths fought on the draftsmen's board, in the machine shop, and by the remotely located ground forces). Less than a tenth of our mobilized warriors in battlefields, factories, and farms ever smell the human enemy or grapple with him. The poetry and romance, the snorting rush of the foaming charger and the wild savage clash of sabers have been machined out of modern and future wars. Most of the thrills for most of us are vicarious. At the height of a hard pressing crisis, we may work at the lathes some fifty-four hours a week—with time-and-a-half for overtime, of course, and we only temporarily modify our squealing about renegotiation.

Our material gains in war are therefore not so elemental as those which made war a national business for earlier tribes. It is now not so much for food, loot, and glory that we fight, as (if we judge by our successes) for the great social gains: for widely distributed prosperity, the education of the masses, large wealth for a new set of capitalists, the provision of work for everybody, and good pay for good work. Socially uplifting is this war, as well as materially profitable, for more than a hundred million Americans.

Up to this point, it sounds as though it would be folly not to adopt World War as the national policy. The amazing advantages and dividends must be balanced somehow, or even written off in some way; otherwise we are at a loss to understand another equally amazing situation, namely that practically everyone wants this beneficent war to end immediately, and fervently hopes, apparently, that there will never be another such war in the future history of the world. (Undoubtedly there exist a few friends of war, scattered among the officers of the armed forces, the politicians and government officials, the magnified personalities of press and radio, and especially among profiteering business men—a considerable number altogether who secretly hope that this war will continue and that others will come. These people must be watched, but I choose to consider such individuals as low moral perverts, and not as a part of the American citizenry.)

To enumerate briefly the chief objections to war, we note first that it is making nearly all of our regularly trained army and navy personnel important, and perhaps overweeningly arrogant. The same is true for hundreds of Washington bureaucrats. To these few thousand individuals, the war is a great immediate advantage, and probably therefore a disadvantage to the American political and social system. It may be pretty hard to demobilize the pride and spirit and habits of many of the war-enriched glory-inflated citizens.

The war is building a much greater American Legion—again, a two-sided sword, disadvantage and advantage.

The war has decreased the normal care of children, and probably their morale. The bull-market boom of the late '20's, of course, tended to do the same.

The usual type of college education has been interrupted for a few years for many boys. Presumably that should be listed as a disadvantage.

Although the war has improved the business of newspapers, of the radio, of manufacturers, of the transportation and communications industries, and of most small businessmen the country over, there were some enterprises temporarily ruined by the war (although the corresponding businessmen themselves have landed on their feet elsewhere). And the white collar classes have, as usual, suffered disproportionately, because the take has lagged behind the increased outgo.

Some would list "the economic waste of war" as a frightful price to pay for our full employment and full stomachs and purses.

Finally, taxes have become atrocious; but hardly any of us regret that others pay the government heavily, to meet a part of the costs of the war and to help in moderating the inflation natural to the existence of prosperity. In fact, we almost cheerfully pay our own taxes as a part of the healthful national discipline.

It is obvious that I am reaching around desperately to find sufficient disadvantages of war; it must be discredited somehow. It seems fairly clear that our antipathy to war is not based on worry about the postwar effects. Good times frequently follow successful wars. We are rather blindly hopeful that the government this time will meet the unusual emergencies without too much trouble; we trust that capital will not be too greedy, or labor too insistent, and that a bearable compromise between decreasing taxes and proper rehabilitation of our returning soldiers and factory workers will be worked out. Such is our somewhat vague hope. We are just that simple!

As I see it, there are two major comments on our aversion to adopting war as the best national or international business. One is very obvious, the other leads toward hope.

We in America are on the winning side of this war, and from the first we have known that we are winning; also the war is not on the home grounds. Those obvious factors explain much. Practically none of the war advantages cited above have been available to the French, Dutch, Norwegians, Czechs, and other conquered states. Only a few advantages (like full employment and perhaps unity of spirit) have been available to the now defeated Axis countries; and by no means all of our advantages have come to Great Britain and the Dominions. This time we have kept a winning war at a distance. It is relatively very profitable, and all the profits are not temporary. We have reasons to suspect, however, that a future war might eventuate otherwise.

It remains to make the hopeful comment that the basic reason why a hundred and thirty million Americans and untold hundreds of millions of others want an end of this war, and of all similar world struggles, is that war is immoral. The Moral Values in the situation more than balance the immediate material and social advantages, more than balance the prosperity, the glory and excitement—even for us, a winning nation. This is a fact of highest encouragement to all who are solicitious for the further evolution of the human race. It is inspiriting that we, who are temporarily gaining so many worthwhile social and personal advantages, are nevertheless conscious of the cosmic error of it all.

We owe our present consciousness of the long-range tragic penalties of war to two widely different causes. One is the remarkably dramatic news coverage by press and radio, which has not concealed from the happy Americans the bitter blood and tears. The other is the religious and secular education of past centuries, which has gradually built an intellectual heritage and a universal ethics that link peace with social justice, international good-will, and human progress. Through moral education, peace has become an inherent human desire; it is almost an instinctive good, for educated men, and war an instinctive evil.

Possibly there are other important factors that tend to cancel or minimize the social and material gains of successful war at a distance—mass anxiety and regret over economic waste, for instance. But we also had deep prewar anxieties. Personally I am content to accept the contention that the moral gain of abolishing war is the best reason for such a policy. The arguments based on economics and demography are too often specious and circular; usually they involve merely postponements and short-term compromises. The inherent moral antipathy, moreover, is a factor most clearly associated with the mental and spiritual development of mankind. I am gratified that we can rate it highly.

At this point I should remark that the review of the profits and losses of human warfare are really relevant to the theses I am attempting to develop. A political and military background is necessary for the scientific and scholarly Designs for Fighting that are to be presented for your consideration. To fill in the background further, I should like to digress again and ask a rather embarrassing question: What is the present Design for Fighting? Just why are we in this war? The soldiers and sailors continue to ask this embarrassing question.

"Nonsense, it's all perfectly clear to everyone"—but not to the next expert you meet! The Germans and Russians, the French and Austrians know why they must fight, but too many Americans are not sure. Perhaps we need not be, at this stage of the conflict. The individual combatant might say he is fighting (if you should ask him and he would honestly and seriously reply) because he has been drafted—drafted either by the Selective Service or the equally potent public opinion (however camouflaged under words like duty, patriotism, etc.). A few, of course, are in the war because of their natural spirit of adventure. Fortunately not many soldiers set out solely in the hope that they can commit a legalized murder.

Here follows my list of specific reasons for human warfare, which may be much like yours, if you have thought about it:

1. Ambitious leadership
2. Economic necessities or ambitions
3. Public education awry (either through misplaced nationalism, religious short-sightedness, or otherwise)
4. Absence of effective international law
5. Desire to maintain a power balance in Europe and Asia
6. A combination of many of these reasons

There is nothing very complimentary to civilization in any of the listed causes of war.

It should be noted that we fight not because we were attacked. There was a trigger action on December 7, 1941, that set us off in a war to which we had been definitely committed for a couple of years. There's no need in fooling ourselves that self-defense is the sole reason we are fighting.

In some comprehensive but vague way—a way made vague by detailed rationalizations—we are fighting for a civilization. Let us leave it at that, and receding from contemplations of the present and immediate past, look toward some of the future wars: their necessity, advisability, the new alignments, the strategy and campaigns.

As the current strife draws to a conclusion that seems to be satisfactory for the continuance of a Western culture, we may profitably turn our thoughts first toward postwar peace plans. And when the world gets stabilized politically and economically, or even before then, we should begin planning for the next war. In the remainder of my talk I hope to make some progress toward inciting you to consider plans of new martial activities. It will then become clear why I have taken time to consider both the advantages of successful war and the moral and material costs thereof. We shall have standards of comparison.

In 1918-19 more than four times as many Americans were killed by influenza as by our enemies of the First World War. Twenty million humans perished of that ruthless disease. The economic loss in the worldwide battle with the influenza organism was also tremendous. Moreover, sad and shameful to say, we lost that war. We, the highest and most resourceful animals on the face of the earth, came off battered and disgraced, with the enemy hardly scratched. Only when it became satiated with its successes did the savage foe recede into the invisible realms where it normally dwells, and from which it has at times made further minor forays with murderous and economically destructive results. Even yet, that adversary is not defeated; our Maginot lines of defense against it are permeable and insufficient.

Clearly we have right here a dangerous enemy for our next war. Why are we not all arming ourselves against this treacherous foe that does not hesitate to make sneak attacks, and has no respect for armistice? There were several millions of us engaged in those influenza battles of 1918-19; we are the casualties who recovered. I now wonder why in heaven we who returned from those battlefields did not form an American Flu Legion, don our old face masks and march in parades, brandish our voting strength, and influence Congressmen. With our political power, under the leadership of General Doctor, Captain Laboratory Technician, Lieutenant Nurse—all who fought valiantly with us millions of private sufferers in the great influenza war—with that power we might have got the government to fortify research laboratories munificently, drill the citizens in epidemic prevention and control, enforce the care of body and mind, and turn the powerful mass psychology into a fervent patriotic assault on the enemies of mankind that have always been more deadly than the soldiers of European fanatics and tyrants. So prepared, when the next attack comes along, we would be ready for it. We could sell Health Bonds, pay taxes luxuriously, work like the devil, and perhaps we would, this time, win the war, conquer our great enemy and keep him subjugated for as long as man remains civilized and sanitary.

But, alas, we did not organize. Medical investigators and public health officers continue to do their best, without much government or public support, while the undertakers year after year continue to tuck us away prematurely.

But the Design for Fighting I want to sketch for you tonight is not so simple and obvious as would be a defensive war against some major decimating epidemic. To fight defensively means admission of intellectual defeat. I want to go deeper. We should remember that it is only the bodies of men and women that the gravediggers inter and the cremators oxydize. Our influences, our contributions to knowledge and to the art and beauty of human living—our spirits, if you will—escape the mortuary. Our works live after us. Why not, therefore, seek out some of the enemies that assail those human qualities that we group loosely under the term civilization; let us look up the opponents to the evolution of those human characteristics that seem to differentiate men from other animals and plants. We may discover that an enthusiastic warfare against such opponents, even if only partially successful, is a fair substitute for warfare against fellow men. At least it would emphasize the absurdity of world war or national wars where life and property are wildly squandered, while these greater enemies—the enemies of the soul, mind, sometimes body—are almost completely ignored.

Instinctive and acquired human morality, as we have already noted, seems to oppose the promotion of man-kill-man war; but I believe this same inherent morality must unquestionaly be vigorously pro-war, war to the death, if we define our enemies as those that obstruct or challenge the social and intellectual growth of man and of human society.

In designing a fight, it is comforting to know that right is on our side. Such a claim has a familiar ring. It is the conscience-salve of provocateurs, everywhere and every time. Kings, kaisers, cardinals, cutthroats, and even we minor squabblers have always taken comfort in the benign assistance of God, the eternal righteousness of our cause, and the justice of our murderous actions. Very well, we shall leave over-used Omnipotence out of this. Rather we shall put in Nature, or Creative Evolution, or the

Primal and Persisting Urge of the species man to evolve during the billions of years that the stars appear to have allotted him.

We could, of course, betray this innate evolutionary struggle, deliberately refuse to grow, and go turtling through the ages, dull and static; we could even regress, like a petered-out biological species, by way of recurrent world wars and social degradations. But it will be better cosmic sportsmanship to go to the top, to the limit of our abilities and aspirations; for, who knows, there may be something at that rainbow's end that will make even the galaxies look incidental.

Whatever the postulates in which we clothe ourselves, whether our tailors are religious prophets, pagan philosophers, modern scientific cosmogonists, or the still striving spirits of jungle-born curiosity, the majority of Americans are already amply dressed for the uphill climb. We can put on varied armor to suit the fight. This readiness of the citizen-soldiers is a challenge to those who venture to make plans. They must choose opponents worthy the steel and spirit of determined and intelligent men. No boastful pacification of a restless island will suffice, no capture of a distant market for the enriching of a few traders, no gloating superiority in armored flying battleships. Those are goals of an old-fashioned type, unworthy, unsuited to human dignity in this time of a New Renaissance. No, it has got to be good, this set of plans; and those whom we have trained to be the long-range social thinkers should heed well the ways and means, the details of joining battle with the real enemies. These new conflicts, moreover, must not be local wars, for a few scientific laboratories, or for one country or one county. The fight must be at least nationwide. Perhaps over the borders are potential allies, willing, well armed, and similarly star bent.

As a simple preliminary, I shall mention four national or international problems, the resolution of which seems to lead in the right direction. And one of them I shall commend especially to the attention of this scientific association as its most natural opponent. I shall also offer timidly the introduction to a preliminary sketch of a Design for Fighting this greatest of foes.

Education, as you know, is well spoken of. Although it is perverted at times, and in places, into anti-social channels, it is by and large both good and necessary. It is indeed indispensable, if democracy is to prevail and the dignity of the individual man is to be respected and enhanced. Literacy is basic for it. Notwithstanding the rapid rise of auditory education by way of the radio, and of pictorial education by moving pictures and oncoming television, there is no reasonable escape from the general necessity of knowing how to read and write. Even a tabloid requires a modicum of literacy, and the comic strips carry printed materials.

The point I am driving at is that illiteracy can and should be wiped out. The basic equipment (reading and writing) for general and special education should be universally provided. It is not a job for the regular school teachers alone. It is a national job, for the public and the local governments. Ten years from now the existence of illiteracy between the ages of ten and sixty should be reckoned as a community disgrace. The shame should be on the community, and not on the unfortunate individuals. In many communities, perhaps most, volunteer teachers, performing a sympathetic rather than a patronizing task, could take care of this business without difficulty. In Mexico, the enlightened president, General Manuel Avila Camacho, has recently requested educated adults to undertake, as a part of their national service, the elementary education of at least one unschooled neighbor. Must we lag behind in social progress? Must we await a presidential order? A command from the conscience of the community should suffice. The people can do this work with pleasure and with justifiable pride. And once the first battle for universal literarcy has been won in the community, city, county, or state, the level can be raised and a further step taken toward an enlightened citizenry. The second goal might be: "80 per cent of those older than fifteen years to have a completed grammar school education"; and there should be a ceremonious bestowal, to the successful community, of an "E" for Excellent, or Education, or Evolving.

Teachers' associations have no doubt worked locally on this important problem of illiteracy; but it should not be left wholly to educators. We are all involved. I wonder if sufficient thought has been given to rewards for community successes, to enlisting the interest of Service Groups, and to the expert selling of the enterprise to the general public.

There may be, of course, an irreducible minimum of illiteracy of perhaps 1 per cent, because of the existence of insurmountable physical disabilities, and the presence of illiterate transients. But the occurrence of foreign-language elements in a community should be no excuse for not undertaking or solving this problem; rather it should be a challenge, and an opportunity, by the way, for mutual education.

As a second martial enterprise, let us organize ourselves and declare war on Premature Senility. The more we study the life span and the death causes of Americans and Europeans, the more we realize that a few maladies and a few bad habits cut off too many useful people prematurely. Most of us say that we would dread the prolongation of useless old age; but who can object to the adding of ten years to the active lives of men and women to whom the years have brought augmented wisdom, and in whom experience has produced nobility of character?

I look forward to the time, perhaps in a century or so, when an adult caught with a communicable disease will be heavily fined, and one indulging in afflictions like cancer, tuberculosis, arthritis, and neuroses will be branded as a social pariah, and put in jail. I would like to hope that the names of some of those diseases will become so little known that one would find them only at the bottom of the dictionary page—"cancer: obsolescent name for a rare disease, rampant in the dark ages, when, about 1940, it was killing 150,000 Americans annually." But my hope is perhaps too wild. Certainly there will need to be some hard fighting and heavy expense and further education before that Utopia dawns.

The Western world is not too crowded; there is useful work to be done, joys to be shared, fine thoughts to be meditated, sunsets for everybody. The proper balance for a diminishing but healthily controlled birthrate could be the prolongation of adult life. Already the medical and health sciences have done astonishing work on the diseases of infancy. The average age has risen spectacularly in America and elsewhere. But mature men and women will live and work happily half a generation longer when, as the result of a sincere and widespread war, we conquer or control arthritis, cancer, nephritis, diseases and disorders of the circulatory system, the respiratory system, and the brain. These six are the chief disablers. There is reason for the high hopes of continued advance against all of them.

The battles must be fought, to be sure, largely by the specialists, but in three ways the public can contribute notably; and without this public help, complete victory is impossible. We can inspire brilliant young scientists to enlist, preferably as volunterrs, in this great war in the interest of human life and happiness. We can provide directly by gift, or indirectly through influencing governmental support, the necessary funds for the hospitals, research laboratories, and field studies. We can cooperate in controlling some of these scourges by care of personal health and by seeing to it that our communities are provided with appropriate health programs.

Let us comment quickly on each of the six:

1. In the United States five million people suffer from the various forms of arthritis, and hundreds of thousands are prematurely disabled thereby. Yet, with minor exceptions, there are no appreciable funds for the basic study of this disease, and no specific research army or institution. Arthritis rarely finishes off its own victims; it prepares them painfully for the kill by some more lethal assailant. The average mildness of the malady is probably the reason that it is commonly overlooked as one of man's great enemies.

2. Some further comments on the cancer war. The first eleven days of the recent critical and bloody invasion of Normandy took an average of three hundred American lives a day; cancer averaged to kill four hundred Americans on each of those days. And it does not stop; it offers no armistice. In the next twelve months there will be the customary hundred and fifty thousand deaths in America from this one source, preceded in general by great suffering, sorrow and expense. Why do we not do something about it? But we are! Yes, we spend *annually* in cancer research in all the universities and medical research institutions (not including the recently established National Cancer Institute) a little less than the receipts of one major football game! For the current "War of the Tyrants" we spend 300 billion dollars of public money. For the war against cancer, the greater man-enslaving enemy, one-millionth as much!

Of course we need more research men and more ideas for the fight on cancer, but both will be forthcoming if ample funds are supplied for numerous full-time research positions in leading hospitals and medical schools. The cancer investigators must also explore the possibilities in neighboring fields, with no more worry about wasted efforts and money, in following faint trails, than we now worry about the expense of exploratory scientific researches for the present war. Four hundred American lives a day justify an expensive fight.

3. Hard arteries and the associated consequences stop in mid-career too many important workers in business, in the professions, in public service. A career of high nervous pressure is tough on the circulatory systems of those men who respond too generously to the call of duty and opportunity. As yet no real defense, but worried sermons from harassed wives and family doctors. More than half a million Americans die each year from disease of the circulatory system; and if you are over ten years of age, more than half of you are to die of these maladies, unless something vigorous and drastic is done about it. How much do we spend in basic research on the ravages of this enemy? Practically nothing at all!

4. Tuberculosis is still a most deadly enemy to those important people between the ages of twenty-five and forty years, notwithstanding modern progress in care of the afflicted; and also unsolved as yet is that other respiratory affliction, the expensive common cold. We have already grimly saluted the goliath influenza, and in a sense we are sparring for time, hoping to load our slings with some new effective ammunition.

5. Nephritis buries nearly a hundred thousand Americans a year. We lose the lives, but save a little money, for again there are negligible funds earmarked for research on kidney diseases.

6. But perhaps our greatest enemy among the major maladies is the group of physiological and psychological factors that disorder and spoil the human mind. Some of the many forms of mental diseases are already yielding to the various therapies. Epilepsy is pretty well under control. The depressions are better understood than formerly and that new knowledge is a necessary preliminary to successful treatment. The plight of the schizophrenics is no longer a hopeless mystery. The alarmingly large number of neuropsychiatric cases coming out of the armed forces (approximately one half of the total discharges for disability!) emphasizes dramatically the great importance of fighting this ruthless enemy, fighting hard for the sanity of the race, fighting, also, for the prolongation of mental power. With the mind senile, a virile body is rudderless; the centenarian's closing days should be bright, but not balmy!

Without further documentation, let us acknowledge the need for a concerted national attack on the recognizable causes of Premature Senility—the ailment that sooner or later will be of personal interest to practically all of us. Would you like to have a tenth of one per cent of your future federal income tax devoted to the elimination, or at least the great diminution, of the ills that prematurely weaken and destroy? That's all the cash it would require. There is a highly sponsored National Science Fund with committees that could administer grants for medical research.

Would you participate in a national "one meal fast" to pay for research on the major maladies? If all took part, and contributed the equivalent, about fifteen million dollars, we would win both happiness and years, because several deadly diseases would die.

Universal literacy is a goal the average citizen can help attain; longevity is a problem chiefly for the specialists to handle. I would like to isolate another conflict in which everybody can take part. We can name it the Fight against Cultural Uniformity. It would take long to elaborate fully the need for this movement, and longer to specify sample procedures in detail. A brief summary must suffice for the present.

Life, I have found from experience, is the dullest thing one can live; and it would be vastly duller but for variety among the people one meets, diversity in their habits, manners, and intellectual reactions. To maintain and increase the diversity, to the end of enhancing the degree of satisfaction with life and the opportunity for intellectual and artistic growth, requires immediate fighting against real foes.

I assume you all realize that a world state is in prospect for the near future—geologically near—perhaps not in this decade or generation, but soon. By world state I mean the organization of practically all terrestrial men. The quality and degree of the internationalism of the coming world state should be examined. Aviation and radio, and similar modern arts, force the unification. A world-wide economic association, that encompasses all states that do business, seems so inevitable, ultimately, that one wonders why we go ahead trying half-way substitutes. And the unified political organization that will include all the present nations, super-nations, and sub-nations, is also rapidly developing, notwithstanding some stubborn and perhaps bloody resistance, and in spite of the temporary dominance by political cartels of major powers. The world state, however, will come long before Pluto returns to Aries, two centuries from now. That is my prediction. Some would probably predict that the political unity will be obtained and stabilized before the end of the present century; and others may hold out for a thousand years of strife and political individualism. But we all would probably agree, if put to it, that either we sink to savagery, or rise, perhaps slowly, to a world unity, however drab this last prospect may appear.

But is a world-wide common culture an inevitability of the new order? I believe not. A political inter-nation and a universal economic agreement need not lead to a sterile uniformity in the cultural world. Local languages perish slowly; and many local customs can persist because they are linked with local geography. Hills, valleys, deserts, mountains, the seashores, and the various belts of latitude will remain, notwithstanding the ingenuity and deviltry of man. And the climates, soils, waters, and scenery in these various types of geographical localities can and will have a basic effect upon the folkways of whatever inhabitants choose to remain, or are permitted to remain, in such relatively specialized domains.

That localized cultures change slowly (whether of man, plant, or animal), and with some care might be made almost permanent, is demonstrated in nearly all the large countries of the world by the present social and domestic differences in contiguous groups. Only if the world maintains these cultural human varieties, these endemic cultures, will it provide natural opportunities for evolution. I mean evolution in taste and art, as well as growth in industry and natural science. For it is well known to the biologist that a uniform population changes but little.

We must, therefore, oppose, if I am right, those tendencies that are working toward standardization and cultural homogeneity. We must strive against chain-thinking and acting. As one contribution to this objective, the small community must continue to live, to play, and to think by itself. It must be our fervent hope that the local American community will grow in cultural self-sufficiency, not only for the delight of the people in being doers rather than in being done for, but also because of the importance of endemic cultures to general welfare.

We are quite willing to give over to international organization the responsibility of the larger political and economic management, if such delegation means peace, efficiency, and progress. But let us work toward a colorful new world through the development and maintenance of local customs.

And it is high time we got started on a program of deliberate cultivation of community life. For we must admit that much of our thinking and feeling has now been delegated to others through the predominance of chain newspapers, broadcasting syndicates, and movie theatres. It is alarming to realize how many of us hear the same news commentators, the same comedians and music analyzers; and to realize how many of us read the same comic strips, eat the same food, announce the same profound observations on passing events. Unconsciously we have delegated our thinking, our feeling, much of our tasting, and even the intonation of our trite comments, to a few score of men and women, mostly mediocre, who have gained access to our broadcasting studios, our newspapers, and our food-jobbers.

All of this standardization and mental goose-stepping has gone so far that escape seems impossible. Chain-thinking has linked our brains. The radio serves simultaneously ten millions of us parrots. Originality of thought and expression have been sold down the river for the joy of hearing a hot gag.

Possibly we cannot retrace and start over; and most of us would not want to; we are mentally lazy, and too willing to follow leaders. But can we not counteract a little the deadening effect of this national centralized domination by emphasizing the activities and the contributions of localized natural communities?

Some of us have cheerful hopes about the more methodical encouragement of craftsmanship in country, town, and city. Already much is done, and it has been tremendously worth while. Art and science often blend in the craftsman. Local group work in the sciences is an entering wedge for community collaboration. In less than two years, the club membership in Science Clubs of America has increased 600 per cent, and now we have some five thousand active groups that are doing things, with a maximum of inspiration and a minimum of centralized direction. Much of the work of the Science Clubs, in the schools, and among the adults, deals with the biology, topography, and archaeology of the community. Such interests foster pride in the community. Before long, many counties or valleys are going to be proud, for instance, that the herbarium of the home county valley is well known and has been related to the flora of larger regions and to the community's horticultural and agricultural problems.

The rise of small symphony orchestras and choruses, and the growth of amateur musical performances, are signs that we can develop genuine loyalties to the striving home folk, and really enjoy them, notwithstanding the superior excellence that could be ours by the turning of a dial. These musical movements, especially when they can be related to the folk songs and folklore of the community, are a challenge for all of us who recognize the importance of the independent life of the community, and the heightened likelihood of the evolution of taste and intelligence is homogeneity is opposed.

The responsibility for the fight against cultural uniformity devolves finally on the community itself. The local leaders should not leave to remote practical politicians, or to uniformity-producing centralized broadcasters and writers the shaping of the future, either for the individual or for natural social areas. In this connection it is well to study the goals and triumphs of our Tennessee Valley Authority, the progress of the community theater movement, the future of Frequency Modulation broadcasting as a new tool in community development, and the spirit and procedures in those few American communists that already stand out as individualistic.

In the contest against deadening centralized manipulation of the minds and mores of the people, we have a happy fight that all can join; and, paradoxically enough, nationally working artists and scientists can help to incite diversity and direct the development of local cultural projects; the radio and press syndicates can assist in spreading the gospel of community self-sufficiency.

I come now to the fourth scheme for combat. The three proposed struggles for community individualism, for useful and happy longevity, and for universal literacy, are all of interest to the working scientist, and in these days of widespread social responsibilities these great problems should be at least irritating to the social conscience of everyone. But my next, and final, proposal is directly in the line of the professional interest of scientists and scholars.

I may be obsessed, or suffering from anthropocentric illusions, but I cannot escape the feeling that the human mind and human curiosity are significant in this world—even perhaps in the cosmos of geological time and intergalactic space. With this impression (or illusion) that the mind is the best of us, and the best of biological evolution, I cannot escape (and neither can you!) the feeling of a responsibility to glorify the human mind, take it seriously, even dream about its ultimate flowering into something far beyond the primitive muscle-guider and sensation-recorder with which we started.

It is, possibly, naive to deduce that the acquiring of knowledge and sensations, and the judging and correlating of such knowledge and sensations, is a human necessity; and also rather elementary on my part to observe that in the short time that the race has had for reasoning about things, it has been impossible to learn much. But pointing out such elementals gives us background, and perhaps modesty. We are still embedded in absymal ignorance of the world in which we live. Relative to the total surmisable extent of knowledge, we have advanced very little beyond the level of wisdom acquired by many animals of long racial experience. We are, to be sure, no longer afraid of strange squeaks in the dark, nor completely superstitious about the dead. On many occasions we are valiantly rational. Nevertheless, we now know "how much the unknown transcends the what we know." The unrevealed seriously oppresses us as men of mind. We are tyrannized by the unanswered, more than by governmental restraints or social taboos. This tyranny shadows the brightness of the explored realms of nature and of man. To use again the battle cry of the cornered, the war slogan of the ardent social fighter, "Let's do something about it!" Let's exorcise these tyranical spirits of the surrounding darkness. Let's declare a methodical and elaborate war on the Tyranny of the Unknown.

Already, in our quiet way, most of us are mildly opposing this tyranny. We do it in our spare time, sometimes apologetically, and sometimes with rather brave and hopeful sanction by our institutional chiefs. But, of course, except when we have war-urgency assignments, we do not let the fight get in the way of comfortable living, routine duties, and our ordinary neighborliness.

Now please do not get the impression that I have with large words simply advocated the continuity of research. That is not at all what I have in mind. I said, *"a methodical* and *elaborate* warfare on the Tyranny of the Unknown."

It is time we quit treating the acquisition of new knowledge as the luxury of a special class, or as the precursor to profit-making new gadgets or nostrums. It is time we quit leaving the explorations beyond the horizons to the long-haired professors and the workers in a few government bureaus. The contest against the Tyranny of the Unknown is a job for the people of America, if they are going to keep up in the competition with other countries. It is their job if they are planning to participate in either the practical or the idealized progress of mankind. It should be the concern of the businessman, the labor union, the fruit grower, and the farmer. This war can be an affair for the Popular Front, if the proper leaders properly blueprint the campaign. Practically every community in America that can produce an ensign or a sergeant could produce a boy or girl who could be trained to effective, even if modest, service in these new armies. Once the attack is briefed and the skills are sharpened, finding new facts and checking old interpretations are no more difficult than making an automobile from blueprints, or managing intership communications, or unravelling the mysteries of an income tax form. Yes, certainly the increase and spreading out of scientific and other research is a national concern, and, in making this a national issue, respect for fundamentals need not be sacrificed to the utilitarian. But how far we now appear to be from an aggressive governmental interest in this particular fight!

Some months ago (April 19), the British House of Commons debated "Sir Granville Gibson's motion calling for a bold and generous government policy towards research. . . . The debate itself ranged over a wide ground, and no scientific worker could desire to have so many of his points made more effectively or trenchantly than was done in its course. The case for adequate remuneraiton of the scientific worker was pressed even more forcibly than in the House of Lords debate [the preceding July], and the arguments on this point . . . would have seemed incredible in a Parliamentary debate ten or twenty years ago. The credit for this change of outlook must be attributed in no small measure to the work of the Parliamentary and Scientific Committee, the reports of which have done much to prepare the ground for the debate." I am quoting from *Nature* for May 6, 1944. To me it seems that that particular session of Parliament was epochal, not only for science in Western civilization, but for the British Empire.

Can you imagine our own Congress sympathetically and understandingly considering research as a national issue of high importance? Almost inconceivable, you would say; and unfortunately there are many smug scientists entrenched in Washington who would say "Thank God, Congress is keeping out of this." And I fancy that among you here are many who have been shaking your wise heads and saying "Nonsense. This enlisting of the common people in a war against the unknown! They can't understand research, to say nothing of doing creditable creative work. They would only mess up the profession."

How transparent you are! Even if you won't think straight and thoroughly, you can, we grant, do some research; but by denying the ability of ordinary mortals, you are merely indecently strutting your own foolish personal vanity. (You understand, of course, that I do not mean you personally; I am referring to the man who sits beside you.)

But fortunately only a few of you feel that the increase of knowledge is for the elite alone. To the rest of you, I go on to say that we are not yet ready to open the systematic national or international campaign against Enemy Number One. There must be several preliminary preparations, all of which take labor, thought, and time:

1. The selling of the crusade to the average citizen, through skilful propaganda (or education, if you prefer that term). We must dis-

cover appeals to the imagination and the emotions. We need systematic research on the methods of creating understanding and sympathy for research. We must discover the way to make the fight against the Tyranny of the Unknown a national issue, like good government and individual freedom.

2. Local and national governments must be convinced of the merit of this cause, and of the importance of increasing official support for the mobilization of appropriate forces and resources.

3. The schools and colleges must recognize the importance of producing critical scholars and creative thinkers. They must see that one man fired with curiosity is worth much more than two solid and stolid citizens.

4. The Design for Fighting must be prepared. It must be outlined and published to the collaborating workers. It may require the leadership of a new institution—an Academy of Intellectual Exploration.

It is this fourth preliminary preparation of the fourth proposed national combat that I shall now commit to your further contemplation.

Among the citizens of America are several thousand who are the special agents of the people and of the civilization they compose. These agents or servants of society have been trained, mostly at the expense of the public, to know what is known and what is not.

It is to these several thousand servant-thinkers that I now put the question I set out to ask: Would it be advisable and possible to list *in extenso* for each of scores of special fields of knowledge the unsolved problems immediately before us?

The question requires elaboration. The proposed listing would be for technical specialists chiefly, and less directly, or only incidentally, for the non-specialist. Probably in all fields there are many able workers who for one reason or another do not have a grasp of neighboring areas, or even a full picture of their own subject. These workers may be young and as yet inexperienced, or they may be isolated scholars, away from discussion groups or large laboratories and libraries. Important fields often are thoroughly comprehended by only a few intense workers who have favorable temperaments and opportunities and for such fields even highly competent investigators in adjacent areas are unacquainted with the problems solved and unsolved.

Everybody gains if the obstacles to enriched research—namely, the unclear pictures—are removed. Would not such detailed clarification through problem-listing be worth doing, for the benefit of beginner and professional? What are the immediate unknowns, practical and theoretical, which might be subdued, if they were fully recognized and if there were an abundance of thinkers and resources available, in, for example, mammalian anatomy, in atomic structure, in the amelioration of insanity, in regional planning, in pre-Cambrian stratigraphy, in the history of printing devices, in the phylogeny of the anthropoids, in aeronautics, group tensions, meteorology, and the use of leisure?

An example might clarify my inquiry. Suppose I should take some weeks or months for the careful and thoughtful listing of the unsolved problems in the field of galaxies and related sidereal organizations. I could start my report with a "cushion" introduction to ease, perhaps, the shock of the subsequent technical presentation of scores of unanswered questions, pregnant puzzles, observational and mathematical desiderata. My picture might be amazing because of its succinct presentation of what is really known, and more amazing for what is not known but seems potentially knowable. My listing would perhaps provide a guide to the immediate researches of myself and my colleagues. It would give the inquisitive philosopher an indication of the situation in practical cosmogony, and an intimation of the hopes for the future increase of our knowledge on space and time. It would give to the physicist, if he were curious or needed the knowledge for his own work, an indication of the astronomer's contribution to the interpretation of space, time, entropy, and atomic aging. To the young astronomer and the isolated worker I hope I might provide incitation, and increase his personal efficiency. Such a listing of galactic unknowns should be out of date in a decade. It should sow the seeds of its own speedy obsolescence, if it were successfully done. But would it be worth doing, as a part of the great blueprint? Personally, I believe it might be highly useful, especially if it were reinforced by a general listing by half a dozen astronomical experts of the unknowns (which are perhaps knowable) in all astronomical and astrophysical fields. And I am still more confident of the usefulness of such designing, if it is also properly done in other subjects, scientific and otherwise. (For many years in the Harvard Observatory we have informally made similar surveys, to our considerable advantage; and spottedly they have been made elsewhere, as in geology—with what success, I should like to know.)

I visualize a great impetus to research through the methodical listing of the problems. Several biologists and physicists have told me that the project should be both feasible and highly profitable in their own fields. No doubt in economics, sociology, administration, philology, and the like, it would be possible to prepare essays on the detailed problems that should be attacked. The evaluation of the unknowns would perhaps become more personal and possibly less valuable, the farther one goes from the physical sciences. But surely, in almost any field of the humanities or social sciences, there would be gain from an attempt to tell the world which unknowns (that time and intense study might liquidate) now seem most to bedevil the advance of knowledge and constructive theory. The various surveys could not well be homogeneous in formulation or presentation; and they need not be, to attain the desired end.

In practice, there would be the aforementioned danger of narrow or personal views of the major and minor problems. And another handicap is the natural one that a scholar, forgetting his social responsibility, might hesitate to show his cards; he might want to reserve the brightest battles for a test of his own personal valor. He might be selfish. In the natural sciences a worker's connections with industrial research might stop him from presenting in detail some problems that have commercial value.

And among you, no doubt, are those who, having not watched closely the modern trends of investigation, may worry that a bold public listing of the unknowns, and of the possibly obtainable goals, would spoil the spontaneity of the true investigator, who gropes and finds and refinds; or you may worry that in some way a survey would tend to regiment the young. Perhaps we should not teach calculus to the young, but let them figure it out as Newton did! If there is anything whatever to this argument of "Better leave us all alone," I believe that the compensating gains would far outweigh the disadvatanges. The lone wolf investigator, with a string and an old corkscrew, has pretty well disappeared, except from romantic journalism; and one surmises that in the humanities and perhaps in the social studies, a frank, full statement or two of the basic problems, made by competent scholars, might discourage a lot of second-rate rag-chewing.

The campaign to list systematically, and with bibliographic reference, the visible problems in a special field will require the judgment and ingenuity of a leader in that area. Of this I feel sure. The work cannot be done by popular science writers. The big question then arises—is the light worth the candle? Are the survey of the field, the guidance and acceleration of other investigators, worth the time and effort of the expert? You will need to help him find the answer. You will need to ask yourself whether we in America are still young-minded enough, and socially minded enough, to work in this way for a common national and human good. Or should we leave dreams such as this to those national groups where there is no hesitation in making five-year plans, social, economic, scientific, and where the plans are carried out and progress made premeditatively toward the transformation of a nationl culture?

Whether or not the American Association for the Advancement of Science, or the National Research Council, or any other organization of scientists or scholars in America, thinks well of an organized, expedited, and national program of research. I do want you to think well and hard of the necessity that has come to American scientists and other scholars of taking an active part in searching for intelligent substitutes for war. America and Americans will never retreat to the prewar sociology and economics; need we retreat to the prewar indifference of the academic specialist to the national social problems? To me that seems impossible, especially for scientists. There is not an officer or private among the ten million in our armies and navies who does not know that we are winning this war, not alone through personal valor, but very largely because of our superior engineering and scientific activities. We would be devoid of vision if we did not take advantage of these new contacts with practical science and new respect for it.

We would be shortsighted if we did not proceed now to build up a national understanding so that, with the tools of science and cultural education, we can undertake holy wars here at home against our non-human enemies, which have long held us down physically and frustrated our social evolution.

EDUCATION AND THE PEOPLE'S PEACE [8]

ALEXANDER JERRY STODDARD [9]

Superintendent A. J. Stoddard of the Philadelphia schools, and Chairman of the Educational Policies Commission, gave this address at meetings of the American Association of School Administrators in New York, Chicago, Kansas City, in the spring of 1944, at the National Education Association meeting in Pittsburgh in the summer of 1944, and before meetings of many state and local teachers' associations, as well as lay groups in various sections of the country during 1944-45. The address "was prepared and delivered to help promote support for the establishment of an international office of education as a part of the peace machinery." [10]

The address is an example of a closely reasoned, fully developed argument, with statement of the problem, clear definition of terms, and a solution and program of action specifically laid down. The linking together of the parts, the frequent use of questions to further the analysis and provide assent to his suggestions, the frequent summaries, and the plausible specificity of the entire discourse invite study of it as an example of effective argumentation.

Dr. Stoddard has long been recognized as one of the outstanding speakers on educational themes. He has heartiness of delivery and platform geniality as adjuncts to his logic.

Some day this war will end and we shall try again to make peace. But this war will not end as the last war ended. That was a war along a big ditch, or a whole maze of ditches, on a continent. This is a war in the streets, over the fields, on the beaches, in the passes, on the snow-capped mountains, in the trees, in the fox-holes, in the trackless jungles, in the seas, and in the skies. *This is a world war.*

The last war stopped suddenly with an armistice that began at a split second after eleven o'clock one morning in November. But the end will be different this time. It may take days or even weeks to throttle down the present gigantic war machine. Whether the end comes in a certain second, or during a certain

---

[8] By permission of Superintendent A. J. Stoddard. Text furnished through the courtesy of Dr. Stoddard and the Educational Policies Commission.
[9] For biographical note see Appendix.
[10] Letter from the author to the editor of this volume, May 23, 1945.

day, or month, or year, what a glorious time it will be when the boys come home again!

Millions will dance in the streets for joy. They will tear up a billion books and shower the confettied paper down from skyscrapers and the clouds; they will tie any tin cans that are left to any old cars that may still be able to run and drive hilariously down the main streets of a thousand towns and cities; they will dash wildly along the marching columns of returning soldiers throwing roses in their paths and kisses to their lips. They will shout and sing until the piled up chorus of ecstacy mounts to the throne of God!

Other millions over the world will stand numb and silent, too tired to weep, as if in a trance, unable to comprehend. Whether laughter or tears or merely dry-eyed staring into space, never before will so many have welcomed the end of a war, and never before will so many have suffered and lost so much to make it come true.

The war will end, but will peace come? That is now and ever has been the one supreme question confronting mankind. Always the human race has made the fatal assumption that peace naturally follows war, that the alternative to war is peace.

What *has* followed every war throughout the ages? Not peace but an armistice which should not be confused with peace. An armistice is a suspension of hostilities, a period when the machinery of war, the arms, stand still for a while. The time may be short or long during which an armistice lasts. But *peace* has the characteristic of permanence—it abides as do faith and hope and charity. We must not make the mistake of assuming again this time that the inevitable consequence of war is peace. In the 1920's and '30's we thought that a peace had been made. We did not realize that we had run out on what we had made, and it turned out to be only one more in a seemingly endless series of armistices.

At one of the great national educational conventions immediately following the First World War, one of the speakers cried, "Imperialism as a world force is dead! The funeral was but yesterday." The United States Commissioner of Education declared, "All isolations, splendid or otherwise, are gone forever."

Who would dare think otherwise? Had we not just finished winning the war to end war?

And then almost before the boys of World War I had folded their uniforms and stored them away with moth balls and sacred memories, the American people ran out on them. Almost before they had looked up their old jobs, we turned back to our classrooms, our offices, our newspapers, our politics, our pulpits, our automobiles, our golf courses, our night clubs. Heaving a gigantic sigh of relief that the war was over and peace had come we turned our backs on the past and sometimes even upon those who had won the war for us. We did not mean to be unkind; we were just tired of war and we assumed that peace had come because the war had ended.

Complacency is the most baffling and challenging of all human traits or attitudes. Complacency is a way of retreat, a smug excuse for justifying inactivity, a self-satisfying alibi for lack of concern about meeting and solving problems. In science, complacency takes the form of superstition, unwillingness to study cause and effect, objection to experimentation, and belief in all the varied forms of witchcraft, ancient and modern. Complacency seizes upon the highest motives of religion and distorts them into intolerance, dogmatism, and bigotry. In the area of social relationships, complacency leads to self-patriotism, with its evil offspring of chauvinism and of international, racial, and class hatreds. In human psychology, complacency breeds a satisfaction with the status quo and, like the opiate, lulls the human organism into a sweet tranquility in the midst of strife and storm.

Complacency has caused every war that the world has known. Complacency is the arch-foe of peace. The glib generalization that we always have had war and therefore we always shall have war and the philosophy of the survival of the fittest are the answers of complacency to the universal call for the brotherhood of man and a world dominated by good will.

As Francis B. Sayre said, "What the Allied victory in 1918 did achieve was to give statesmanship an unparalleled opportunity at the conclusion of the War to work out and apply solutions upon which a stable civilization could be built. Military victory gave us our chance, but we lost it." We failed to realize once more that peace, like freedom, must also be bought at the price of blood, sweat, and tears. What a deadly tragedy it is to assume that peace can be bought for a lesser price!

Everyone admits that *war* involves marching and fighting and dying, but it is assumed altogether too often that *peace* means quiet, rest, sleep, and pleasant dreams. But this is *not* true. Peace is no less dynamic than war; peace has its marching heroes just as has war; peace involves conflict and struggle just as much as war; peace requires red blood just as much as war.

If we are to have peace, we must win it even as war must be *won*. We could call a million witnesses to this fact. The lives of the saints and all who have died that we might have life more abundantly present a mountain of testimony that the ways of peace call for as much real courage, noble sacrifice, high adventure, and a willingness to die for a cause as does war. Even after the world rids itself of war between nations, there will still be an endless succession of battles to establish a decent world and the kind of man qualified more fully to live in that world.

The mistaken assumptions that men make, either consciously or unconsciously, get them into their worst troubles. Witness the pay-off on the idea that the world always has had wars and therefore always will have wars. Several of the world's greatest leaders have told us time and time again that this present war could have been prevented. They have even placed their pointing fingers on the dates and places. Wars are not like the inexorable succession of events that we call the seasons. Wars are made by man. They represent a stage in our development as human beings. Wars are the effect of causes and these causes are within the control of man.

No matter how much we may vary in conviction on the question of the prevention of war, nothing but gain can come from striving toward that hypothesis. It is one of those bets where only the size of the winning is in doubt. Who knows what generation of men and women may live in the last days of war? Maybe we are that generation—the last generation before peace.

I offer no pet formula for ending war. Probably there is no one formula and certainly there is no simple formula. Possibly all that any one person can do, especially if he feels very humble when contemplating the word "peace," as I do, is to suggest some steps or make some proposals that may seem to reasonable men to offer some hope. And none of us should hesitate to do that. Ending war is such a complex and vast problem that everyone, everywhere, should accept the responsibility of trying to help.

We have finally succeeded in waging a war so vast that all people in the world are either in it or affected by it. Maybe we can conceive a condition under which all the people everywhere might contribute toward peace. A people's peace may be possible if a people's war is possible.

In this spirit that we may soon have one more chance to try to end war, and that this may possibly be our last chance, and feeling that we all have a right and a responsibility to try to postpone or prevent another war, I submit these propositions for your consideration:

1. The people must roll up an avalanche of demand that cannot be denied that their voice be heard in making the armistice and the treaties of peace after this war. The framework of the treaties should provide a long enough armistice so that the processes toward peace might get rolling.

2. Some means must be provided for an intensive and yet worldwide battle on intolerance, selfishness, superstition, and exploitation so that cooperation, intelligence, respect for human personality, and the spirit of live and let live have a chance to become the bases of human relationship. Some machinery must be provided through which the forces of good will—burning now feebly, now brightly, but always burning—may find expression.

3. Finally, there must be provided an agency, or complex of agencies, that will wage an eternal battle for peace, even when individuals who planned and constituted the agencies are gone. The watchtowers must be manned continously and eternally, even though the people may sleep.

Never before were as nearly all the people engaged in any war as they are in this war. There is scarcely a home anywhere in our land from which the long ribbon does not reach out to some camp here or there, to some battle front in the faraway nooks and crannies of the world. We are all paying for the war in one way or another. Our play has lost much of its zest, our laughter its ring, our smiles their optimism, and even the entertainment of our night clubs has a metallic ring to it. How can life be the same with our young men gone! But we who have stayed at home are all fighting too. Never before has the expression "home front" had the deep significance that it has today. This *is* a people's war and we the people are *all* in it together.

Why then should we not have a right to think of the possibility of a people's peace? What is meant by the expression, "a people's peace"? Two things are meant most of all. One is that the people themselves shall have as direct a part as possible in the making of the peace. If we are to think again in terms of peace commissions and peace treaties, there should be as many channels as can possibly be provided through which the thought of the American people on the peace can be made articulate.

There should be many types of people, representative of different racial backgrounds, different religious points of view, different national streams, different economic levels, different social status, as can possibly be gathered together on commissions.

There should be included men who know what it means to labor with their hands or at a machine, for who pays more for war than such men? Businessmen should be included, for who knows more than they do about the terrible waste of materials involved in war?

There should be educators on the commission because who knows more about the cost of war in human life than those who give most of their lives that others might live more abundantly? Religious leaders should be on the commission because will peace ever be made except by men who believe that there was some power before they were, is now, and will be after they are gone?

And there should surely be one or more women on the commission! And I know to whom I am speaking! If the women of America allow this peace treaty to be made by a commission without a woman on it, they will almost deserve to go on generation after generation going down into the valley of the shadow to give life to boys to be killed on battlefields! You say, "Mr. Speaker, don't you understand, there never has been a woman on a peace commission in the history of the world?" Sure, I know it, and that is why I am suggesting that there ought to be one!

The politicians and the statesmen will be there too—I have no doubt of that—and we have no objection to their being there if they are not the only ones who are there, as has been the case up to now.

But, someone will ask, "Do these laymen, do we the people know enough to help make a treaty of peace?" The record on peace-treaty making up to date does not provide convincing evidence that some other formula of peace-treaty personnel might not be given a trial! And it might not be amiss to suggest timidly that the pages of history are not exactly strewn with brilliant records of peace-treaty making. We can at least be comforted by the possibility that the whole people are not likely to commit any more colossal blunders than have the professional peace makers of the past.

It is not suggested that the commission charged with making the armistice or peace after this war should be composed of delegates or mere representatives of the various groups, large and small, powerful or weak, that make up our society. But there should be enough laymen on the commission who will insist that the people be heard, who will provide channels through which the people *can* be heard, who will be able to understand the people as they do speak, and who will insist that the interests of the whole people in the peace shall be paramount to any partisan or selfish interest or any minority or majority part of society.

What kind of peace treaty do the people want at the close of this war? Certainly the treaty must give attention to minority rights, certainly it must prohibit colonial exploitation, certainly it must heed the cries of the naked, the hungry, the destitute. Problems of international economics, national boundaries, balance of power, buffer states, freedom of the air, control of airports, location of gasoline stations—all of these and an almost infinite number and kind of other problems and issues must be dealt with fearlessly and fairly and, even to a degree, unselfishly.

But the people of America have one paramount interest above all others in this treaty—we want a treaty that has some decent chance of being kept, and kept for a long time. We want this to be a treaty of peace—not just an armistice. The philosophy, the supreme objective, the over-all criterion that must be applied to every part and to the treaty as a whole must point to the maintenance of peace as the supreme goal of every stage in the deliberations. Peace should be the one and all upon which the treaty is to be judged and approved.

We must do a lot of getting ready for peace. The armistice should be long enough to make this preparation possible. Any abiding peace will involve machinery, and there must be adequate provision made for that machinery to be established and put into action. There may be much in favor of a long armistice and plenty of time to make the peace treaty.

Do we really mean what has been said, that this war is to end with unconditional surrender on the part of our enemies? If so, the armistice should not be an agreement between two contractual parties, one party the victors and the other the vanquished. It should rather be a definition of terms or specification of directions for the surrender of our enemies. Any making of terms with the leaders of Germany or Japan will be an insult to every boy who has died in this war and a defalcation on the honor of every decent citizen of every Allied Nation! So it will be with the treaty of peace itself.

It is very likely that for many years there will not be responsible governments in the enemy countries with which to make treaties. So it is proposed that both the terms of the armistice after this war and of the treaty of peace to follow should be beween and among the Allied Nations and not between the Allied Nations on the one side and the enemy peoples on the other side. Why should we degrade ourselves by trying to enter into treaties or contract with what we know as Germany or Japan? Would we be fools enough to believe again that the subscription to a treaty by any of their present leadership or any that might be substituted for the purpose would be anything other than a travesty and a joke?

No, this time our treaties should be between those who fought together on the same side. They should define clearly the rights and responsibilities of the respective Allied Nations in building the peace. And the guaranties and binding promises should be definitions of the part that each Allied Nation should play in establishing the new day. In time it may be possible that nations that may again be called Germany and Japan will grow far enough beyond national adolescence to be allowed to assume a share as adults in building the brave, new world that is to be. But they should be required to win that right and to demonstrate that their people have developed to that stage and have established control of the means of their own actions before they are given the right to be accepted as parts of the family of nations.

Cooperation, tolerance, and respect for human personality were mentioned as essentials of peace and as if they are attainable human characteristics—and they are. Despite our wars, there never was a time in the history of the human race when so many people everywhere hated bigotry, superstition, exploitation of the weak by the strong, ignorance, filth, disease, and hunger as much as do people today. Never before in the history of the world have the faith which makes us strong and the hope which makes us brave been the possession of such a large proportion of the human race.

But the best treaty of peace that could possibly be devised is after all and at its best only a formula for action, a chart for steps that must follow. The means must be provided for carrying out the formula, for giving effect to the plan of action. Treaties of peace do not implement themselves; peace must be won continuously and perpetually or it is not peace.

It is not within the province of this address and certainly not within the prerogative nor the ability of the speaker to define or even suggest a complete formula for peace. But two proposals can be offered with a certain degree of assurance.

First, it may be possible for the treaty of peace by the Allied Nations to contain a memorandum of understanding on the subject of peace. This may be somewhat in the nature of a philosophy of human relationship and the respective roles that national and international organizations might play in maintaining peace. Second, there might be a further memorandum on education as the basis for peace. The kind of education that enables men to achieve the status that we call freedom should be defined clearly.

Then as part of the treaty itself should be established an international office for education, charged with the responsibility of giving continuing reality to the educational philosophy of the memorandum.

Many organizations and groups and individuals are now advocating the establishment of an international office for education. While it is difficult to choose any as more important than others, it is suggested that no one should regard himself as informed on the subject unless he is familiar with:

1. The activities of our own professional organizations pointing up in *Education and the People's Peace,* published by the Educational Policies Commission, and in the objectives and program involved in the N.E.A. War and Peace Fund Campaign.

2. The program of the Liaison Committee for International Education, representing more than thirty educational organizations, and its publication, *Education for International Security,* presenting the highly significant proposals resulting from the now famous Harpers Ferry meeting last September.

3. The organization and objectives of the *American Association for an International Office for Education,* composed primarily of laymen interested in a program of action that will result in the establishment of an international office for education.

4. The pamphlet series on *Post-war Problem Analyses* by the Universities Committee on Post-war International Problems in association with the World Peace Foundation.

The proposal for the establishment of an international office for education as a part of the peace machinery and procedure is not made with the assumption that this would be any more than one of a large number of steps that must be taken. Many other agencies of peace must and will be established if there is to be any real hope for preventing or postponing the next war. Many individuals and groups will contribute toward establishing these agencies.

The *teachers of America* will have met their responsibility, at least in large part, if they are instrumental in, first, bringing about the incorporation in the peace treaties of a recognition and definition of the role of education in the armistice and the peace, and second, the establishment of a permanent international office for education to carry out that role, not only in the days immediately following the cessation of hostilities but, far more important, down through the years to come. The critical period in the life of the peace will come after most of us here today are no longer active in the cause.

The accomplishment of these two objectives will not be an easy task. After the last World War we cried out for peace and the establishment of a machinery to effect peace. The school administrators of the nation met in Chicago in the spring of 1919, and the N.E.A. met in Milwaukee that summer. Speakers at these conventions voiced the universal happiness that the war had ended and pride in the great military victory that had been won. They said, "In the crisis of war the schools were a mighty agency for victory" and they pledged the continued devotion of public education in the days of peace to "true Americanism and world democracy." The president of the N.E.A. rejoiced that during the war "education has become the chief concern of the statesmen of the world."

These conventions passed strong resolutions in favor of the League of Nations and urging "the creation of an International Commission on Education . . . to provide for a world education in the elements of democratic citizenship and the extension of the privilege of education to all people and to all classes."

And then what happened? Even the educators of America, who of all people should know better, left the peace to the caprice of chance. Even we who were the teachers of history and the writers of the history textbooks turned our back on the inexorable lessons of the past and devoted our attention to school building construction and per capita school costs—highly significant but relatively unimportant problems as the events of the last five years have demonstrated. How long, oh, how long will it take us to learn, how many millions must die to teach us, that peace will come only as the result of careful planning followed by determined, continuing, and consecrated action which recognizes peace as the supreme objective of mankind whatever price may be the cost?

It should be remembered at this point that all organizations and groups did not run out on the last attempt at peace. As a part of the Treaty of Peace there was established, to the surprise of the world at large, the International Labor Office. We may well study the forces and conditions that made this action possible. More important still is the history of the activities of the Office since that time. In the month of April 1944 there was held in Philadelphia the International Labor Organization Conference at which some forty countries were represented and participated. It is significant that no similar international educational convention has been held, although one could yet be planned and held before it is too late. There is little doubt but that labor will be represented at the next peace table. Nor is there any doubt that labor will again be included in the peace treaty.

In fairness to education it should be mentioned that in 1922, four years after the Armistice, the League of Nations, of which we were not a part, did create a Committee on Intellectual Co-operation. However, this committee had "neither the authority nor the resources to make a direct attack on the problems of general education as these relate to international relations." [11] But let it be said to the credit of this committee that it did demonstrate that intellectual cooperation on an international basis was both possible and practicable. The story of its accomplishments and the stories of other attempts made by individual countries toward international educational cooperation should encourage us not to be afraid to dare on even a greater scale to write an international office for education into the coming treaty of peace.

Let us consider more fully what should be the nature of the memorandum on education proposed as a part of the treaty of peace.

First, the memorandum should express the faith of the Allied Nations in the role that education can and should play in establishing and maintaining peace.

Second, it should be made clear that the Allied Nations have faith that no political and economic provisions of the Treaty can and will be effective without parallel and continuous educational programs of action to support the peaceful reorganization of the world. Resolving the problems of national sovereignty and empty stomachs will not alone guarantee peace.

[11] Quotations not otherwise credited are from: National Education Association and American Association of School Administrators, Educational Policies Commission. *Education and the People's Peace*. Washington, D. C.: the Commission, 1943.

Third, the memorandum should condemn the use of education within nations to promote chauvinistic attitudes and activities or the use of the schools as the agencies for developing highly nationalistic faith in war as the means of solving international questions.

Finally, the memorandum should provide for the establishment and maintenance of an international office for education as a part of the treaty of peace.

While all nations might be equally represented in the organization of which the international office would be the agency, the financial support should be relative to the varying economic resources of the nations included.

The international office should not be delegated *administrative powers* over education in the several nations, but should have specific research, publicity, and advisory powers and functions given in the memorandum. It should not be an integral part of any political or other organization of nations that may be established as agencies of the peace machinery. While it should be officially constituted and maintained, it should be entirely free to appraise and criticize, if necessary, the very international power that created it.

The duties which would be performed during the period of readjustment immediately following the war would be related to reconstruction of education in the conquered and devastated territories and would vary considerably from the long-term program that would evolve as peace became established more securely.

What functions should be performed by this international office for education? This is a question that cannot be answered fully here. I refer to the publications formerly mentioned for a more comprehensive treatment of this question. But these suggestions can be made here!

First, one of the immediate postwar functions of the office should be to help bring about the educational disarmament of Germany, Italy, and Japan. In an address in October 1942, Madam Chiang Kai-shek said:

When victory is won we should see to it that the evil which has brought about the world catastrophe is attacked at the source—in the schools. If the minds of millions of children had not been poisoned in the schools of Germany, Italy, and Japan, their young men would not have allowed themselves to be led like beasts to the slaughter for a cause contrary to all ideas of humanity and justice.

To fail to give our attention to the schools of these nations would be as foolish as to leave their armament factories in good working order. All Axis teachers who functioned willingly during the war should be removed and forever barred from teaching again. New teachers from *within* these countries must be found or trained or both. If this cannot be done at once, let the schools be closed until teachers can be provided from within those countries to do a trustworthy job. For the peace of the world it is better that the children of Germany and Japan have no schooling for a while than to have their minds twisted again as they were in the years before and during this war.

The task of planning for the reeducation of the youth and younger men and women of Germany and Japan will challenge the best efforts and the ingenuity of the international office for years to come.

Second, the international office for education should promote in every way practicable the "complete academic freedom and complete academic responsibility and accountability for the teaching staffs of schools in all parts of the world."

Third, the international office for education should provide assistance and leadership in many fields of intellectual cooperation. It should "stimulate and encourage the fraternal contact of scholars, librarians, and teachers in various fields of specialization. It should assist in the international exchange of research materials, technics, and findings in the natural sciences, the social sciences, and the humanities. It should encourage international art exhibits, music festivals, and dramatic performances."

Fourth, the international office for education should have "one clear-cut appraisal function. It should be solemnly charged with the duty of studying textbooks, syllabuses, and teacher materials, used or proposed for use in any and all countries, in order to determine whether their effect would be aggressive, militaristic, or otherwise dangerous to the peace of the world. *All nations* should agree to refrain from such instruction and to submit copies of all textbooks and teaching materials to the international agency. As a permanent policy, the United Nations should not ask any of the defeated nations to submit to any educational appraisal which they are not prepared equally to undergo."

Fifth, the international office for education should define minimum standards of education recommended for all peoples everywhere. It should make available expert advice for countries desiring to improve their educational systems. Proper precautions should, of course, be taken to safeguard the pride and independence of action of the nation receiving these suggestions for help. It should provide, on the proper basis, for the exchange of students, teachers, and representatives of all areas of culture. It should offer definite factual instructional materials at every level in all school systems concerning the history, culture, psychology, and problems of other peoples, and concerning the world organization and problems of international relations—such materials to be factual and free from recrimination.

Sixth, the international office for education should maintain a "division of radio and visual aids in education, with the presentation of occasional multilingual radio and motion pictures direct to all the schools of the world that wished to listen or look."

To summarize, this international office for education should not only attempt to prevent and remove the causes of war, but even more its efforts should be devoted to the development of those positive educational philosophies and procedures which make for international good will. As the powerful forces of technology draw the peoples of the world closer and closer together, they must, if they are not to die, learn how to respect the right of the peoples of the world to be different from one another. It may be that we can learn how to understand and appreciate one another's differences in place of hating everyone who is different from us. Our salvation lies not in trying to remove all the differences among the peoples of the world or killing those who are different from us, but rather in learning how to live peacefully together in spite of our differences.

The increasing officially documented evidence concerning the atrocities perpetrated by our enemies in this war has shocked us beyond expression. It is difficult to keep from despising our enemies. Their contemptible acts make us realize that peoples at war sooner or later in the way they fight and in their relations toward their enemies reflect the stage of civilization which they have reached. While we may despise Germany and Japan for the way they act in war, let us not hate them. If we allow ourselves to hate them we may drag ourselves down to their level. Let us rather hate the conditions that led to this war. Let us resolve that we *will* prevent those conditions from arising again.

What can *we do* to help bring the peace that may come? Three things at least:

First, insist at the proper time in not a few but in tens of thousands of petitions to the Department of State, to the President, and to the Senate that any arrangements for world order after the war, as defined in the treaty of peace, shall specify the role that education can and should play in establishing and maintaining peace.

Second, insist in these petitions that there be established an international office for education whose function it shall be to give effect to the role of education in the peace.

Third, support *even with money* the promotion of strength and organizational machinery within our profession to give the schools a dynamic voice at the peace table and a part in the arrangements established to keep the peace.

Fourth, demand that our great national professional organizations provide continuously through the years some method of reporting at least annually to the teachers of America on the subject, "How goes the peace?" Possibly an annual monograph on the subject would be desirable, informing the world concerning plans and procedures for keeping the peace and the progress, or lack of progress, that is being made year by year. Also, through our professional organizations and as individual citizens, we can demand of every person who represents us in strategic public office, state or national, that he give an accounting on the question, "What have you done to prevent the coming of another war?" before he asks our support for reelection.

Who will be the last generation of war and the first generation of peace? Those who are worthy so to be. We pray for peace, but are we willing to be and to do what it takes to make peace? We know that wishful thinking will not bring peace. We wait for some power above us to give us peace, while knowing full well that peace cannot be given to or had by a people who are not prepared to pay the price that peace entails.

We *might* implore some power greater than we to give us the grace to cherish peace, the humility to believe it is possible for us, and the will to discipline ourselves so that we may win it. Peace in our day is not so much a matter of fate and chance as it is a matter of deliberate planning and the determination to make the plans come true whatever may be the cost. The last generation of war will be the first generation of people big enough to reach for peace and strong enough to attain their reach.

The supreme test of an educated man, the supreme test of a cultured man, the supreme test of a civilized man is the manner and extent of his care about what happens after he has gone. It will be relatively easy to make an armistice for our time, for 1945 or 1950. Are we ready, able, and willing to take the steps that will be necessary and likely to insure peace in 1975 or 2000? To what extent are we willing to sacrifice now that they may have peace then? Will the story of 1975 be that of 1918 and 1944 over again?

In 1944 there is nothing for us to do but pay the price that unqualified victory entails. It is a bitter price to pay when we think of what we might have done but did not do in the generation preceding 1944. Too little and too late is a new expression but an old, old story. Must history always go on eternally repeating itself? The fact that it has not done this in so many areas of human endeavor gives up hope.

The time to determine the question of war and peace in 1975 is now. It is not too late to prevent the next war now. When and if the next war comes, it will again be too late to prevent it. Then the only choice that will be left will be to fight through to victory, just as now, regardless of the cost. Americans have never been afraid to take a chance, to try a course of action even though failure may be one of the alternatives. An abiding peace will be established some day only if those who lived before were willing to have enthusiasm for and confidence in whatever next steps they were able to take. The teachers of America are confronted again with the choice between complacency and determined action in the direction of peace.

We shall never have peace in the world until we are willing to pay for it with sacrifices at least somewhat comparable in size with those we are willing to undergo to win war. We will pay hundreds of billions of dollars to win the war. Are we willing to pay at least tens of billions if necessary to win peace? Until we *are* willing to do so we *shall not have* peace. How long will we continue to refuse to pay what peace costs and then continue to pay many times more for the war that might not have been?

The only way in which we, the teachers of America, can ever partially amortize the debt which civilization owes to those who have already died and who are yet to die in this war is to establish now in our day at least a *beachhead for peace* that has a decent chance of being extended beyond our time.

I call upon my fellow teachers of America to resolve here tonight that from here on out, as long as we live—both personally and as members of a great, marching dynamic profession—the supreme objective of our lives will be to do what we can in our day to build a beachhead for peace that may be some later generation will consolidate into a permanent peace!

AMERICA AND RELIGION

THE CHRISTIAN CHURCH—WHAT OF ITS FUTURE?[1]

John D. Rockefeller, Jr.[2]

This address was delivered on January 31, 1945, at a dinner given by the Protestant Council of the City of New York. The dinner marked the launching of a campaign to raise $800,000 for the Protestant Council and its six constituent organizations.

The Council was formed to "promote the coordination of different religious and welfare activities in New York, looking toward better co-operation among the churches and agencies of the Protestant faith and a more effective affirmation of the great principles of that faith."

President Roosevelt and Governor Thomas E. Dewey both sent messages to the dinner endorsing the campaign. Speakers included Newbold Morris, representing Mayor La Guardia; Charles H. Tuttle, chairman of the campaign; Dr. Henry Sloane Coffin, president of Union Theological Seminary; and Mrs. Frank L. Babbott, a leader in Protestant women's activities.

Interdenominationalism and religious idealism were long established principles preached and practiced by John D. Rockefeller, Jr. Throughout his boyhood and later in his student days at Brown University he followed the strict religious tenets of his Baptist family. According to the record at Brown, he "did not drink, smoke, or gamble," and seriously applied himself to studies and religious activities. After 1899 he took charge of a men's Bible class at the Fifth Avenue Baptist church, New York City, which, under his tutelage, became well known throughout the country. In 1910 he began to study and accept the "new theology and broader denominational cooperation." He emerged as "a most ardent religious progressive and advocate of the inter-church movement."[3]

From 1914 to 1918 he was active in United War Work campaigns and in movements to unite the churches in war and other work. Some of this thinking may have been influenced by Dr. Harry Emerson Fosdick, the Baptist clergyman of Union Theological Seminary. Mr. Rockefeller sponsored Mr. Fosdick when the latter became pastor of two New York

[1] Permission to reprint through the courtesy of Mr. Rockefeller, and of Mr. Burnham Carter, New York City. Text is from the pamphlet furnished by the speaker. For text see also the *New York Times*, February 1, 1945.

[2] For biographical note see Appendix.

[3] Current Biography: 1941.

zhurches that merged into the First Presbyterian Church of New York City. Later the pastor, under attack from the Presbyterian prebytery, resigned, and became pastor of the Park Avenue Baptist church. Mr. Rockefeller was one of the sponsors and heavy contributors to the erection of the large Gothic Riverside Church, costing some $4,000,000, built expressly for Dr. Fosdick.

Mr. Rockefeller's address was an expression of his consistent religious philosophy and his record of activity for church unity.

Not many weeks or months had elapsed after this World War began before there was presented to our vision a picture so horrible it hardly seemed that it could be true. It appeared that hell had broken loose and that millions of evil spirits had become incarnate in human form and were going about the earth committing atrocities and acts of cruelty beyond belief. In the face of this awful picture it is not strange that we should ask ourselves the question: "Has Christianity failed?"

But there is another picture which the war has painted. In it we see millions of men and women who are exemplifying in their daily lives, in the most commonplace fashion, unselfishness, generosity, loyalty, self-sacrifice and other characteristics and qualities which command the admiration of the world. Unconsciously these people are reflecting Christ's spirit. Whether they know it or not, their inspiration comes from the God of all good deeds. Yet many of them have no church affiliations, for too often the church seems to them quite apart from their lives, an institution which has little contact with or understanding of their problems, since theirs is fundamentally a religion of deeds, not of creeds; expressed in life, not in words.

We turn from this picture with a glow in our hearts and say with renewed faith, "Christianity has not failed; churches may have failed, but not Christianity! For never in the history of the world was Christianity a more vital force in human life than it is today."

In the presence of this great host of noble men and women, who, generally, have not come from the church, although directly or indirectly all have been more or less influenced by it; who, many of them, have faced death, have lived a life far worse than death, have sacrificed their all, we ask, "What of the future of the Christian Church?"

Will these people, after the experience through which they have passed, find in the church generally as it exists today the recognition, the association, the guidance and the inspiration which they need and have a right to expect? Regretfully we must answer, No. For the church has learned too little to speak their language, to think in terms of their environment, to meet their needs.

If this be true, one of two things is inevitable. Either this unorganized spiritual force which is silently dominating millions of lives will not be conserved, or the church must have a new birth if it is to meet this marvelous opportunity and great human need.

Let us picture, for a moment, this reborn church. It would be the Church of the Living God. Its terms of admission would be love for God, as He is revealed in Christ and His living spirit, and the vital translation of that love into a Christlike life.

Its atmosphere would be one of warmth, freedom and joy, so sympathetically and distinctly manifest as to attract and win into its fellowship all those who are striving to live useful and worthy lives. It would pronounce ordinance, ritual, creed, all non-essential for admission into the Kingdom of God or His church. A life, not a creed, would be the test. Its object would be to promote applied religion, not theoretical religion.

As its first concern it would encourage Christian living seven days a week, fifty-two weeks a year. It would be the church of all the people, of everyone who is fighting sin and trying to establish righteousness; the church of the rich and the poor, the wise and the ignorant, the high and the low—a true democracy.

Its ministers would be trained not only in the seminaries, but in some form of work-a-day life, so that they might acquire a personal knowledge of practical problems. Thus they would live in closer touch with humanity, would better understand and sympathize with human difficulties, and would exert their influence as much in living as in preaching.

Would that I had the power to bring to your minds the vision as it unfolds before me! I see all denominational emphasis set aside. I see cooperation, not competition. In the large cities I see great religious centers, wisely located, adequately equipped, strongly supported, ably led, inspiring their members to participation in all community matters. In smaller places, instead of half a dozen dying churches, competing with each other, I see one or two strong churches, uniting the Christian life of the town; great economy in plant, in money, in service, in leadership; the money thus saved available for home and foreign mission.

I see the church, through its members, moulding the thought of the world and leading in all great movements. I see it literally establishing the Kingdom of God on earth. Shall some such vision as this be realized? Upon the answer to that depends in large measure the future of the Christian church.

We have been considering the demand for a united Christian church from the point of view of the world's need for Christian leadership. There is another motive, not less compelling, urging the churches on toward that end. It is the necessity for cooperation if the forces of righteousness are to triumph in the eternal warfare against the forces of evil. The forces of evil, united on the common ground of their nefarious interests, are ever ready for aggressive action; while the forces of righteousness, although seeking a common goal, are frequently so preoccupied with their individual interests and petty differences that their attack upon the common foe is too often belated, and not infrequently scattered and ineffective.

Christian men and women must come to see that only by the fullest cooperation and the setting aside of emphasis on nonessentials can the many branches of the Christian church, standing together on the common ground of Christianity, hope for victory in this great warfare against sin.

When Christ came into the world, He found the church loaded down with ritual and formalism. Every minutest detail of daily life was regulated by religious enactment. In the eyes of the church the most religious man was not he who gave to the poor, who helped the unfortunate, who was unselfish, meek and lowly, but he who kept most punctiliously every jot and tittle of the law. The *spirit* of religion had been displaced by empty form.

To establish spiritual righteousness in the world, to build up an internal rather than an external religion, to emphasize the responsibility of the individual to his Maker, was Christ's mission on earth. Few and simple were the forms He set up or sanctioned, such as baptism and the Lord's Supper, but they were wonderfully beautiful and filled with sacred inspiration.

Baptism is an ordinance of profound symbolic meaning. Christ Himself was baptized. He did not, however, make baptism a condition of church membership. The Lord's Supper is a sacrament, also rich in symbolic beauty. In this day of materialism, far be it from any true follower of Christ to minimize the spiritual value of these symbols; rather should they be preserved and guarded.

On the other hand, in the face of the great problems of sin, of evil and of spiritual hunger which confront the world today, can we imagine that, were Christ to come to earth again, He would regard the observance or non-observance of these and other ordinances and individual beliefs, or the manner in which they are observed, as of sufficient importance to justify controversy among His followers, and their separation into rival factions? Can we fancy Him giving His approval to such a course, resulting as it does too often in relaxing the warfare against the common enemy, sin, and in causing men to forget their common responsibility, the needy brother?

Let ordinance, creed, ritual, form, Biblical interpretation, theology, all be used to enrich worship, and to bring the believer into a fuller understanding of Him Whom we worship, as each individual or separate church may find them helpful toward that end. But God forbid that they should ever, any of them, divert the attention from, or be regarded as a substitute for, that personal, spiritual relation between the soul and its God which is the essence of true religion.

God forbid that they should be allowed to cause divisions among the followers of Christ or be set up as barriers at the door of any branch of the Church of the Living God.

What the world craves today is a more spiritual and less formal religion. To the man or woman facing death, great conflict, the big problems of human life, the forms of religion are of minor concern, while the spirit of religion is a desperately needed source of inspiration, comfort and strength.

I plead not for a modification of form, but for its subordination to the spirit; not for the abolishing of ordinance and sacrament, but for their voluntary rather than obligatory observance.

As we face, then, the world's need of great spiritual leadership, that humanity may be brought into vital, daily relationships with a living God, and that all the forces of a righteousness may be united in an eternal warfare against the forces of evil, we ask again the question: "What of the future of the Christian Church?" This is the answer which I give you:

If the various divisions of the church as it is organized today catch the vision, have the breadth, the tolerance, the courage, and, setting aside all non-essentials, all barriers, will stand upon the bedrock principles of God's love and Christ's living spirit, "not satisfied," as Donald Hankey has said, "until the church is the church of all good men and women, until all good thoughts and deeds are laid at the feet of the Lord of all good life," the Church of the Living God will come into being, ushering in a new era of Christian unity.

What an opportunity! What a privilege! What a duty! In God's name I ask, does anyone dare let it pass?

What I have said thus far is the substance of an address which I made during the First World War. The convictions then expressed have only grown upon me with the passing years. I voice them tonight with even greater assurance as to their timeliness and present applicability. The bitter lessons taught by World War No. 1 have not saved us from the vastly greater conflagration of today. Nor has the church during the past quarter-century put its house in order and with unity of action opposed the advancing hordes of the godless.

Today, as always, humanity craves the substance of religion; while churches too often emphasize the form. Men have long looked to the Christian church for religious training and spiritual inspiration that they may acquire both the knowledge and the will to make wise decisions and to take right actions in their daily lives. Their natural craving for religious guidance must not be repelled by alphabetical lists of denominational churches and agencies, when what they seek is so fundamental, and sectarian differences are so superficial. Rather should they be able to get in any Christian church, whatever the style of its architecture or the shade of its belief, the spiritual wisdom and strength which they need to fit them for practical daily living.

To say that no progress has been made toward the resolving of denominational barriers during this quarter century would be unjust to various groups which have made earnest efforts along those lines and definite advance. But to say that any broadly conceived, concerted movement to that end is under way, which is generally participated in, would be equally untrue.

Toward religious cooperation more progress has been made, although it has been too slow and too little. The movement in the interest of which we are gathered here tonight gives promise of significant possibilities in cooperation. Six interdenominational groups representing Protestant interests in Greater New York have come together in the Protestant Council of the City of New York to confer together, to plan together, to finance their needs together, and let us hope increasingly work together. The relationship is as yet only partially developed. There are many questions to be worked out. How successful and effective the organization may become, time only will tell. But granting its weaknesses and imperfections, like the Dumbarton Oaks conference in the political field, it is a start in the right direction. It is an important experiment in religious and welfare cooperation on a significant scale.

On Feb. 3, 1943, the cargo transport Dorchester was torpedoed at 1:15 A.M. and sank within twenty-five minutes in iceberg waters, ninety miles from Greenland. As the ship went down, four chaplains—one a Catholic, one a Jew, two Protestants—were on the deck encouraging the men and passing out life belts. When there were no life belts left, they took off their own and gave them away. These chaplains were last seen standing arm in arm praying.

As they went to their death, united in the service of their common Lord, so let us, the living members of the great religious faiths they represent, go forward, shoulder to shoulder, as a united army, fighting evil, establishing righteousness, brothers in service, sons of the one God and Father of us all!

THE INESCAPABLE CHRIST [4]

BENJAMIN E. MAYS [5]

President Benjamin E. May, of Morehouse College, gave this sermon first during the Lenten Season, at the Albee Theatre, Brooklyn, New York, on April 6, 1944. It was delivered under the auspices of the Brooklyn Church and Mission Federation. Here is an example of an evangelical, highly exhortatory type of sermon, composed and delivered during a special season for a specific audience. It has the textual background, framework, structure, illustrations and other motivating details that reflect the strong convictions and sermonic purposes of its author.

President Benjamin Mays is one of the outstanding Negro speakers and educational leaders of this country. A native of South Carolina, he was graduated from Bates College (Maine) with high honors and was elected to Phi Beta Kappa. He was a prominent intercollegiate debater, president of the Debating Council, of the Bates Forum, was winner of first prize in the Sophomore Declamation Contest, was class day orator, and was elected to Delta Sigma Rho, honorary intercollegiate debate society. He won other honors in public speaking and debating at Bates. He received his M.A. and Ph.D. degrees at the University of Chicago. From 1934 to 1940 he was Dean of the School of Religion at Howard University, Washington, D.C. Since 1940 he has been President of Morehouse College (Atlanta, Georgia).

In December 1944, he was elected as the first Negro Vice President of the Federal Council of the Churches of Christ in America, an organization representing twenty-six million protestants of twenty-five denominations. According to *Time* (December 11, 1944, p. 74), he is a "firm believer in education and patience as cures for racial discrimination."

Some of his skill in public speaking lies in his experience and ability in written composition. He has several books to his credit as well as a long list of published articles in educational and religious periodicals. He has delivered addresses at more than seventy colleges in the United States. Notable was his "The Crisis in Race Relations: Which Way for the Church and Democracy?" at Vassar College on September 29, 1944. He was an American delegate to the World Y.M.C.A. conference at Mysore, India, represented the United States at the Oxford Conference on Church, Community, and State, 1937, and at the Youth Conference at Amsterdam, Holland, in 1939.

[4] Reprinted from *The Pulpit*, v. 15, no. 6:123-5, June 1944, through the courtesy of President Mays and of the Christian Century Press.

[5] For biographical note see Appendix.

Text: "Pilate saith unto them: What then shall I do unto Jesus who is called Christ? They say all: Let him be crucified." Matthew. 27:22.

For nineteen centuries Jesus has been a disturbing element in society. And for nineteen centuries the world has been trying to get rid of Jesus. We don't like him! We don't like him! We don't like him! Nineteen hundred years ago a man by the name of Pilate raised a baffling question, and what turned out to be in subsequent years an embarrassing question—"What shall I do, then, with Jesus which is called Christ?" Almost two thousand years have passed by, yet the question is more pertinent in 1944 than it was then. What shall I do with Christ? What shall the nations of the world do with Christ? For nineteen hundred long years the world has been trying to answer the question, What shall I do with Christ?

Yielding to the demands of the crown, Pilate thought he could save himself and get rid of Jesus by allowing him to be crucified, by washing his hands, saying, "I am innocent of the blood of this just man." But no man can get rid of Jesus by washing his hands and no man can get rid of Jesus by shirking the responsibility which God has placed upon him. We may not always rise to the demands of the hour; we may not always do that which we know we ought to do; we may even excuse ourselves as did Pilate saying, "I am innocent." But no man can ever get rid of Jesus that way. Nearly two thousand years have passed, but the world has not forgiven Pilate. It looks upon Pilate as a man in high office who had the mind to see what was good to do and who had the power to execute the right but who lacked the moral courage to do what he knew was right. And to see the light, to know the good, to perceive the true and not to be able to follow them—and to see the high road and take the low road—that's a calamity, that's a lost soul.

And herein lies the tragedy of our time! We are confused and baffled today not because we do not know the right path, not because we are imbeciles in the mind or morons in the head, but because we are imbeciles in the heart and morons in the spirit. Never before in the history of the world have we developed so many brilliant minds, never before have we unearthed so many vital scientific facts, never before have we made so many physical improvements and brought so much material convenience to the world; yet we are more bewildered today than at any time in the history of the world—primarily because we lack the moral courage to do with our hearts and hands that which we see with our minds. No! It isn't more light we need, as important as light is. It isn't more truth that we need, as important as truth is. It isn't more scientific data, as important as scientific data are. It is more Christ, more courage, more spiritual insight to act an the light we have. Pilate had plenty of light—so much light that he admittted that he found no fault in Jesus; but he lacked the moral courage to live up to the light he had. No! We cannot get rid of Christ by washing our hands, nor by shirking our responsibility, nor by protesting that we are innocent. Jesus is real and he cannot be dismissed with a wave of the hand or a shrug of the shoulder.

Fearing the crown, Pilate sacrificed an innocent man in order to save himself. Too often we sacrifice the right because we fear the immediate consequences of our actions. Right decisions frequently involve physical suffering and the temporary loss of position and prestige. Pilate, no doubt, would have exonerated Jesus if he could have believed that no harm would befall him.

How typical of our day and generation! We know enough about the physical and ethical consequences of sin to live better and purer lives. We know enough about the cruelties and injustices in race relations to approximate the Kingdom of God in that area. We know enough about war, its cause and consequences, to abolish it from the face of the earth. But we aren't willing to take the moral leadership and to run the risks involved in that leadership. Like Pilate of old, we fear the consequences to us if we do what we know is right. We may shirk our responsibility at these points, but we cannot get rid of Jesus that way.

There were others who sought to get rid of Jesus by crucifying him. Both the Romans and the Jews used this method. To the Romans Jesus was a traitor, unpatriotic, disloyal. To the Pharisees he was a heretic. To the Sadducees he was a menace to correct procedure. To the zealots he was a coward and spineless. To the members of his own family he was out of his mind. When asked by Pilate, "What shall I do with Jesus which is called Christ?" they cried out, "Let him be crucified." They thought that they could get rid of Jesus by nailing him to a cross. But Jesus could not be so readily dismissed. Three days after the crucifixion the news got abroad that he was alive. The discouraged disciples who had gone back to their former occupations rallied around him again. A few days later Peter stood up at Pentecost and said that this same Jesus, "whom we have crucified," had been lifted up and made both Lord and Christ. Out from this experience sprang the Christian Church to hold up the name of the crucified Christ. And all the way from Stephen to the martyrs of the church in Germany, people by the millions have gone out to do battle for the Lord. We could not get rid of Jesus by nailing him to a cross. "Truth, crushed to earth, shall rise again."

Other devious methods have been used in our attempt to get rid of Jesus. Some have reduced him to the role of a man— a good man, probably better than the average—yea a prophet, but nevertheless a man. They would classify him along with the great prophets of Israel—Micah, Amos, Jeremiah and others; but beyond that they would not go. They would attribute to him no peculiar role of Savior except the fact that he has indicated one of the ways that may lead to salvation. Therefore his way of salvation is to be taken no more seriously than the ways advocated by other great reformers. There is absolutely nothing divine about him. What he achieved in his life and person, you and I can achieve. But you cannot get rid of Jesus by making him a mere man. Any honest man who sets out to follow Jesus the man and goes with him through the Sermon on the Mount, goes with him through Gethsemane and the cross, with him at the Resurrection, will end up by saying: "My Lord and my God."

There are others who try to answer the question about Jesus by arguing that he is out of date, that his ethics and ideals were probably all right in days when a minority group found itself unable to resist with the sword the oppressive hands of Rome.

The way of Jesus is the way of the weak and the coward, not of the strong and the militant. A weak people, unable to take what it wants, may find it to its advantage to preach a gospel of love and to insist that non-resistance is the only way of life. But only the weakling would subscribe to the ethics and teachings of the Man of Galilee. The ethics of Jesus is the ethics of the underprivileged. Jesus was all right in his day, when life was simple and when civilization was far less complex than it is now. But he lived two thousand years ago when social and political conditions differed widely from those that exist at present. How foolish it is to take the principles and teachings of Jesus enunciated over nineteen hundred years ago and try to make them applicable to modern problems when science has revealed to us a new world of which Jesus never dreamed! We might as well do as the humanists and the communists do—try to lift ourselves by our own bootstraps and sing with Langston Hughes—"Good-by, Christ." But we cannot get rid of Jesus by calling him out of date. It is true now and it will be true a million years from now that the hope for man lies in the direction which Jesus has indicated.

Some have tried to get rid of Jesus by denying his historicity. These argue that no such man as Jesus ever lived. The story of Jesus is a myth, a creation of the imagination. But we cannot get rid of Jesus by denying his historicity. Even if we could prove that Jesus never lived, experience testifies that the things attributed to him are real and inescapable.

But perhaps the most subtle and devastating answer to the question, "What shall I do with Christ?" comes from modern customs and practices. In 325, at Nicea, we made Jesus a God, of one substance with the Father. At Nicea, at Constantinople, at Ephesus, at Chalcedon, and in all subsequent creeds up to the dawn of the twentieth century, we dealt with Christ primarily on the basis of creeds, dogmas and rituals. And the ethical and moral teachings of Jesus were never written into the great creeds of Christendom. On the basis of the creeds, it seems possible to get into the Kingdom of God and hate your brother. We get rid of Jesus today by praising his holy name. We write scholarly books concerning him. We compose beautiful hymns to him;

we sing inspiring songs about him. We paint beautiful pictures in adoration of him. We meet on Sunday and through the week to offer long prayers to him. We send missionaries to foreign lands to convert the heathen and teach them how to worship the God revealed through Jesus Christ. We defend his divinity and split hairs over what he did or did not teach. We magnify his name by erecting beautiful churches. We spend millions upon millions of dollars in the construction of cathedrals in order to make the house where God dwells beautiful, entire and clean. I have seen and worshipped in St. Paul and Westminster Abbey; I have seen Westminster Cathedral and bowed my head in adoration in Notre Dame. I have seen the Cathedral of Cologne and I have seen some of the great churches and chapels of America. And when I see what is happening in the world today, I know we are trying to get rid of Jesus by building costly churches and by praising his holy name.

We talk glibly about the Prince of Peace. We sing fervently, "Joy to the World; the Lord is Come," "Silent Night," "Hark the Herald Angels Sing," and "It Came Upon the Midnight Clear"—and yet, as we sing, we prepare for war. We go out to build the best army, the finest navy, the most durable airplanes, and each nation puts its chemists to work to discover the most deadly gases. The national debt may soar sky high, depressions may come and depressions may go, unemployment may mount on wings, and slow starvation wages may take thousands to their graves, but the preparation for war must go on. And when the war comes, we bless it in the name of Jesus. We call it a holy war, and we ask God to join us in our holy crusade to help kill other men who are his children and our brothers.

Let us hear the conclusion of the whole matter. We cannot get rid of Jesus. The only way to get rid of Jesus is to accept him in mind, in heart and in soul. Jesus represents God and God is the absolute—not man, nor race, nor economic nor political systems—but God. And whenever man in his arrogance and pride sets himself up as the absolute, he will be beaten to the ground.

I think it was Napoleon who said: "The more I study the world, the more I am convinced of the inability of force to create anything durable. Alexander, Caesar, Charlemagne and I have built empires. But upon what did they depend? They depended upon force. But Jesus Christ built his empire upon love and until this day millions will die for him."

Everywhere we turn we meet this man Jesus. When our anger gets out of control and we would enjoy inflicting the death blow upon another, we hear Jesus saying to us "It is not enough not to kill; you must not get angry." "Love your enemies, bless them that curse you, do good to them that hate you, and pray for them which despitefully use you, and persecute you; that ye may be the children of your Father which is in heaven."

Jesus will not let my conscience be at ease. When we take advantage of the poor, the weak and the helpless just because they are poor, weak and helpless, we meet Jesus. He speaks softly but convincingly to us, telling us that when we take advantage of the helpless we take advantage of God, that when we hurt man we hurt God, that when we rob man we rob God, that when we kill man we kill God. Everywhere we turn, we meet this man Jesus. He will not let my conscience be at ease. He haunts me in my dreams, he disturbs me in my business. When man lets his passion get the better of him and he lusts after a woman, he meets Jesus there, saying: "He who looks after a woman to lust after her has committed an adultery already in his heart." Everywhere I turn, I meet him. He will not let my conscience be at ease. When we condemn and criticize others for their shortcomings, we hear Jesus saying to us: "He who is free from sin, let him cast the first stone." Everywhere I turn, I meet Jesus. When we are inclined to exercise our prejudice against a member of another race, we meet Jesus there. He tells us that a certain man went down from Jerusalem to Jericho and fell among thieves; and that it was a member of another race who came to his rescue, setting forth the eternal fact that he who responds helpfully to human need is your neighbor.

Everywhere I turn I meet this man, Jesus. He will not let my conscience be at ease. When we would build peace on war and an economic system on injustice, he whispers to us, "You can't do it that way." "Execpt the Lord build the house, they labor in vain that build it. Except the Lord keepeth the city the watchman waketh but in vain." Throughout the ages, man has tried to do it otherwise, and throughout the ages he has failed. There is something in the nature of the universe which says you can't do it that way and thrive.

God has decreed through the resurrected Lord that the world will never be what it ought to be until we develop an international ethics and learn that the fear of the Lord is the beginning of wisdom. As long as France distrusts Germany and Germany France; as long as Italy looks with suspecting eyes upon England and England cannot rely on Italy; as long as Japan has no confidence in China and China none in Japan—there is going to be war. And as long as we take revenge to the peace table rather than forgiveness, there is going to be war. And a billion armies will not be able to keep the peace. If all the world should turn communist tomorrow, fascist tomorrow; if all the world should develop democratic governments tomorrow—our social and economic problems would be essentially the same, if there were no radical change of heart.

Our trouble is not economic. It is not political. It is ethical and moral. The world is suffering today from spiritual and moral bankruptcy. And no political or economic system can permanently endure unless it is basically ethical and essentially moral. God has decreed that he is the absolute—not man, not races, not nations, not political and economic systems—but God. As long as man moves contrary to these laws, God will beat him down. Kingdoms will rise and fall, races will degenerate, economic system will collapse until we learn that the fear of the Lord is the beginning of wisdom.

Approximately nineteen hundred years ago, a Jew of Palestine hung on a cross, dying between two thieves, because he dreamed a dream—that all men are sons of God, and when we hurt man we hurt God. Some blessed day a stupid world will rise to the divinity of God and acknowledge Jesus as Lord. Then the nations of the earth will know that armies and navies, battleships and machine guns, airplanes and submarines will never bring peace to a suffering world. And that the acquisitions of political, material and commercial powers are not permanent possessions, but are as "the vapors of night. They fade and die in the morning of reality."

"What shall I do then with Jesus which is called Christ?" The only answer is: Accept him—in our minds, in our hearts, in our wills, and in our souls.

NOT TAPS BUT REVEILLE [6]

BERNARD IDDINGS BELL [7]

Dr. Bernard Iddings Bell, preaching canon of St. John's Cathedral, Providence, Rhode Island, gave this sermon before his congregation on Sunday, May 27, 1945. It was presented as a Memorial Day address.

This sermon is a model of homiletic construction and composition. The text, announced at the outset as in the conventional sermon, becomes basic to the thought. The problem is clearly and emphatically presented; the two divisions of the solution are each given proportionate treatment; the most important idea is reserved for the concluding sections. Applications to individual and community association are constantly made. The illustrations and reinforcing details are copious and timely. The author is alive to contemporary problems and saturates his talk with such thinking. Exegetical warmth and religious conviction pervade the discourse and lift it above a merely sociological-political discussion.

Familiar doctrines and injunctions are expressed in original language. Stylistic dullness and conventionality are absent. Notable is the flexibility of the movement. An elaborated pattern of parallel phrasing is interspersed with short sentences. The oral quality throughout is apparent.

Dr. Bell has been in wide demand as a lecturer or visiting preacher before college and university audiences in the United States, Canada, and England. His voice, presence, and compositional power combine to rate him as one of the more effective sermonizers of his denomination.

Text: "Ye shall know the truth and the truth will make you free." St. John. 8:32.

Gradually we begin to emerge from the strain, the horror, of world war. Hitlerism has been crushed; the danger inherent in his ambition to rule the earth according to a vicious ideology and to force all nations into slavery to his mad purpose, is a danger that exists, thank God, no more. Nazi Germany is prostrate, impotent for further evil. There remains Japan to be conquered, restrained from a similar dream of forceful domination. There is also Russia, which joined us in crushing Germany and may possibly join us in reducing Japan but which itself is isola-

[6] By permission of Dr. Bell. Text furnished through the courtesy of the author.

[7] For biographical note see Appendix.

tionist, self-centered, unwilling to compromise its desires and ambitions for the sake of getting on with the rest of the nations, demanding to do as it pleases with the Balkans, with Poland, with the Baltic lands generally, beginning to demand the right to do as it pleases with Iran, Turkey, Manchuria, China. But despite the great endeavor still necessary against Japan and despite the enigmatic threat that emanates from Russia, it is true to say that an exhausted world now begins to fall into a panting peace. We shall soon have a breathing spell from war sacrifices, war destruction, from risk of violent death to our loved ones. We are thinking with a new urgency, as we ought to think, of the millions now in uniform who will be back home again—all of them eventually, except those who can never return. These soldiers, sailors, marines, we at home helping them, will have won the fight, a magnificent fight against diabolically dangerous external enemies.

We begin already to relax, and to long for more relaxation, into the easy ways of peace. We have been patriots long enough, we think, some of us *say,* now let us get on with life as it used to be. We are free once more from danger; therefore let us enjoy ourselves.

Brethren, this is a great and dangerous folly. The tasks of patriotism are not over for us, will not be over when treaties of peace are signed and the armed forces return. The patriotic duties facing us Americans are not so quickly discharged; they are entering now into a different phase, a more difficult phase than that we have had to get through in the years of war, harder in themselves and harder still because there will be in these coming years no thrill of combat against an alien foe to key us up to sacrificed endeavor. There will be reaction from excitement of battles fought or read about into the relative monotony that goes with certain grim, drab labors. There remains the labor necessary for reestablishing home relationships too greatly strained, and for too long, by the sundering of husbands and wives, of parents and children, of friends and neighbors; the labor involved in finding jobs for 7,000,000 veterans plus at least 35,-000,000 more persons now engaged in war work; the labor of reconversion to peacetime production, a long and expensive and nerve-racking business; the labor of carrying a national debt so large as to be unpayable in a hundred years or more, of paying interest charges on it up to $7,500,000,000 annually; the labor of carrying a national tax load which cannot possibly be reduced from the present onerous rates; the labor that must accompany a firm resistance to pressure toward an American totalitarianism, toward interference by the government with the rightful liberties of self-respecting citizens; the labor that comes from facing the plain fact that a large part of our states, cities, counties, towns, school districts, are either bankrupt or precariously near it and urgently in need of greater local taxes; the burden of disillusionment as we realize that the Atlantic Charter and the Four Freedoms were moonshine fed us to pep us up for war, with no root of reality in them, and that "the peace" is only the same rickety make-shift of a thing that we had before 1939, constantly threatening to collapse into new wars for our children to fight. There are other labors beside these; one could go on for an hour, enumerating them; but these will do for now.

Yet people talk of ease, of the possibility to relax our patriotic efforts. Have we Americans lost our minds, that we indulge in wishful thought about easy days to come?

No, brethren, the patriotic task will not be over when the guns cease firing. The war has been the prelude, the overture; now the drama *begins*. All that we shall have won when the peace is signed is a chance for America someday to arrive at greatness. In imagination we may see that day, as Abraham foresaw the day of Christ, and be glad of opportunity to build America, a goodly nation for our children's children's children. That distant day will never dawn upon *our* eyes. As patriots our hardest labor toward that future now begins.

Are we sufficient for it? Can we who are already tired out, almost beyond endurance, stand the necessary strain of postwar years, make of our country that which will become worthy of the sacrifices we have made this past few years, of the greater sacrifices made by our million casualties? We can have the strength we need, but only on two conditions.

First, we must know how America may become free and what is the price of that freedom.

Someone will say, "But we are free already, we Americans. Why, then, do you speak of our *becoming* free?"

To a certain extent we are free. We have political freedoms such as are not to be found in any other country on earth, freedoms guaranteed as long as we preserve the precious Bill of Rights in our Constitution: freedom to worship God in such fashion as we choose; freedom of every citizen to own and bear arms for his protection; freedom from having soldiers quartered in our houses; the right not to have our property searched or our papers seized except by due writ of the civil (not military) courts; freedom not to be held for a serious crime except after Grand Jury indictment; freedom not to be tried more than once for the same alleged offense; freedom not to have the government take our property without just payment for the same; freedom to be tried by jury and not by a bench of judges; freedom of a free vote to choose those who shall govern us; freedom not to be held in prison without trial; freedom to criticise the government openly, by speech or in the press; freedom to hold mass meetings of protest against governmental acts or policies. These are indeed great freedoms.

But in another sense, and a very important sense, Americans today are not free men, free women. Jesus Christ clearly tells us in what respect we are not free. He taught that a citizen who lives for his own selfish advantage is a slave, a slave to *himself*; that a faction which has its eye primarily on its own prosperity and prestige is a slave to *itself*; and that to be a slave to self is a peace-destructive, nation-rending slavery. We are slaves to a false theory of human life. We seek to build a nation on self-seeking, self-expression, self-assertion. We have resolved the commonwealth into a scramble of groups and classes and localities and individuals, each out for what, by hook or crook, may possibly be wangled. If "sin" means "selfishness," and it means just that, then we Americans are not free; we are *slaves to sin. And the wages of sin is death.*

If we Americans are to build with hope of success for our country after the war, we need to be freed from disrupting greeds. Ever since the Civil War we have become more and more in bondage to such greeds. First we had big business, the high and mighty financiers, the robber barons and demanders of profits as heavy as the traffic would bear, the devotees of the gospel of wealth, using every device, including political corruption, to milk the country. Then up rose the embattled masses, angry working people—first the Knights of Labor, then the A.F. of L. and the C.I.O.—determined that they no longer would be serfs under capitalists or slaves of factory managers. "Good!" some of us said, and cheered, and jeopardized our livelihood to help organized labor. But soon we began to discover that organized labor was less determined than we had thought to establish fraternity and cooperation in this land. Rather we found labor seeking to dethrone the old despoiling classes only that its own despoiling forces might in turn control and plunder. Wall Street *et al* had milked the land; now labor would milk it. Strikes, lockouts, violence, breaking of agreements, lobbying and intimidation, every low device from both sides in the industrial battle; the class struggle was on.

The World War now drawing to its close at last broke upon us, threatening our very existence. "Surely now," we said, "this crazy inner battle between groups out each to exploit the nation will cease, and labor and management and finance declare at least a truce." Nothing of the sort! The virus of class greed is in our blood-stream. Wartime Washington became an arena for pull and haul between the various groups, each demanding as of yore its right to grab. Is ours a healthy commonwealth, a nation free to dare great things for God and man? God knows that it is far from that!

We must be saved from class struggle or the nation will go down into ruin, scorned by all the world for large pretension and next to no performance. Can we be saved from that? We shall never be saved until we see that our peril is not so much from outside attack—that we have shown we can repel—as from inner corruption. We have forgotten the wisdom of God, the wisdom Christ taught us—that he who seeks to save himself will perish, that he who loses himself, for the brethren's sake and God's, alone can be free from sin, alone can be preserved and a preserver of his country.

No, America's struggle toward freedom is not over, nor is it nearly over; it is only moving into a new and more crucial stage. That is the first thing that we who love America must understand if these *post-bellum* days are not to fill us first with bewilderment and then with despair.

Secondly, and even more, we who would be patriots need to lay new hold on God. We need once more to remember what most of our people have forgotten, that we belong, that America belongs, to God the Father, who preserves only those nations whose citizens live for one another and destroys the rest of the nations; that it is His mills which, though they grind slowly, yet do they grind exceeding small. We need to see again and love again and follow again Jesus Christ, God the Son, who reveals what it means for man to live as God lives, wholly for the welfare of other than one's self, and by so doing has gained the power to save from the Hell that comes from self-seeking both men and nations that have wit to understand Him and obey. If we do serve God the Father, obey God the Son, then God the Holy Spirit will take possession of our bodies, minds, souls, lead us into all truth, guide us when perplexed, strengthen us to endure hardness with patience, sanctify to us the good that is latent in America, give us that inner peace without which no other peace can last for long, nor matter while it lasts. We need to lay hold on God the Holy Trinity, we patriots.

Ours is a superficial nation. We play with Religion. We think almost never about God, His purpose for America, His power to make us lovers of one another. We have banished the facing of God out of our educational system. Such folly must cease! We *must* remember God, not because some parson tells us to but because life is too hard for us without God, our pressing problems too complex for solution by our own unaided wisdom and virtue. We are mired in the muck of our own desires. We do not know the way. America without God will flounder to ever lower levels of behavior until she comes in the end to those same horrible depths into which we have seen Nazi-ism sink, and perish for its stupidity. We need God's help, each one of us, help to live for God, to cry God's wisdom in an America which, having beaten down its foreign foes, must now decide, in the midst of almost unbearable strains, whether it is to do God's will here at home and go on into greatness or else drift, befuddled, into disintegration.

The modern patriot's labors are not done; in a true sense they only now begin. Blow, bugles, blow—not *Taps* but *Reveille*! GOD SAVE THE STATE!

APPENDIX

BIOGRAPHICAL NOTES [1]

BAUKAGE, HILMAR ROBERT (1889-   ) Born in LaSalle, Illinois; Ph.B., University of Chicago, 1911; student at Universities of Bonn, Kiel, Jena, Freiburg, 1911-13; newspaperman since 1908; Washington Bureau Associated Press, 1914; with Consolidated Press, 1919-32; with the United States News, 1932-37; Washington correspondent Western Newspaper Union since 1940; news commentator, National Broadcasting Company, 1934-42; was broadcasting from Berlin 1939; Washington commentator Blue Network since 1942; served with AEF, 1918; author (with C. L. Baldridge) of *I Was There,* 1919.

BELL, BERNARD IDDINGS (1886-   ) Born in Dayton, Ohio; A.B., University of Chicago, 1907; S.T.D., Western Theological Seminary, 1912, D.D., 1921; Litt.D., Columbia, 1929; LL.D., Colorado College, 1931; other honorary degrees; clergyman, St. Christopher's Episcopal Church, Oak Park, Illinois, 1910-13; held pastorates subsequently in Wisconsin; chaplain, Great Lakes Naval Training Station, 1917-19; professor of religion, Columbia University, 1930-33; preaching canon at St. John's Cathedral, Providence, Rhode Island, since 1933; lecturer and preacher at University of Chicago and at various other colleges and universities in America, England, and Canada; member Phi Beta Kappa; author of *Preface to Religion,* 1935; *Religion for Living,* 1939, and some ten other volumes.

BUTLER, NICHOLAS MURRAY (1862-   ) Born in Elizabeth, New Jersey; A.B., Columbia, 1882, A.M., 1883, Ph.D., 1884; honorary degrees from many American and European universities; appointed president of Columbia, 1901; resigned,

---

[1] The chief sources of these notes are *Who's Who in America, Current Biography, Religious Leaders in America, International Who's Who, Who's Who in American Education, American Scholars* and the *Congressional Directory.*

April 1945; frequently a delegate to the Republican national conventions; received Republican electoral vote for Vice President of the United States, 1913; received 69 ½ votes from New York State as candidate for President of the United States, Republican National Convention, 1920; member or chairman of many committees, associations, and foundations for the advancement of education; awarded half of Nobel peace prize, 1931; president of Carnegie Endowment for International Peace since 1925; author of *The Meaning of Education,* 1898; *Philosophy,* 1911; *A World in Ferment,* 1918; *Looking Forward,* 1932, and numerous other books, essays, and addresses on subjects relating to philosophy, education, government, and international relations.

CHURCHILL, WINSTON LEONARD SPENCER (1874-   ) Educated at Harrow and Sandhurst; entered the army, 1895; served with Spanish forces in Cuba, 1895; service in India, 1897-98; with Nile army, 1898; correspondent with *Morning Post,* South Africa, 1899-1900; escaped prisoner, and in various battles of the Boer War, 1900; Member of Parliament, 1900-22; an officer in the British Army in France, 1916; First Lord of Admiralty, 1911-15; Minister of Munitions, 1917; various ministerial offices, 1918-22; Chancellor of the Exchequer, 1924-29; First Lord of the Adimralty, 1939-40; Prime Minister, First Lord of the Treasury and Minister of Defense, 1940-45; author of a long list of books, including *Marlborough,* (4 vols.) 1933; *Blood, Sweat, and Tears,* 1941; *Unrelenting Struggle,* 1942; *The End of the Beginning,* 1943; *Onward to Victory,* 1944.

DEWEY, THOMAS EDMUND (1902-   ) Born in Owosso, Michigan; A.B., University of Michigan, 1923, LL.M., 1937; LL.B., Columbia University 1925; honorary degree at Tufts, Dartmouth, and other institutions; admitted to New York bar, 1926; chief assistant, U.S. Attorney, 1931-33; special prosecutor, Investigation of Organized Crime, New York, 1935-37; elected District Attorney, New York County, 1937; Republican governor of New York since 1942; defeated as candidate for the presidency, Republican ticket, November, 1944; author of *The Case Against the New Deal,* 1940.

EDEN, (ROBERT) ANTHONY (1897-   ) Educated at Eton and Christ Church, Oxford; D.C.L., Oxford, Durham; LL.D., Cambridge; Conservative M.P. for Warwick and Leamington since 1928; Under Secretary of State for Foreign Affairs in National Government, 1931-33; Lord Privy Seal, 1934-35; Secretary of State for Foreign Affairs, 1935-38; Secretary of State for Dominion Affairs, 1939-40; Secretary of State for War 1940-45; represented Great Britain at the United Nations Security League Conference at San Francisco, 1945; publications include *Places in the Sun,* 1926; *Foreign Affairs,* 1939.

EISENHOWER, DWIGHT DAVID (1890-   ) Born in Denison, Texas. B.S., United States Military Academy, 1915; Army Tank School, 1921; Graduate, War College, 1929; 2nd Lieutenant, U. S. Army, 1915; Lt. Colonel Tank Corps, World War I; advanced through grades to General of the Army, December 1944; Chief of Operations Division, Office of Chief of Staff, 1942; Commanding General, European Theatre of Operations, June, 1942; Allied Commander in Chief, North Africa, November,1942; Supreme Commander of Allied land, sea and air forces in Western Europe, November, 1943; many military decorations and honors, including investment by King George of Order of Merit.

HOCKING, WILLIAM ERNEST (1873-   ) Born in Cleveland, Ohio; A.B., Harvard University, 1901, A.M., 1902, Ph.D., 1904; D.D., Chicago, 1933; Th.D., Glasgow, 1933; studied in Göttingen, Berlin, Heidelberg; teacher of philosophy University of California, 1906-08; assistant professor and professor of philosophy at Yale, 1908-14; professor of philosophy at Harvard since 1914, professor emeritus since, 1943; visiting lecturer at Princeton, Glasgow, Oxford, Cambridge and other institutions; inspector war issues courses United States War Department, 1918; author *Philosophy of Law and of Rights,* 1926; *The Self, Its Body and Freedom,* 1928; *Types of Philosophy,* 1929; *Recent Trends in American Philosophy,* 1941; *Contemporary Science and the Idea of God,* 1944.

HUTCHINS, ROBERT MAYNARD (1899-   ) Born in Brooklyn, New York; A.B., Yale, 1921, honorary A.M., 1922, LL.B.,

1925; LL.D., West Virginia University, Lafayette College, and other institutions; Dean, Yale Law School, 1928-29; President, University of Chicago since 1929; in ambulance service, U.S. Army, 1917-19; Italian Army, 1918-19; decorated Croce di Guerra (Italian), 1918; member of numerous honorary and learned societies, including Phi Beta Kappa, Order of the Coif; author of *The Higher Learning in America,* 1936, and numerous other books and magazine articles.

JOHNSTON, ERIC ALLEN (1896-   ) Born in Washington, D.C.; soon moved to Spokane, Washington; was graduated from high school, Spokane; LL.B., University of Washington, 1917; captain, marines, 1917-22; entered business 1922 and later was co-owner and president of large electrical contracting and electrical manufacturing companies; president of Spokane Chamber of Commerce, 1931-32; director, United States Chamber of Commerce, 1943, vice president, 1941, president since 1942; visited South America, Great Britain, and Russia, 1943; author of *America Unlimited,* 1944.

KING, ERNEST JOSEPH (1878-   ) Born in Lorain, Ohio; graduate of United States Naval Academy, 1901; student, United States War College, 1932-33; LL.D., College of William and Mary, 1942; Midshipman, U.S. Navy, Spanish-American War, ensign, 1903; Rear Admiral, 1933; Admiral, 1941; appointed Commander in Chief of the U.S. Fleet, 1941; Chief of Naval Operations, 1942; twice awarded the D.S.M., also Navy Cross.

MACLEISH, ARCHIBALD (1892-   ) Born in Glencoe, Illinois; educated Hotchkiss School; A.B., Yale, 1915, Litt.D., 1939; LL.B., Harvard, 1919; honorary degrees from Tufts, Wesleyan, Colby, Pennsylvania, Johns Hopkins; captain, First World War; author of *The Plot of Earth* (verse), 1925; *Conquistador* (Pulitzer poetry prize), 1932; *Public Speech* (verse), 1936; *The Fall of The City* (verse play for radio), 1937, and other works; librarian of Congress 1939-44; Director of Office of Facts and Figures, 1941-43; Assistant Secretary of State, 1944-45.

MAYS, BENJAMIN ELIJAH (1895-   ) Born in Greenwood County, South Carolina; A.B., Bates College, 1920; A.M., University of Chicago, 1925, Ph.D., 1935; teacher, Morehouse College, 1921-24, South Carolina State College, 1925-26; Dean, School of Religion, Howard University (Washington, D.C.), 1934-40; President, Morehouse College since 1940; widely traveled in the United States, Europe, and Asia; author of numerous articles and research publications, including *The Negro's God*; member and vice president of Federal Council of Churches in America, 1945.

MUNDT, KARL EARL (1900-   ) Born in Humboldt, South Dakota; A.B., Carleton College (Minnesota), 1923; A.M., Columbia University, 1927; teacher of speech and social sciences, South Dakota public schools, 1923-27; chairman of speech department, Eastern State Teachers College, Madison, South Dakota, 1927-36; member of the House of Representatives from South Dakota since 1939; member of House Foreign Affairs Committee; president of National Forensic League; member, Pi Kappa Delta, Delta Sigma Rho, Tau Kappa Alpha.

NIEBUHR, REINHOLD (1892-   ) Born in Wright City, Missouri; student Elmhurst College (Illinois), 1910; Eden Theological Seminary (St. Louis), 1912; B.D., Yale Divinity School 1914, A.M., 1915; D.D., Amherst, Yale, Oxford; ordained in ministry, Evangelical Synod of North America, 1915; pastor, Detroit, 1915-28; associate professor of philosophy of religion, 1928-30, professor of Applied Christianity, Union Theological Seminary since 1930; author of *The Nature and Destiny of Man*, 1941, and other books on Christian ethics and philosophy.

PRENTIS, HENNING WEBB, JR. (1884-   ) Born in St. Louis, Missouri; A.B., University of Missouri, 1903; A.M., University of Cincinnati, 1907; LL.D., Hampden-Sydney College (Virginia) and other colleges; with the Armstrong Cork Co. since 1907, president since March, 1934; president and director of National Association of Manufacturers; member of Phi Beta Kappa.

REDFIELD, ROBERT (1897-   ) Born in Chicago, Illinois, Ph.B., University of Chicago, 1920, J.D., 1921, Ph.D., 1928; instructor in sociology, University of Colorado, 1925-26; instructor in anthropology, University of Chicago, 1927-28, assistant professor, 1928-30, associate professor 1930-34, professor and dean of the Division of Social Sciences since 1934; research in Yucatan and Guatemala, 1930-42; ambulance driver, American Field Service, 1917; president American Anthropological Association, 1944; Phi Beta Kappa; author of *The Folk Culture of Yucatan,* 1941, and other publications on Central American civilization.

REYNOLDS, QUENTIN (1902-   ) Born in New York City; Ph.B., Brown University, 1924, Litt.D., 1942; LL.B., Brooklyn Law School, 1931, LL.D., 1941; sports writer, *New York World, New York World Telegram;* International News Service, 1932; Berlin correspondent, 1933; associate editor *Collier's* since 1933; war correspondent since 1940; author, *The Wounded Don't Cry,* 1941; *London Diary,* 1941; *Only Stars Are Neutral,* 1942; *Dress Rehearsal,* 1943; *The Curtain Rises,* 1944; radio commentator and frequent speaker before popular and professional audiences.

ROCKEFELLER, JOHN DAVISON, JR. (1874-   ) Born in Cleveland, Ohio; A.B., Brown University, 1897, M.A., 1914, LL.D., 1937; associated with his father in business enterprises; active in philanthropic work; trustee Rockefeller Foundation, 1913-40; president of board of the Rockefeller Institute for Medical Research; Phi Beta Kappa; author of *The Personal Relation in Industry.*

ROOSEVELT, FRANKLIN DELANO (1882-1945) Born in Hyde Park, New York; A.B., Harvard, 1904; attended Columbia University Law School, 1904-07; honorary degrees from Rutgers, Yale, Notre Dame, and other institutions; began practicing law in New York, 1907; Assistant Secretary of the Navy, 1913-20; Governor of New York, 1929-33; President of the United States, 1933-37, 1937-41, 1941-45; inaugurated for a fourth term, January 1945; conferred with Winston Churchill in the North Atlantic, August 1941; in Washington, December 1941; at Casablanca, January 1943; at Quebec, August 1943; at Cairo, November 1943; at Quebec, September 1944; and with both Churchill and Stalin at Teheran, December 1943; and at Yalta, February 1945; died suddenly at Warm Springs, Georgia, April 12, 1945; author of *Whither Bound,* 1926; *Looking Forward,* 1933; *Political Papers,* 1938, and other books.

SHAPLEY, HARLOW (1885-   ) Born in Nashville, Missouri; A.B., University of Missouri, 1910, A.M., 1911, LL.D., 1927; Ph.D., Princeton, 1913; honorary degrees from Missouri, Princeton, Harvard, University of Pennsylvania, and elsewhere; astronomer at Mt. Wilson Observatory, 1914-21; director of Harvard Observatory since 1921; researches in photometry and spectroscopy; member of Council of American Association for the Advancement of Science; officer in other learned societies and recipient of various medals for distinguished contributions in the field of astronomy.

SHEIL, BERNARD JAMES (   ) Born in Chicago, Illinois; St. Viator's College, Bourbonnais, Illinois; ordained priest, Roman Catholic Church, 1910; St. Mel's Church, 1910-17; Chaplain Great Lakes Naval Training Station, 1918-19; Holy Name Cathedral, 1919-23; Auxiliary Bishop of Chicago since 1928.

STASSEN, HAROLD E. (1907-   ) Born in West St. Paul, Minnesota; student University of Minnesota College and Law School, 1923-29; practiced law in Minneapolis since 1929; County Attorney, 1930-38; Governor of Minnesota, 1939-41; reelected Governor for the terms 1941-43 and 1943-45; resigned to enter United States Navy, 1943; keynote speaker of the Republican National Convention, 1940; member of Delta Sigma Rho; selected as one of the seven delegates to represent the United States at the United Nations Security League Conference, San Francisco, 1945.

STETTINIUS, EDWARD R., JR. (1900-   ) Born in Chicago, Illinois; University of Virginia, 1919-24; in industry, 1924;

assistant to the vice president of General Motors Corporation, 1926-30; vice president of General Motors, 1931; vice chairman United States Steel Corporation, 1934; chairman Board of Directors and member of Finance Committee, United States Steel, 1938-40; resigned all positions with United States Steel, 1940; Chairman War Resources Board, 1939; Administrator Lend-Lease Administration, 1941-43; Under Secretary of State, 1943; Secretary of State, November, 1944-45.

STODDARD, ALEXANDER JERRY (1889-   ) Born in Auburn, Nebraska; graduate of Peru (Nebraska) State Teachers College, 1910; studied law, University of Michigan, 1913-15; B.S. in Education, University of Nebraska, 1922; A.M., Columbia, 1923; Ed.D., Rhode Island College of Education, 1933; honorary degrees from Beaver, Temple, Nebraska, Pennsylvania; superintendent of schools, Nebraska, 1910-22; Bronxville, N.Y., 1922-26; Schenectady, N.Y., 1926-29; Providence, Rhode Island, 1929-37, Denver, 1937-39, Philadelphia since 1939; lecturer at Yale, 1923-26; at Columbia, 1929-31; chairman Educational Policies Committee; president of the Department of Superintendence of the National Education Association; contributor to professional journals.

TRUMAN, HARRY S. (1884-   ) Born in Lamar, Missouri; student Kansas City School of Law, 1923-25; Captain, Field Artillery, First World War; judge, Jackson County Court, 1922-24; presiding judge, 1926-34; United States Senator from Missouri, 1935-41, reelected for the term 1941-47; elected Vice President on the Democratic ticket November 1944; sworn in as President of the United States on the death of President Roosevelt, April 1945.

VANDENBERG, ARTHUR HENDRICK (1884-   ) Born in Grand Rapids, Michigan; studied law at the University of Michigan, 1901-02; honorary A.M. from University of Michigan, 1925; LL.D. from Hope College, 1926; editor of Grand Rapids *Herald,* 1906-28; United States Senator, 1928-47; Chairman of Republican Senate Legislative Committee, 1933-34; received 76 votes for Republican presidential nomination, Philadelphia, 1940; American delegate, United Nations Security League Conference, San Francisco, 1945; member of Authors' Club, London, England; author of *Alexander Hamilton, the Greatest American,* 1921; *If Hamilton Were Here Today,* 1923; *The Trail of a Tradition,* 1925.

WALLACE, HENRY AGARD (1888-   ) Born in Adair County, Iowa; B.S., Iowa State College, 1910, honorary M.S. in agriculture, 1920; editor of *Wallaces' Farmer* since 1910; Secretary of Agriculture in Cabinet of President Roosevelt, 1933-40; Vice President of the United States, 1941-45; visited Latin America, 1943; defeated for nomination as Vice President on the Democratic ticket for reelection in 1944, but campaigned actively for Roosevelt; appointment as Secretary of Commerce confirmed in March 1945, after vigorous Senate opposition; author of *America Must Choose,* 1934; *Statesmanship and Religion,* 1934; *Whose Constitution?* 1936; *Paths to Plenty,* 1938, and other books and articles on agricultural, political, and religious topics.

WEAVER, ANDREW THOMAS (1890-   ) Born in Waukesha, Wisconsin; A.B., Carroll College (Waukesha), 1910; A.M., University of Wisconsin, 1911, Ph.D., 1923; instructor, Dartmouth College, 1912-13, Northwestern University, 1913-17; professor of English and Speech, Wisconsin State Teachers College, 1917-18, Assistant and later Associate Professor of Speech, Wisconsin, 1918-23, Professor since 1925, chairman of department since 1927; visiting professor at University of Hawaii and elsewhere; president of National Association of Teachers of Speech, 1927; editor of *Quarterly Journal of Speech,* 1930-33; member of Delta Sigma Rho; author of *Elements of Speech* (with J. M. O'Neill), 1933; *Speech, Forms and Principles,* 1942, and other well-known texts.

CUMULATED AUTHOR INDEX

An author index to the volumes of *Representative American Speeches* for the years 1937-38 to 1944-45. The date following the title of each speech indicates the volume in which it appears.